TIM COOPER

Tim Cooper is a prominent figure in Britain's fast expanding Green movement. He is Joint National Co-ordinator of Christian Ecology Link (formerly the Christian Ecology Group), the main organisation linking Christians and Greens, which he helped to form in 1981. A member of the Green Party for over a decade, he has been a candidate in parliamentary and local elections and is a past Co-Chair of the Green Party Council.

He has made numerous appearances on radio and television and has written extensively on the Green movement. This is his first full-length book.

An economics graduate, he now works as a writer and adviser on economics and environmental issues.

SPIRE

Tim Cooper

GREEN CHRISTIANITY
Caring for the whole creation

**For young Jamie,
Christopher and Edward,
who will inherit the Earth
in whatever state we leave it.**

Copyright © 1990 by Tim Cooper

First published in Great Britain 1990
Second impression 1990

Spire is an imprint of Hodder & Stoughton *Publishers*

British Library Cataloguing in Publication Data
Cooper, Tim
Green Christianity:
1. Environment. Conservation. Christian viewpoints
I. Title
261.836

ISBN 0-340-52339-5

Part of the royalties from this book
will be given to tree-planting projects.

*Printed in Great Britain for Hodder and Stoughton Limited, Mill Road, Dunton
Green, Sevenoaks, Kent by Richard Clay Limited, Bungay, Suffolk. Photoset by
Rowland Phototypesetting Limited, Bury St Edmunds, Suffolk.*

Hodder and Stoughton Editorial Office: 47 Bedford Square, London WC1B 3DP.

CONTENTS

INTRODUCTION

Few topics have attracted more publicity in recent years than the state of the global environment. The emergence of a Green movement in many countries throughout the world promises to have a crucial impact on social, economic and political life in the 1990s. How should we respond?

As scientists have warned of many long-term threats posed by environmental damage, people have become much more concerned about the future. Uncertainty fuels our fears. By how much will skin cancer increase as a result of damage to the ozone layer? What will be the impact on food supplies of the climatic change through the greenhouse effect? How many people in low-lying coastal areas will suffer from flooding as a result of sea temperatures rising? And how much will we suffer from the loss of rainforest when species of great potential value as food or medicine become extinct?

Closer to home, many aspects of the environment in the industrialised world are deteriorating, despite our greater affluence. More and more traffic congests and pollutes urban areas. New building developments lead to fewer green spaces in towns and cities. Rolling hills in the countryside are no longer patterned with fields edged with hedgerows, but replaced instead by huge, bare, mono-cropped fields. Beaches are so often polluted that prospective swimmers use guide books to find the safe ones. Air pollutants cause respiratory diseases and other illnesses and rise up into the atmosphere, later to fall as acid rain and destroy trees. A constant growth in economic output does not hide people's awareness that their quality of life is in decline.

With this background, *Green Christianity* is written in

the firm conviction that the Green movement's growing influence represents a bright ray of hope in a world where millions needlessly suffer, and even die, because of environmental degradation arising from abuse of God's creation. The book's aim is to explore the inter-connections between Christianity and ecology. My intention is to develop a Christian view of the whole creation which is appropriate to an industrialised world very different from that of over two thousand years ago. In contrast with the slogan of today's Friends of the Earth, in the days of Jonah it was the whale which had to proclaim 'Save the Human'!

The first five chapters of the book trace the sources of today's problems, the impact of Christian teaching and practice, and the emergence of the Green movement. In the remaining three chapters some contemporary issues are addressed from a Christian perspective, including nuclear power, genetic engineering and factory farming. During the course of the book practical examples are given of Christians who are taking steps to protect God's creation from abuse, and ideas given to help people choose a Greener lifestyle.

Green Christianity is particularly intended for Christians who feel a need to understand more about the nature of the Green movement and how its ideas fit in with the Christian faith. We have much to learn about ecology. Many Christians still believe that they need not be overly concerned about global environmental problems, pointing to biblical passages relating a call to 'subdue' the Earth and promises of 'a new heaven and a new earth'. Some even believe that it is an unnecessary waste of time to protect our earthly home. *Green Christianity* is a direct response to this challenge. It argues that, although Christianity must share some blame, the ecological crisis cannot be attributed to the fundamentals of Christianity. It is perfectly possible, as this book seeks to show, to develop a 'Green' Christianity.

My starting point is a belief that the Earth is neither self-regulating, nor the product of chance, but the creation of a loving God whose supreme expression is through

Jesus Christ. I hope, however, that the book will be read by some of the many people I have come across in the Green movement who have had some past connection with the Church but have left, dissatisfied because so few Christians appeared to share their concern for the fate of the planet. Such readers will, I trust, accept that many of the basic assumptions which underpin the Christian faith cannot be explained here in detail.

I am acutely aware that many of the issues raised are worthy of more lengthy and detailed discussion. Being 'the study of the structure and function of nature', ecology involves considering the environment of people, other living species, and even institutions. In other words, it embraces the whole of life. By necessity, a selective approach to this theme is taken, but I hope to show that Green Christianity has more to offer than recycled sermons and organic communion wine!

What of my own background? My involvement in the Green movement stretches back over fifteen years, to the time when I was first alerted to the scale of the crises by *The Limits to Growth* report and then came into contact with Friends of the Earth members campaigning on the streets of Bath against nuclear power. I soon became active myself, joining Friends of the Earth and what was then the Ecology Party, later to become the Green Party. In 1981 I helped to set up a nationwide network of Green Christians, the Christian Ecology Group – now known as Christian Ecology Link – as a means of encouraging people to relate Green commitment to Christianity.

Although rather reluctant to add labels to my Christian faith, I should perhaps explain that although I am somewhat more at ease theologically with evangelicalism than liberalism, my faith has been enriched by Christians of both persuasions and neither label seems particularly appropriate. Similarly, although a member of the Church of England, I support believers' baptism, appreciate the commitment to justice and caring for the Earth of many Roman Catholics, and have latterly gained valuable insights from Eastern Orthodox thought! In heaven there will be many mansions, but I hope that they will be unlabelled.

Throughout the book I use the term 'Green' in its proper sense, to describe a school of thought based on ecology and not simply to refer vaguely to one or other environmental concern. I do not restrict the 'Greens' to members of the Green Party, as some Greens express their beliefs through other channels. It is also common for the term 'environment' to be used loosely. I have tried to qualify it where appropriate as 'natural', 'living' or 'built'.

Much of the thought behind *Green Christianity* has arisen through my work with Christian Ecology Link. It has also benefited from the input of several people who have kindly provided advice on draft chapters. I wish therefore to express gratitude to John Peck, Bob Tatam, Rosalind Tatam, Edward Echlin, Michael Crowther-Green and Elizabeth Cooper, who kindly read and commented upon the complete text, Michael Schluter for comments on Chapter Three and Andrew Linzey for comments on Chapter Seven. In addition, during the course of my research numerous other people provided invaluable help, to whom I owe thanks. Any shortcomings in the final text are, of course, my personal responsibility.

The encouragement given by Carolyn Armitage and Christine Plunkett at Hodder and Stoughton is much appreciated. Last and by no means least, I am deeply grateful for the constant support of Bess, who during the course of this book's publication became my wife.

Tim Cooper   January 1990

Christian Ecology Link is the leading organisation for Christians interested in the Green movement. Details can be obtained from the Secretary, Christian Ecology Link, 17 Burns Gardens, Lincoln L2 4LJ.

1

CREATION UNMADE:
The ecological crisis

Not so long ago a picture of a fatherly-looking God peering through a hole in the Earth's atmosphere appeared in a cartoon. The hole represented the gap in the ozone layer. God seemed to be questioning whether prayers would somehow reach Him more quickly without the obstruction of ozone.

People who are scared by a serious threat often do one of two things – they laugh nervously and hope that it will go away, or turn to God for help. The hole in the ozone layer will certainly be no laughing matter for anyone who, as a consequence, suffers skin cancer or an eye cataract. But neither are people turning to God – in the industrialised West the number of Christians appears to be in decline.[1]

Damage to the ozone layer is one of many signs that environmental damage has reached crisis proportions. An unprecedented warming of the Earth's atmosphere, the 'greenhouse effect', threatens to disrupt world food production and displace the millions of people living in regions susceptible to flooding as sea levels rise. Huge tracts of tropical rainforest, rich in animal and plant species, are being systematically cleared for agriculture or harvested for fuelwood. Throughout the world soil is being eroded or losing its fertility and rivers and seas are being polluted. Problems of such magnitude may initially appear rather distant, but ultimately they will affect the lives of each one of us. How are we to respond?

A first step is to identify their ultimate source. There are some significant connections between the ecological crisis and disillusionment with Christianity. Many practices which degrade the environment arise out of the dominant 'world view' in the industrialised West, which is neither Christian nor ecological. A world view is characterised by people's faith, their *ultimate* concerns. The faith in God of Christians and faith in nature held by pagans have largely been replaced in modern times by faith in the individual 'self'.[2] In other words, faith which once was directed *outwards* has been rejected; people trust only themselves.

People's relationship with God and with nature has consequently become fractured. The dominant world view in the industrial West is fundamentally *materialistic* and *human-centred*. Freedom of the individual has come to mean freedom to live without any external constraints.

Most people have until recently tended to disregard the warning of Greens that living on a planet with finite resources demands limits on consumption. But nor have people been attracted to Christianity, with its God-given norms of behaviour, which are often seen as inhibitive rules. They prefer not to see themselves as interdependent with nature or dependent upon God; both bring potential restrictions to human autonomy.

The truth is, however, that we are *not* autonomous beings. People depend on the living environment for the food and energy that sustains life. And ultimately we depend on the Spirit of God, which breathes life into the whole creation. We are bound to certain biological principles and to divine truths.

The aim of this book is to explore how these vital connections are made through Christianity and ecology. There is a multitude of relationships, 'a web of life', by which different parts of God's creation are interconnected. The healing of people's relationships with God and with the rest of creation are thus part of the same urgent task. In this opening chapter the meaning of ecology is explained and, after some of the problems are described, a response is given to the frequent accusation that Christianity is primarily to blame for the environmental crises.

Perceptions of the planet

How do we view our earthly home? Many environmentalists have said that there was a key 'turning point' in their relationship to the Earth after it was photographed from outer space for the first time. The visual image of the Earth floating in space, like a blue pearl surrounded by darkness, seemed very powerful. It conveyed a sense of solitude and fragility, loneliness and vulnerability. In everyday life it is difficult to avoid seeing the marks of human activity upon our environment, but from space the Earth and its surrounding atmosphere is seen as a mix of cloud, oceans, greenery and soil. At such a distance humans appear of less significance. In an excellent historical study of ecology, *Nature's Economy*, Donald Worster recalls: "That lonely planet, we now understood in a way no previous epoch of man could have shared, was a terribly fragile place. Its film of life – man's sole means of survival – was far thinner and more vulnerable than anyone heretofore had realised."[3]

Seeing the biosphere – the Earth and its surrounding atmosphere – as a connected whole, the first astronauts spoke of their relationship to the Earth in terms of 'global consciousness' and being a 'planetary citizen'.

An analogy portraying the Earth itself as a 'spaceship' became popular following a speech in 1965 by the US Secretary of State, Adlai Stevenson, in which he described the Earth as a little spaceship on which people travel together, dependent on vulnerable supplies of air and soil. In their popular book *Only One Earth* Barbara Ward and René Dubos wrote: "We are indeed travellers bound to the earth's crust, drawing life from the air and water of its thin and fragile envelope, using and re-using its very limited supply of natural resources."[4]

Many people thus share a sense of awe at images of the planet from outer space. Indeed the influential World Commission on Environment and Development has suggested that the initial impression of such images might prove to have a tremendous influence on human thought, perhaps even greater than the scientific revelations of the six-teenth century, when it was first accepted-that the Earth is not the centre of the universe.[5]

The starting point of ecological analysis is that our impact on the environment is strongly affected by how we view our earthly home. In other words, how we *perceive* the world around us influences how we *treat* it.

Behind such an assertion lie important questions concerning the nature of the universe, our ability to 'change course', and our accountability. Does the universe exist through divine creation or chance? Do we have free will, enabling us to change direction? Is our accountability to our consciences, to future generations, or to God? If ecology is to enable us to enhance our relationship with our surroundings, we need to consider these most fundamental religious questions.

This is to say that any interpretation of ecology has profound implications. An example of how a view of the world arises out of religious assumptions is that of the words of Mother Julian of Norwich, written some six hundred years ago in one of a series of visions:

And he showed me more, a little thing, the size of a hazelnut, on the palm of my hand and round like a ball. I looked at it thoughtfully and wondered, "What is this?" And the answer came, "It is all that is made." I marvelled that it continued to exist and did not suddenly disintegrate; it was so small. And again my mind supplied the answer, "It exists, both now and for ever, because God loves it." In short everything owes its existence to the love of God. In this "little thing" I saw three truths. The first is that God made the earth; the second is that God loves it; and the third is that God sustains it.[6]

In Mother Julian's view of 'all that is made' she identified three important spiritual realities. Likewise the poet Gerard Manley Hopkins saw the world as 'charged with the grandeur of God.' To Bishop Berkeley nature was 'the visible language of God.'

In the contemporary world, however, scientific thought processes have tended to crush any such mysticism and we look at the world in other ways to make sense of it. Many scientists and industrialists see it very differently and, believing that the Earth is not sacred, treat it with profanity. To these scientists its most immediate characteristic is that it consists of mechanically operating interconnected particles, while, similarly, some industrialists seemingly look upon it as simply a stockpile of potential raw materials. God is forgotten and our scientific and technological power enable us to plunder the planet to meet our greed. The value of nature is measured solely in terms of its usefulness to humankind. It is not considered to have intrinsic value, but only instrumental value.

Our view of the planet is thus important. Do you see the Earth as indestructible and resilient, or do you first think of its fragility? Do your thoughts turn to the dense richness of the Amazonian rainforest, or to the barrenness of the Sahel desert? Do you think of scientific processes at work? Is your image of the Earth one of beauty and joy? Or is it of a creation "groaning as in the pain of childbirth" (Rom. 8.22)?

As the twentieth century draws to a close, new visual images of the Earth enable us to see our world as never before. We have a new-found potential to appreciate it, but we must recognise that with our greater knowledge and understanding comes an awesome responsibility to take care of it.

Ecology and the 'integrity of creation'

Ecology is 'the study of the structure and function of nature'. Although some scientists define it very strictly as the study of living organisms in relation to their environment, its more common definition is broader and even includes the study of institutions in relation to their environment; hence it is possible to speak of the ecology of the Church. Some people also speak of our 'inner ecology', meaning the relationship between mind, body and spirit.

One of the basic lessons of ecology is that all life,

ultimately, is interconnected. To quote American biologist Barry Commoner, "everything is connected to everything else" and John Muir, who founded America's leading environmentalist body, the Sierra Club, "when you try to pick out anything by itself, you find it hitched to the universe."[7] Christians might express this kind of connection in terms of an *order* in God's creation through which nature operates consistently according to ecological laws. These make life possible by, for example, allowing for the regulation of cycles of food, water and carbon, and maintaining adequate stability within and between ecosystems. Indeed many of the early ecologists sought to 'find the hand of God in nature' through which they could explain this order and harmony within creation.

It is only because there *is* this overall order in creation that life is intelligible to us and we find it possible to survive and make sense of our life and surroundings. Ecology thus provides the basis for scientific *and* philosophical study. The significance of interdependence within creation has led to the concept of '*the integrity of creation*' coming into use, notably in a major World Council of Churches initiative. 'Integrity' in creation means 'wholeness' or 'entireness'. The idea is to express the unity within creation which cannot be disregarded; if even a small fraction of the environment is abused there is a sense in which the whole of creation suffers.

From a Christian perspective, ecology is an exploration of how 'the structure and function of nature' fit into God's purpose. The biblical story of creation conveys an understanding of the origins of life in which a move from *chaos* to *harmony* is most significant. To begin with, "the earth was formless and empty" (Gen. 1.2). Each of the six days represents a step taken by God to piece together the *structure* of nature, within which each part is given a *function*. He sets all the boundaries in nature (Job 38.8–11; Ps. 74.17; Prov. 8.27–9). Thus in creation there is an order, or harmony, for all space and for all time, and also a transcendent purpose: "The Lord works out everything for his own ends" (Prov. 16.4).

The norm of creation is that it is responsive to its Creator, evolving into the right order according to His will. Theologian William Dyrness writes: "All of God's work involves the earth, humankind, and divine purposes in intimate relationship. All involve creating order in place of chaos."[8] This is what *ought* to happen, but when people are disobedient to God the intended order begins to disintegrate because the whole creation is influenced by human behaviour.

Disobedience leads to disorder; there is an inevitable retribution in the structure of nature. However God does not wish the created order to return to *total* chaos and so He *positively reacts against this*. Thus, writes Albert Wolters in *Creation Regained*: "God does not allow man's disobedience to turn his creation into utter chaos. Instead he *maintains* his creation in the face of all the forces of destruction."[9]

God's hope for His creation is summarised in the Hebrew word *shalom*. Usually translated somewhat crudely into English as 'peace', *shalom* more accurately describes a state of right relationships between people and their God, each other and the environment. This is the ideal 'order' in creation. (In the New Testament the Greek word *eirene* has a similar meaning.)

The concept of a covenant describes how relationships are regulated with the intention of bringing about *shalom*. Thus God established a covenant with Noah, and with his descendants and all living creatures, in which He pledged never again to destroy the Earth through a flood (Gen. 9.8–11). A covenant was also initiated by God with the Israelites, declaring that they would be special to Him (Exod. 19.5–6). Obedience to His laws would be rewarded with healthy crops and freedom from disasters such as drought and disease (see below).

A covenant may involve either one-sided or mutual obligations but, more crucially, it is not simply between God and people but includes the whole creation. It binds all together. Numerous passages throughout the Bible point to a 'planetary covenant' in which the fate of the whole creation is found to be linked to our response to God (Job 5.22–3; Ezek. 34.25; Hos. 2.18). Thus the scope of redemption extends beyond humankind (see Chapter Two).

A covenant of right relationships is the exact converse of the rampant individualism which is so increasingly prevalent, a political trend based on a belief that people can only be fulfilled *as individuals* (in Mrs Thatcher's famous phrase, 'there is no such thing as society'). In contrast the Bible suggests that we will be content only when we learn to live *together* in right relationships with God, one another and the rest of creation. We cannot properly live in isolation.

The fundamental importance of relationships in making sense of life is underlined by Orthodox theologian Paulos Gregorios:

> A person exists only in relation – in relation to other human persons (his/her father and mother, to begin with) and to non-human realities (light, air, water, food, etc.). It is not possible for a person to come to be or to grow without relation to other persons and things. The earth and the sun as well as other people are an essential part of our existence. Without them we cannot exist.[10]

God's intention is that these relationships are characterised by loving care, justice, peace and righteousness. Christians worship the source of all true ecology, who created a universe full of relationships in which all living things are intended to co-exist harmoniously, each with its own structure and function. An inspiring example of one man who sensed a kind of harmonious 'Earth community' was St Francis of Assisi. In the 'Canticle of Brother Sun' St Francis expressed his experience of a total universal reconciliation which was directed towards God. Such was the depth of harmony between St Francis and his environment that he felt that the sun, moon, wind, water and fire were like brothers and sisters, each offering an invitation to praise God.

Naturally good

In more recent times there has been a trend of people wishing to 'escape' to the countryside and, particularly in recent years, to buy 'natural' products. They sense a desire to be close to nature. How we relate to nature – whether we see ourselves as above nature or part of it – will affect how we value nature and treat it. Such questions will be explored later at more length, but it is necessary first to consider how we *understand* nature.

People use the words 'nature' and the 'natural' in several ways. 'Nature' is often used to define our living environment, but may either include or exclude the human species. This is significant. In the latter case there is an implied separation of humans from the rest of nature and this is often blamed for our abuse of the environment. If humans see themselves as *separate* from nature they are more liable to imagine that they can destroy nature with impunity.

Another understanding of 'nature' is in terms of its laws of operation, to refer to that which exists or occurs without either human activity or divine intervention. In this definition the impact of human activity is considered 'artificial' and intervention by God 'supernatural'. A third usage of 'nature' is in terms of behavioural patterns or character. For example, it is in the nature of owls to fly and of lions to be ferocious.

Taking the first of these definitions, it is notable that nature as a separate vast entity existing without reference to a Creator is a concept alien to biblical thought. In the Old Testament God's action in producing and sustaining creation is always recognised. Indeed, no Hebrew word exists for nature in the sense of an entity; the closest term in common use is *bara*, a verb meaning 'creating'. (Hebrew has a feminine noun for the whole creation, *beriah*, but its usage is rare.)[11]

Similarly, nowhere in the New Testament is *physis*, the Greek word for nature, used to refer to the whole of creation, or its non-human aspect. In the rare instances where the concept of nature is used, it is to communicate 'God-givenness' or constitutive characteristics. There are references in the New Testament to the whole creation, but these invariably describe it in relation to God and different Greek words are used (e.g. *ktisis* or *ta panta*). For example Paul, in his epistle to the Romans, writes:

> For since the creation of the world God's invisible qualities – his eternal power and divine nature – have been clearly seen, being understood from what has been made, so that men are without excuse. For although they knew God, they neither glorified him as God nor gave thanks to him, but their thinking became futile and their foolish hearts were darkened. (Rom. 1.20–21)

In other words, people's knowledge of God may derive from "what has been made" or, more literally, 'the works of the craftsman's art' (the Greek word used here is *ktisis*).

With God as our primary reference point in making sense of our surroundings, people in the Judaeo-Christian tradition *ought* to view the natural world in the context of His actions. But this relationship has been fractured and instead many 'objectify' nature, seeing it as separate from themselves. The Western world has discarded any sense of a sacred dimension to nature (in a Judaeo-Christian, or even pagan, sense) and nature has consequently been devalued (see later).

When the Earth is fertile this is considered *natural*. The Bible speaks of the Earth in its original state, newly created and untouched by human activity, as fundamentally *good*. Goodness and fertility are thus linked as the natural characteristics of the Earth.

Similarly, it is *natural* for human beings to communicate with and obey God. According to Bishop Kallistos Ware, another Orthodox writer:

> To believe that man is made in God's image is to believe that man is created for communion and union with God, and that if he rejects this communion he ceases to be properly man.

There is no such thing as 'natural man' existing in separation
from God: man cut off from God is in a highly unnatural
state.[12]

In this sense, humankind in a fallen state is not 'natural'. If we are failing to live in a right relationship with
God, we are not the people that we ought 'naturally' to be.
We are *truly* natural when we freely respond positively to
our Creator.

This is not to say that nature is necessarily benevolent
to humankind, nor that human behaviour which seems
natural is always right. 'Natural disasters' take place and,
though having a moral conscience, we often find ourselves
behaving contrary to it. As the apostle Paul found, "I do
not understand what I do. For what I want to do I do not do,
but what I hate I do" (Rom. 7.15). Inclinations which
appear natural are not always those which God desires us
to follow. The whole of creation is fallen.

Such apparent contradictions may be understood not
just in terms of personal morality but in a political context. Supporters of capitalism, for example, argue that it
works precisely because it recognises and accommodates
people's 'naturally' selfish behaviour. The free market is,
it is said, a market operating 'naturally', without intervention. Indeed, the capitalist principle of progress
through 'survival of the fittest' originates from observation by Charles Darwin and others of the processes of
nature. Alternatives to capitalism which involve political
intervention are, in contrast, deemed 'unnatural'.

However such thinking draws wholly unwarranted parallels between human behaviour and the instincts of other
animals, and makes an assumption of biological inevitability which implies that humans lack free will. It provides an insight into how people's faith in nature or
natural processes may be exploited and taken too far.

Broken relationships – creation unmade

In contrast with other creatures people may disobey God
and disrupt His intended order and purpose for creation.
The Old Testament prophet Jeremiah contrasted the
limits of the freedom of the sea and sand with the free
choice of humans to reject God's norms (Jer. 5.22–3).

Right relationships exist only if people respond obedi-
ently to God and so the whole creation is subject to human
behaviour. Dyrness writes: "One is continually brought
up against the fact that morality, response to God, and the
fertility of the earth are interrelated . . . the very stability
of the created order is dependent upon Israel's faithfulness
to the covenant."[13]

For example, the Bible records that on Mount Sinai, and
again just before the Israelites enter the Promised Land,
God promises Moses that He will reward obedience by
providing them with favourable conditions. If the
Israelites obey His commands He will send the season's
rain so that "the ground will yield its crops and the trees of
the field their fruit" (Lev. 26.4). The Israelites will be
rewarded with grain, new wine and oil, and their offspring
and that of their livestock will be blessed (Deut. 11.13–15;
28.1–6).

But they are told that, if disobedient, they will be
defeated and ruled over by their enemies and the "soil will
not yield its crops, nor will the trees of the land bear their
fruit" (Lev. 26.20). Moses warns: "The Lord's anger will
burn against you, and he will shut the heavens so that it
will not rain and the ground will yield no produce, and you
will soon perish from the good land the Lord is giving you"
(Deut. 11.17). In addition, the Israelites' offspring and
that of their livestock will be cursed and "the Lord will
strike you with wasting disease, with fever and inflamma-
tion, with scorching heat and drought, with blight and
mildew, which will plague you until you perish" (Deut.
28.22).

With certain specific laws instituted by God, regarding
the use of natural resources, the consequences of disobedi-

ence would be felt directly. For example, breaking the law to keep the land fallow periodically would eventually cause it to lose fertility (Lev. 25.3–5; 26.34–5; 2 Chron. 36.21). However, many of the prophets also believed that the living environment would be affected in a more indirect manner, according to whether or not the people were obedient. Isaiah was written in the eighth century BC, a time when the Israelites lived in fear of the powerful Assyrian Empire. In Isaiah the following warning of their failure to trust and obey God is issued:

> See, the Lord is going to lay waste the earth and devastate it; he will ruin its face and scatter its inhabitants . . . The earth will be completely laid waste and totally plundered. The Lord has spoken this word.
> The earth dries up and withers, the world languishes and withers, the exalted of the earth languish. The earth is defiled by its people; they have disobeyed the laws, violated the statutes and broken the everlasting covenant. Therefore a curse consumes the earth; its people must bear their guilt. Therefore earth's inhabitants are burned up, and very few are left. (Isa. 24.1,3–6)

Likewise the prophet Hosea suggests that a healthy environment is dependent on the Israelites' behaviour. Warning that God was angry with them for turning away from Him and worshipping idols, Hosea conjures up the image of the Earth mourning:

> There is no faithfulness, no love, no acknowledgement of God in the land. There is only cursing, lying and murder, stealing and adultery; they break all bounds, and bloodshed follows bloodshed. Because of this the land mourns, and all who live in it waste away; the beasts of the field and the birds of the air and the fish of the sea are dying. (Hos. 4.1–3)

Amos, too, witnessing hypocrisy and injustice, speaks of God using 'natural disasters' in urging the Israelites to repent. He withholds rain, causes blight and mildew to damage gardens and vineyards, and sends locusts to destroy fig and olive trees. In consequence there are "empty stomachs in every city" (Amos 4.6). Yet despite this the Israelites failed to pay heed and within a few decades the Assyrians destroyed Samaria and took them into exile.

Around a century later the Assyrian Empire began to crumble and, as the Babylonian army grew in strength, prophets such as Zephaniah and Jeremiah cried out warnings of God's judgement upon His people for their disobedience and idol worship. Again, nature is involved.

Zephaniah pictures God's judgements as an exact reversal of His creative acts. Just as God populated the Earth He may equally choose to depopulate it: "'I will sweep away everything from the face of the earth,' declares the Lord. 'I will sweep away both men and animals; I will sweep away the birds of the air and the fish of the sea'" (Zeph. 1.2,3). Significantly, the order in which animals, birds and fish are swept away is the reverse of that in which they were first created. In effect, creation is 'unmade' because of people's unfaithfulness.

The prophet Jeremiah pleaded with God: "How long will the land lie parched and the grass in every field be withered?" (Jer. 12.4). He believed that it was because of people's wickedness that animals and birds perished. Pleasant fields were turned into a desert wasteland: "The whole land will be laid waste because there is no-one who cares . . . They will sow wheat but reap thorns; they will wear themselves out but gain nothing. So bear the shame of your harvest because of the Lord's fierce anger" (Jer. 12.11,13). Apparently it was only the exile of the Israelites to Babylon that enabled the land to enjoy the fallow periods which God instituted through the sabbatical laws (2 Chron. 36.21; Jer. 25.11).

The story of the Israelites is traditionally told with great emphasis on the battles; the fate of the living environment is less frequently described. But God's response to the Israelites' faithlessness and disobedience is not only to allow invasion by armies, but to permit disease, pestilence, famine and attack by wild beasts. All this might be regarded by some as poetic myth, assuming that no such natural disasters ever materially took place. But this would involve making a dangerously false division between the spiritual and material content of the Bible. It would follow from such reasoning that the invasions, too, were myths, which is, historically, untrue. Similarly, some people might argue that God no longer works in this way. This, however, would shed doubt on much else that may be learned from the Bible.

As noted earlier, in the Judaeo-Christian tradition nature is properly viewed in relation to the Creator within a covenant relation which binds all creation. Jesus Christ reveals the same God who made the Israelites His chosen people and who operates through nature today, just as in Old Testament times. The implication of the planetary covenant is therefore plain. The current environmental pressures reflect the judgement of God upon a world which rejects Him and worships instead idols of materialism and militarism.

Earthwreck

Experts have long warned that in the absence of radical change, the planet will face serious stresses involving population, resources and the environment by the turn of the century. The Green movement may only relatively recently have hit the news headlines, but a succession of authoritative reports over the past twenty years have highlighted the serious threats which lie ahead.[14]

Human abuse of God's creation extends from the depths of the sea to the atmosphere many miles above the Earth. We are guilty of using natural resources which are in finite supply with thoughtless profligacy and causing unnecessary pollution of air, land and water. The effects of this bad stewardship will be felt not just by ourselves, but by people in other parts of the world and in future generations. The quality of many people's lives will diminish as the benefits of the Earth's rich and varied natural resources are lost for ever. Greater injustice may well arise, as the affluent attempt to hold on to their power. Military conflicts may increase as nations seek control over vital raw materials, energy supplies, land, river basins or sea passages.

Some Christians may question the significance of the environmental threat. The Bible tells of Noah who, many years ago, built an ark upon which to escape the fate of other creatures, to perish through a great flood (Gen. 6.9–8.22). Some interpret God's covenant after the flood, mentioned earlier, as a clear promise that He will never again allow the Earth to be destroyed. Others believe that He ultimately intends to annihilate the Earth, thus making attempts by humans to protect it rather pointless. And other people think that the Earth will never end because within it is a kind of 'global brain', internal self-regulating controls which will prevent its destruction.

Such views will be explored later, together with important questions relating to responsibility for environmental damage, such as the extent to which Christianity is to blame and the role of individuals and governments. Our first task is to survey recent evidence of the state of the global environment. Is the problem really as serious as scientists such as David Bellamy and Norman Myers and Greens such as Jonathon Porritt and Sara Parkin are making out?

Most of the data by which to judge the severity of the situation is compiled by international agencies such as the United Nations.[15] The latest research by United Nations Environment Programme (UNEP) officials has led them to the stark conclusion that environmental destruction threatens the world with unprecedented human suffering:

If the world continues to accept disappearing tree cover, land degradation, the expansion of deserts, the loss of plant and animal species, air and water pollution, and the changing chemistry of the atmosphere it will also have to accept economic decline and social disintegration. In a world where progress depends upon a complex set of national and international ties, such disintegration would bring human suffering on a scale that has no precedent.[16]

To many people in the industrialised world such problems may appear rather distant, though they attract increasing attention in the media. However we have the greatest responsibility because, though accounting for only one quarter of the world's population, we consume roughly 80 per cent of the world's resources. Moreover, we have the technical and financial ability to overcome many environmental problems. Significantly, the most affluent countries are in the industrial West (with the exception of certain oil-rich nations) and in these Christianity is at its most influential. What would happen if Christians took more seriously the words of Jesus warning of the dangers of accumulating riches on Earth (Matt. 6.19–21)?

Instead, although scientific evidence of the vulnerability and fragility of the Earth is mounting, people's response has so far been wholly inadequate, as if we were sailors moving deckchairs around on the *Titanic*. The sailors failed to avoid a shipwreck; what we face is an ecological catastrophe, an *Earthwreck*.

Hidden dangers

When a new motorway is built over farmland, or effluent is seen in a river, the environmental effect of human activity is clearly visible. Changes currently taking place in our atmosphere are all the more disturbing because they are not visible. Consider some examples. Global warming through the so-called 'greenhouse effect' poses the greatest environmental threat and has been likened by scientists to a gigantic unplanned experiment. The Earth's atmospheric temperature is rising because the amount of carbon dioxide and other gases has been increasing. Due to the burning of fossil fuels and changes in vegetation, especially rainforest destruction, the amount of carbon dioxide in the atmosphere has risen by 25 per

cent since the 1850s. The emission into the atmosphere of
nitrous oxide, methane and other polluting gases has
contributed further to the problem.

Over the past eighty years the Earth's average surface
temperature has risen by about 0.5 °C. The consensus
forecast among scientists is an increase of between 1.5 °C
and 4.5 °C by the year 2030. Such an increase could have a
devastating effect. Sea levels could rise by up to 50 centi-
metres, and as much as 2 metres in the longer term,
because sea water expands when warmed and the ice caps
would melt. Many low-lying regions in Egypt, Holland
and Bangladesh would be flooded even by a 50 centimetre
increase. Serious problems would arise. For example,
around a sixth of Egypt's population would need to be
relocated. The warmer climate and associated changes in
rainfall patterns would affect agriculture, with worrying
implications for world food supplies. A greater incidence of
extremities in weather, such as hurricanes, might occur.

No nation would be unaffected. Low-lying cities such as
New York, Bangkok, Tokyo and London are threatened.
In London, for example, the Thames Barrier, intended to

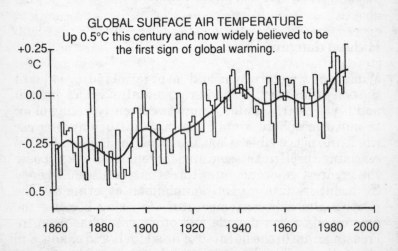

FIG. 1 GLOBAL WARMING
Source: *Nature* Magazine

prevent relatively minor flooding, might instead become nothing more than one of the world's largest underwater monuments. The House of Commons could end up submerged in the River Thames (an unforeseen advantage, some may argue!). Serious flooding in coastal towns and in regions such as East Anglia would only be averted by rehousing and expenditure of billions of pounds on upgraded sea defences. Crop losses throughout the world would push up food prices. Urgent action is needed *now*, by individuals and governments alike, to reduce the emission of carbon dioxide and other greenhouse gases in order that such a scenario can be averted. This should include a major energy conservation initiative, a tree-planting programme, and measures to reduce the need for car journeys.

A second problem relates to the ozone layer in the upper atmosphere, which prevents harmful ultraviolet radiation from reaching the Earth's surface. This causes skin cancers and cataracts. A threat posed by chemicals known as CFCs (chlorofluorocarbons), used in aerosols, foam packaging, insulation products, refrigerators, air conditioning and dry cleaning solvents, has been known about since 1974. By the end of the 1970s most scientists agreed that a serious problem existed, but only after a hole in the ozone layer was discovered in 1985 were practical steps initiated to reduce the use of CFCs. Two more years elapsed before a major international agreement was signed in Montreal. The delay was costly – between 1979 and 1986 the global average total amount of ozone fell by about 5 per cent. The problem is worst over Antarctica, where during the past decade there has been a 30 to 40 per cent reduction in the spring; the Arctic area, too, is now suffering serious depletion. Research into alternatives to CFCs has yet to offer a satisfactory solution, especially for refrigeration purposes.

Similar delays occurred in responding to acid rain. Forests around the world are dying as a result of sulphur dioxide, nitrogen oxides and other gases released into the atmosphere through, in particular, the burning of fossil fuels by industry and in vehicles. These gases combine with rain and snow and fall to the ground as chemically weak, but biologically deadly, sulphuric acid or nitric acid.

The prominence of recent headlines might suggest that acid rain is new, but it was first identified over one hundred years ago and scientists from Sweden and Norway warned of it at the major United Nations environment conference in Stockholm in 1972. Many European countries now have visible damage to more than one-third of their forests. One-half of the forests in West Germany are now dead, dying or in decline. Other countries in central and northern Europe are faring little better. For example, in Scandinavia hundreds of lakes are now too acidic to support fish and other aquatic life.

Buildings, too, suffer serious pollution damage. Friends of the Earth have reported that St Paul's Cathedral, Wells Cathedral, Lincoln Cathedral and many historic buildings in other European cities such as Florence, Cracow, Seville and Cologne have been severely corroded by the cocktail of chemicals in the typical urban atmosphere.

Exposure to sulphur dioxide pollution increases the risk of people suffering from respiratory illness. Latest findings indicate that around one billion of the two billion people living in urban areas suffer levels of sulphur dioxide above or close to those officially regarded as unacceptable. In cities such as New Delhi, Tehran, Wroclaw and Hong Kong the situation has been deteriorating. Although in general air pollution in cities in industrialised countries appears to be on a downward trend, there are notable exceptions. For example, emissions of nitrogen oxides have been increasing in London and Vienna. (Nitric oxide contributes in particular to urban smog and acid rain, and nitrous oxide adds to the greenhouse effect.)

Many of the problems cited above could be substantially reduced if more power stations had flue gas desulphurisation equipment, cars were fitted with catalytic converters, and energy conservation was given a much higher priority.

INTENSITY OF DEFOLIATION IN EUROPEAN COUNTRIES, 1987 (ALL SPECIES)

Intensity of defoliation	Country	% of trees damaged
None	Ireland*	4.1
Low	Hungary	15.0
	Italy	15.3
	Bulgaria	18.3
Moderate	France	31.7
	Yugoslavia	32.2
	Sweden*	32.7
	Finland**	33.4
	Austria	33.5
	Luxembourg	34.6
	Norway*	35.9
	Spain	37.0
	German Dem. Rep.*	37.0
	Belgium	46.5
Severe	Czechoslovakia	52.3
	Germany, Fed. Rep.	52.3
	Liechtenstein	55.0
	Switzerland	56.0
	United Kingdom	56.0
	Netherlands	57.4
	USSR*	58.5
	Denmark	61.0

* conifers only
** preliminary estimate

FIG. 2 TREE DAMAGE IN EUROPE
Source: United Nations Economic Commission for Europe

Plunder and pollution

The planet is constantly being polluted and plundered. Chemical accidents at Seveso in Italy and Bhopal in India, the Chernobyl nuclear disaster in the Soviet Union, and the *Exxon Valdez* oil spill in Alaska are but extreme

ESTIMATED STATE OF RAINFORESTS, 1989

ALREADY GONE:

World total	Over 40% of all tropical forests destroyed
India	All primary rainforest destroyed
Bangladesh	All primary rainforest destroyed
Sri Lanka	All primary rainforest destroyed
Haiti	All primary rainforest destroyed
Ivory Coast	Forest almost entirely logged out
Philippines	55% forest loss between 1960 and 1985
Thailand	45% forest loss between 1961 and 1985
China	50% loss of forest in southern province of Xishuangbana

PREDICTED TO DISAPPEAR:

Brazil	Will lose 63 million hectares by 2000 (an area two and a half times the size of Portugal), 8% of remaining forest
Nigeria	Complete deforestation expected by 2000
Malaysia	Peninsula forest will be exhausted by 1990
Congo	68% of rainforest scheduled to be logged
Thailand	60% of forest remaining in 1981 will be destroyed by 2000
Honduras/Nicaragua	Will lose over 50% of remaining forest by 2000
Ecuador	Will lose over 50% of remaining forest by 2000
Guatemala	Will lose at least 30% of remaining forest by 2000
Columbia	Will lose at least 30% of remaining forest by 2000
Guinea/Madagascar	Will lose 30% of forest by 2000
Ghana	Will lose 26% of remaining forest by 2000
Indonesia	10% of forest remaining in 1981 will be destroyed by 2000

FIG. 3 TROPICAL FORESTS
Source: World Wide Fund For Nature

examples of the abuse which takes place daily. Oil reserves are running low and known reserves of around a quarter of the eighty key minerals in regular use are inadequate to meet anticipated demand over the coming century, including copper, lead, sulphur, tin, tungsten and zinc.

Trees are vital to human survival. Up to two billion people rely on fuelwood for cooking and heating. But widespread forest clearance is bringing a swift end to hundreds of millions of trees each year. The world's forests are disappearing at a rate of 15 million hectares annually, of which over 11 million hectares are in tropical regions. In Brazil alone an area of rainforest the size of Belgium is being destroyed in a single year. Forest clearance is stimulated in the Amazon region through a cattle ranch development programme. Anyone who eats burgers is partly responsible, as this destruction takes place partly to meet the global demand for beef. It is therefore no exaggeration to say that every time that a person bites into a hamburger, a chunk is taken out of the rainforest.

Elsewhere, in once-productive dryland, the process may seem more gradual, but where trees are cut down and not replaced the result is an expanding desert. By the mid 1980s, 230 million people were living on land severely affected by desertification.

No-one knows precisely how many species there are on Earth, but scientists estimate there to be over 30 million, about which detailed knowledge currently extends to a mere 1.4 million. The destruction of important habitats in forests and elsewhere, combined with the trend towards monoculture farming, threatens many species which could well improve upon those presently used. According to most experts, around one hundred species may currently be lost each day and up to a quarter of the Earth's total biological diversity, equivalent to about a million species, faces a serious risk of extinction over the next twenty to thirty years.

Only a small fraction of species with potential value for food, medicine and other uses have so far been utilised.

According to the World Wide Fund for Nature, only 3,000 out of 75,000 plants known to be edible have ever been used for food. Many of our drugs are derived from plants: for example, digoxin and digitoxin from certain foxglove species are used in heart treatment, anti-tumour agents derived from the rosy periwinkle help sufferers from Hodgkins disease and childhood leukaemia, and aspirin is modelled on compounds extracted from white willow bark and fragrant meadowsweet. A mere 5,000 out of 250,000 species of flowering plants have to date been tested for their medical value.

Although tropical forests cover barely 6 per cent of the world's land surface, within them live more than a half, and perhaps nine-tenths, of all animal and plant species. An example of this fecundity is a single tree in Peru which was found to be inhabited with as many species of ants as are in the entire United Kingdom. Thus rainforest destruction is not only contributing to global warming but is seriously threatening global biological diversity.

A less publicised example of environmental degradation is soil erosion. Fertile soil is absolutely vital to other forms of life, and a single inch of topsoil takes hundreds of years to develop. America's 'dust bowl' storms of the 1930s should be a painful reminder of the effects of failing to protect the soil, but even today the planet's outer layer is being scooped off, like icing taken from a cake. This loss of soil, caused by the elimination of tree cover, over-intensive land use and poorly managed irrigation or terracing, amounts to literally tens of billions of tonnes annually. As a result land often becomes no longer fit for growing crops, sometimes desert. In Ethiopia, for example, forest cover has declined from 25 per cent to 3 per cent since 1940 and annual agricultural output is now one million tonnes lower as a result. Elsewhere, rainforests are biologically rich above the surface, but the soil below is relatively poor and on sloping land after deforestation heavy rainfall quickly washes away topsoil.

Rivers and seas are so often treated as sewers or rubbish dumps that it is hardly surprising that so many are unhealthy. Significant pollution affects about 10 per cent of rivers monitored by the UNEP Global Environmental Monitoring System and in many major rivers throughout the world the level of nitrates has been increasing. In Europe levels of nitrates in some rivers are forty-five times the natural average for unpolluted rivers, primarily as a result of 'run-off' from chemicals used in farming. Frequently drinking water is affected, posing a health threat, particularly to children. The seas often fare little better as they are the ultimate destination for much industrial waste, including heavy metals and persistent pesticides. Chaos prevails in the transportation of hazardous waste by sea; ships visit ports only to be refused permission to offload it. Britain has proved more willing than most to act as the world's toxic dustbin – imports of waste material increased tenfold during the early 1980s.

One outcome of our 'throwaway' society is the generation of many kinds of waste; people in Britain on average dispose of waste equivalent to ten times their body weight each year. In Britain nearly 4.5 billion drink cans are thrown away in a single year; if placed end to end they would reach the moon! London seems bad enough, but in Los Angeles people are responsible for creating three times more waste than Londoners!

Consider a simple High Street example. A shopper may buy disposable razors wrapped in disposable plastic packaging which is stapled to a disposable piece of card marketing the product. This may then be placed in a small plastic bag and the shopper offered a further large plastic bag (advertising the store) for this and any other purchases. Though, like the razor, 'disposable', the bags will probably not be biodegradable (i.e. when discarded they will not easily decompose).

Excess waste arises partly because of overpackaging, disposable products and unnecessary purchases, but also because of the inadequate incentives given to repair and recycling activities. For example, used aluminium drink containers can easily be collected for scrap through a deposit scheme. Currently under 30 per cent of aluminium comes from scrap, while experts say that 80 per cent of aluminium could be recycled. Similarly, only one-quarter of the world's paper is recycled, although with greater commitment this could be doubled by the year 2000.

However, of all environmental pollution threats the most dangerous is the nuclear industry. The effects of the Chernobyl nuclear reactor accident in 1986 are still being felt thousands of miles from the site of the accident and will continue for many years to come. A thirty-kilometre evacuation zone had to be established around the site, and around 135,000 people have permanently lost their homes. A disproportionately high number of young children nearby suffer thyroid problems and many mutated farm animals are being born. Even in Britain hundreds of farms are still under Government restrictions because of the radioactive pollution.

Yet as long ago as 1976 a major investigation by the Royal Commission on Environmental Pollution concluded that there should be no significant expansion of nuclear power until a safe means had been found for dealing with nuclear waste, some of which remains radioactive for *250,000 years*. No such means has been found, but the nuclear programme continues, a costly and dangerous extravagance.

We are treating God's creation with such contempt that it is a monumental blasphemy. In energy policy, as elsewhere, consumption is put before conservation. Instead of investing in energy conservation, billions of pounds have been squandered over several decades on nuclear energy, although awareness by private investors in Britain that it is not economic has now forced a long overdue halt to expansion.

The human connection

In considering examples of such abuse it is sometimes too easy to think of the environment as separate from us. But the quality of human life is invariably affected by our treatment of the planet. Any *environmental* problem is equally a *human* problem. The idea that there are 'Green issues' which are separate from 'social issues' is a myth which has persisted for too long.

Nowhere is this seen more starkly than in impoverished countries. As environmental degradation has persisted, and often worsened, increased poverty has followed. People's most basic needs are sufficient food and clean water, though millions lack either or both. More than half of the world's rural population do not have access to clean water and over four-fifths lack adequate sanitation services. All too often the key problem is that families lack adequate land upon which to grow food. In some places the land no longer supports them, through over-use and poor management. Elsewhere it has been unfairly distributed, forcing the poorest people to live on land where long-term cultivation is not possible. The consequence is that at least 500 million people are estimated to be undernourished, and the figure may be even as high as 950 million.

The growth in the world's population puts an accelerating strain on the Earth's resources. The global population rose above five billion in 1987 and current estimates suggest that there will be *an extra three billion mouths to feed* by 2025. However the total amount of land suitable for cultivation is in decline, as the amount being lost through desertification and urbanisation exceeds that newly brought under cultivation. In Africa the problem is most acute, with population growth accelerating, agriculture suffering major problems, and food production per head in decline in many regions.

Prospects of an end to appalling poverty will be in sight only when the affluent have the courage, humility and vision to provide help by demanding a major programme to help those in desperate need.

Many of the problems described in this chapter are brought vividly to life in a recent book by Sean McDonagh, an Irish Columban missionary who for several years worked in the rainforest in the Philippines. *To Care for the*

Earth, one of surprisingly few Christian books on the environment in recent times, is a stimulating study of past insights from, and recent developments in, Roman Catholic thinking. While watching the natural world being – in his own, vivid words – 'torn apart', 'poisoned' and 'raped', McDonagh writes passionately of his experience:

> In the T'boli hills one becomes conscious of the fragility of what is often considered to be a luxuriant environment. Where the tropical forest bloomed in the very recent past, I see today eroded and scarred hills which will only support cogon grass. When I move down from the hill to the plains of South Cotabato I see huge monocrop plantations growing pineapples and bananas. Once again severe erosion caused by torrential rain, wind and sun ensures a very limited life-span for these plantations. The massive use of pesticides, insecticides and herbicides further depletes and poisons the soil. As I drive by, one question is always on my mind – where are the people going to get the land on which to grow food? Above all, where are the children and future generations going to grow the food that they need for an expanding population if these fertile lands are turned into deserts? . . .
>
> Further down the coast I see marine resources being squandered and destroyed. Mangrove swamps and coral reefs, the breeding grounds for a variety of fish, are dynamited, overfished, drained and destroyed. Fish and rice are now staple food for many Filipinos. Yet the supply of fish will dry up unless these destructive practices are reversed.[17]

Seeing these problems at first hand McDonagh concludes that the natural environment can no longer be taken for granted as in the past. We have reached a critical point in time: "If present trends continue, by the turn of the century we will face an ecological catastrophe as irreversible as any nuclear holocaust."[18]

Many other books describe at greater length the issues outlined above and as this book's purpose is to explore the connections with Christianity it is time to turn to a question which Christians in the Green movement very frequently face. Has Christianity been *responsible* for causing this destruction? And if so, have we learnt from our errors, or is Christianity reinforcing negative attitudes to the environment?

Positive or negative?

Christians in the Green movement often appear on the defensive, faced with accusations that Christianity is at least significantly to blame for the present crisis, if not its main source. Among them are many who sense that, even if not primarily responsible, they have at least failed to set a proper example of caring for the Earth.

Attacks on Christianity became increasingly common after 1967, when a lecture was published in the influential magazine *Science* in which Lynn White, an American professor of history, strongly criticised past Christian attitudes to nature.[19] Coming barely a few months after the *Torrey Canyon* oil tanker pollution disaster, his criticism received substantial and prolonged attention. In the late 1960s and early 1970s people were searching for explanations for the emerging environmental crises. White's argument gave attacks on Christianity a certain intellectual credibility.

As a result, several prominent environmentalists voiced public criticism of Christianity, especially of its traditional understanding of the place of humans within the created order. Max Nicholson, for many years Director-General of the Nature Conservancy (now the Nature Conservancy Council), wrote that it was time to "scrub out the complacent image of Man the Conqueror of Nature, and of Man Licensed by God to conduct himself as the earth's worst pest."[20] Others rejected the emphasis of many Christians on individual human salvation. In more recent times leading Green campaigner Jonathon Porritt has addressed the lack of urgency among Church leaders and called for a new understanding of human 'dominion' in terms of ecological responsibility.[21]

In examining the extent to which Christianity is to

blame for environmental damage two questions are particularly important. To what extent has Christianity been the dominant cultural force in the West and so shaped people's attitudes to the rest of nature? And if Christianity is indeed guilty as charged, to what extent are its negative influences essential to a Christian world view?

Lynn White's intention was to show that the disruption of the global environment arose from Western science and technology, and that the development of this stemmed from a Christian view of humankind's relation to nature. Christianity, he argued, had taught that humans are separate from nature, and nature has no purpose other than to meet human needs. Furthermore, it was responsible for overcoming pagan or animist beliefs in independent 'spirit beings' in the natural world, and this meant that nature could more readily be exploited. Moreover, he argued, Christian teaching on the final cause and purpose of life encouraged 'linear' as distinct from 'cyclical' thinking, and so created the basis for an underlying faith in perpetual progress, which was necessary for industrial development.

Without doubt, an essential element in scientific discovery and technological development was the assertion of humankind's power over nature, a willingness to objectify, control and dominate nature. This marked a radical and long-lasting change in humankind's relationship with the rest of the natural world. What is under dispute is the extent to which Christian attitudes enabled the transformation.

It is notable that industrialisation first emerged in countries shaped by Christianity, which motivated scientists such as Isaac Newton and inspired scientific development by, for example, the essayist and Lord Chancellor of England, Francis Bacon. Bacon believed that the purpose of science was to restore to humankind the dominion over creation which was partly lost at the fall. Christianity also found an uneasy tension in attempting to counter the pagan belief that nature is divine without, at the same time, devaluing it and encouraging its exploitation (see later).

But while there is a degree of truth in White's argument, its credibility is weakened by the fact that he and other environmentalist critics have overstated Christianity's impact on Western culture and failed to provide convincing evidence of the causal relationship. In reality Western culture was profoundly influenced by the Enlightenment, which elevated human reason as the arbiter of truth and only accepted Christianity in so far as it could be proved by reasoned argument. Enlightenment thought also laid the basis for optimism about the possibility of progress and the potential of the autonomous individual.

Lynn White, however, asserted that no new set of basic values had been accepted in Western society to displace those of Christianity. This is a serious error. As Wesley Granberg-Michaelson, Director of Church and Society at the World Council of Churches, has argued, "our problem lies in the Church's historical captivity to Western culture, rather than the reverse."[22] No simple description can adequately portray our contemporary pluralist culture but it most definitely cannot properly be labelled 'Christian'. The world view which most accurately describes dominant values in the West is secular humanism, a faith in human autonomy and the essential goodness of humankind. Christianity retains an important, but essentially minor, influence.

One factor which must share any blame is the impact of dualistic thought, attempting to understand the world through two radically different and independent elements. In dualism, more specifically, 'spirit' is regarded as entirely separate from 'matter' and the material world is consequently devalued. Although some people may claim, with some justification, that Christianity has encouraged this distinction, a more considerable influence on Western culture in this respect was the seventeenth-century deist philosopher René Descartes.

Many Greens are thus as critical of Descartes' influence as they are of Christianity.[23] It was through Descartes that a dualistic framework of thought began to penetrate Western culture at the crucial period when the conditions for scientific advance were being established and industrialisation was on the horizon. According to Descartes it was the mind which identified true being: "I think, therefore I am." Only rational beings could have a soul. He believed there to be no purpose, life or spirituality in matter, and imagined that the material world operated like machinery. He compared animals to clocks, with wheels and springs, and even saw the human body as a machine, though he considered human beings to be unique by virtue of their mind and spirit.

Several leading Christian scholars have exposed crucial flaws in the attempt to prove a definitive causal relationship between Christian belief and the destruction of the environment. Apparent connections between Christianity and the scientific development which preceded industrialisation demand careful examination. Professor Thomas Sieger Derr, for example, has contended that Christianity is not a prerequisite for scientific advance, noting that science flourished without its influence in China, ancient Greece and medieval Islam.[24] Indeed scientific leadership only shifted to the West from the Islamic world after Arabic and Greek scientific works were translated into Latin in the late eleventh century. Other scholars have questioned why, if Christianity stimulated technological advance, there were no such developments through the Hebrew culture, which was equally based on Old Testament teaching about human dominion. They also queried why people in non-Christian cultures, which had advanced nature religions or mythologies, made remarkable technological advances, an obvious example being the pyramids built by ancient Egyptians.

Another important response has come from Professor Arthur Peacocke, who drew attention to the fact that exploitation of the natural environment has occurred "from the time of primitive man" and is not specifically associated with Judaeo-Christian societies.[25] French biologist René Dubos argued along similar lines that almost every civilisation, including Hindu and Buddhist cultures, had abused their environment to some degree by deforestation and overgrazing.[26]

Furthermore, there have been different attitudes to life even *within* Christian traditions. Cultural temperament and tradition make a difference to how theology develops and attitudes to science and technology are determined. As Christianity is inevitably understood within a particular cultural context, certain elements of Christian understanding (though not foundational truths) vary throughout the world. For example, the Eastern Orthodox Church has a different, more mystical understanding of the material world compared with the Church in the West. But Christians in the West, so often wary of philosophical influences perceived to be of Eastern origin, have tended to ignore non-Western Christian perspectives. This is unfortunate, as the Eastern Orthodox tradition can offer a helpful perspective on the relationship between God, humankind and the rest of creation and provide fresh biblical insights into our relationship to the natural environment.

A penetrating historical study of Christian teaching, Paul Santmire's *The Travail of Nature*, reveals two contrasting strands within Christianity, one of which affirms the value of nature, the other viewing nature negatively.

In the nature-affirming tradition there is an understanding of the human spirit's rootedness in the world of nature and a recognition of people's instinctive desire to celebrate God's presence in and with the biosphere. Santmire cites as examples of theologians in this tradition Irenaeus, the 'mature' Augustine, St Francis and 'to a significant degree' Luther and Calvin.[27] Many early Christians, notably those in the Celtic tradition, are reputed to have lived with a particular respect for animals, birds and other species; often they chose to live in wild and remote areas. Some of the legends are scarcely credible. In one such legend Colman, described as a 'well organised Hibernian', was said to have a cock to announce his devotional hour, a mouse to nibble his ear if he overslept, and a fly to mark his place on the page where he stopped reading!

On the other hand, there *also* exists within Christianity a nature-denying tradition, in which nature is regarded as of no intrinsic worth and the world is not considered humankind's 'proper' home. A commonly used image or metaphor is the human spirit rising 'above' nature in order to attain communion with God. Origen, Bonaventure, Dante and, more recently, Barth and Teilhard de Chardin, are suggested by Santmire as theologians in this tradition.[28]

It is significant that this negative nature-denying strand of Christianity tended to be dominant at the start of the Industrial Revolution, being more easily accommodated with the prevailing dualistic philosophy, which itself devalued the material world. Christianity is thus not entirely without blame, although, as Santmire's study shows, this negative tradition is only one interpretation of the Christian faith and its validity is under dispute.

To conclude, Lynn White's claim that Christian belief was an essential factor in industrialisation is disputable. The application of scientific thinking stemmed as much from the optimistic climate of secular Enlightenment thought. Thus the fact that industrialisation first occurred in the West was as much the result of *cultural* factors as of factors constitutive to Christianity.

Throughout the modern industrial era, Christianity has very often been interpreted in terms of the relationship of God to *people* as distinct from the whole creation. Humankind has been placed at the centre of God's universe.[29] This continues despite the grave ecological crisis. If this is to be solved Christianity must become less human-centred and more concerned with relationships in the whole of creation. It is this to which we now turn.

Summary

This opening chapter has introduced some preliminary ideas about ecology, nature and the natural environment. These suggest that our perception of the Earth and whether we see ourselves as part of or separate from nature affect how we treat it.

We are wrecking the Earth. Evidence of a wide range of global environmental crises suggests that it can no longer be assumed that life on Earth will inevitably continue much as in the past. We are witnessing what an eminent theologian recently referred to as a 'life and death struggle' for the future of creation.[30]

No real purpose can be served in dwelling unduly upon whether Christianity has been the major factor behind this damage. A combination of influences have been at work, and the assumptions of secular humanism which also have influenced our modern industrial culture cannot escape blame. It is, ultimately, more constructive to consider whether Christianity can become a positive force for change.

This change must take place at all levels – in our households, churches and the local community, in local and national government, and through international agencies. We should, in particular, reflect upon the processes by which our wealth is obtained and used.

1 Declining church membership may be considered an indication (if not proof) of smaller numbers having a Christian faith. See D. Barrett, *World Christian Encyclopedia*, New York: OUP, 1982.
2 The term 'pagan' is used here as belief in the inherent self-regulating and self-perpetuating powers of the Earth. For a fuller discussion, see Chapter Five.
3 Donald Worster, *Nature's Economy*, p. 342.
4 Barbara Ward and René Dubos, *Only One Earth*, p. 31.
5 World Commission on Environment and Development, *Our Common Future*, p. 1.

6 Mother Julian of Norwich, *Revelations of Divine Love*, p. 68.
7 Cited in Wesley Granberg-Michaelson (ed.), *Tending the Garden*, pp. 15–16.
8 ibid., p. 59.
9 Albert M. Wolters, *Creation Regained*, p. 49.
10 Cited in Granberg-Michaelson, p. 85.
11 I am indebted for Hebrew and Greek translations in this section to Paulos Mar Gregorios in Granberg-Michaelson, op. cit., p. 86, and in his own *The Human Presence*, pp. 20–21, and to Albert Wolters, op. cit., p. 25.
12 Kallistos Ware, *The Orthodox Way*, p. 67.
13 Cited in Granberg-Michaelson, pp. 57, 61.
14 These have included *Blueprint for Survival* (1972); *The Limits to Growth* (1972); *World Conservation Strategy* (1980); *The Global 2000 Report to the President* (1980); and *Our Common Future* (1987).
15 Most of the data in the following section is taken from World Resources Institute/International Institute for Environment and Development/United Nations Environment Programme, *World Resources 1988–89*; the United Nations Environment Programme, *The State of the World Environment 1989*; the World Commission on Environment and Development, *Our Common Future*; and Norman Myers (ed.), *The Gaia Atlas of Planet Management*.
16 United Nations Environment Programme, *The State of the World Environment 1989*, Nairobi: UNEP, p. 16.
17 Sean McDonagh, *To Care for the Earth*, p. 9.
18 ibid., p. 11.
19 Lynn White Jr, 'The Historical Roots of Our Ecologic(al) Crisis', *Science*, Vol. 155, No. 3767, 10th March 1967, pp. 1203–7.
20 Max Nicholson, *The Environmental Revolution*, p. 303.
21 Jonathon Porritt, *Seeing Green*, pp. 209–10.
22 Wesley Granberg-Michaelson, 'Why Christians Lost an Environmental Ethic', *Epiphany Journal*, Winter 1988, p. 43.
23 See, for example, Fritjof Capra, *The Turning Point*, pp. 41–8.
24 Thomas Sieger Derr, *Ecology and Human Liberation*, pp. 18–19.
25 Cited in Hugh Montefiore (ed.), *Man and Nature*, p. 156.
26 See Sean McDonagh, p. 137.
27 H. Paul Santmire, *The Travail of Nature*, p. 217.
28 ibid., p. 216.
29 Lynn White described Christianity as "the most anthropocentric religion the world has seen." Lynn White, op. cit., p. 1205.
30 Jürgen Moltmann, *God in Creation*, p. xi.

2

TO RULE THE EARTH:
Dominion and stewardship

Humans have a powerful position within the created order. We can mould and shape the environment to an extent matched by no other living species. We have the potential to destroy the world in a nuclear war. Our activities can affect the upper reaches of the Earth's atmosphere or pollute the deepest ocean; we can leave the land rich in species or barren desert.

Those who blame Christianity for encouraging negative attitudes to the environment argue that it explicitly sanctions the destructive power of humankind over nature. With justification, it is pointed out that much Christian teaching is focused almost exclusively upon individuals and the impression is given that nature has no purpose other than to serve humankind.

However, the appalling plight of the environment is leading many Christians to reconsider the place of humankind in relation to the rest of nature. We reject the fallacy that God lacks interest in the wellbeing of other parts of His creation. As this chapter will show, although we may regard ourselves as, in a sense, above nature and separate from it, nonetheless we are living within nature as part of it and are thus dependent on the biological life-support systems created by God.

Creating with the Creator

The Bible and Church tradition bear witness to the essential Christian belief that God is the creator and provider of all things. A psalmist wrote: "You open your hand and satisfy the desires of every living thing" (Ps. 145.16), while the apostle Paul acknowledged "God, who richly provides us with everything for our enjoyment" (1 Tim. 6.17). The same belief is conveyed in the traditional creeds used by the Church. The Nicene Creed affirms Christian belief in "one God, the Father almighty, maker of all things visible and invisible"; the Apostles' Creed starts with the words: "I believe in God the Father almighty, creator of heaven and earth."

In the past when Christians have discussed creation, the debate has tended to dwell at undue length upon whether the six days referred to in Genesis are meant literally or whether humans evolved from apes. Obviously this question of interpretation is of significance, especially as regards alleged conflict between science and religion, but it has diverted Christians from other important insights in the early chapters of Genesis. For example, if Christianity is to make any sense at all of current trends on our planet, environmental change has to be seen in the context of our response to God's *continuing* activity and *constant* interaction with creation. Creation has been wrongly treated as a single historical event. In fact it is less appropriate to use the past tense than the continuous present. Thus, writes Orthodox Bishop Kallistos Ware: "We should say, not 'God made the world, and me in it', but 'God *is making* the world, and me in it, here and now, at this moment and always.' Creation is not an event in the past, but a relationship in the present."[1]

Only through the sustaining power of God does life continue. God did not make His creation in such a way that it is autonomous and self-sustaining. Contrary to deism, He is not merely *first cause* of our world, a cosmic clockmaker who wound up the machinery of the planet and lets it run, but a '*continual Creator*', actively present today. Creation continues because "the Lord is the everlasting God, the Creator of the ends of the earth" who "will not grow tired or weary" (Isa. 40.28). Just as the Spirit of God was present at the very beginning of time, so the

Earth remains full of creatures only because God breathes life into them through His Spirit (Gen. 1.2; Ps. 104.24–30).

There is a tale of a proud head gardener showing some distinguished visitors around the estate. One of them remarks, "It is indeed marvellous what God and man can do together." Another, rather less impressed, retorts, "Yes, but you should have seen it when God had it to Himself." It is humans who are responsible for the ongoing destruction and therefore obviously necessary to look at how humankind fits into the picture.

People are inextricably part of nature, being formed from dust (or, more precisely, the surface matter of the ground), into which God breathed "the breath of life" (Gen. 2.7). This established two significant links in the chain of being; people are made by the power of God, in His image, and are made from the Earth.[2]

Made in His likeness, we have minds with which to make sense of the world around us and free will with which to choose whether to create with, or against, the will of God. We are creative beings who constantly change the world from one state into another, bringing His creation to its fulfilment.[3] Made from the Earth, we form part of the living community of species interlinked with the soil. Harming other species in the community is thus like threatening to cut off our personal life-support system.

Christians in the Eastern Orthodox tradition speak of humankind's role as *mediator* between God and creation and see Christ as our model, as the supreme mediator.[4] When we respond positively to God a bridge of mutual love is formed between Creator and creation which is life-sustaining. The Church is called to offer creation back to God, "to love the world, creation, and to show it the way back to God, the creator."[5] It is through us that God manifests Himself to creation and redeems it, and at the judgement creation responds by rejoicing, as when Christians are 'revealed' matter will be set free from its 'bondage to decay' (Ps. 96.10–13; 98.4–9; Rom. 8.21).

Through exercising our free will to choose whether or not to act in line with the will of God, we determine the immediate fate of the Earth. People may thus be thought of as co-workers with God in creation. One person plants a seed, another waters it, while God makes it grow (1 Cor. 3.7). God created in such a way as to allow humankind the ability to shape the future condition of the universe. What an awesome responsibility!

Control and freedom

If humankind has this great freedom, however, to what extent is God actually in control of His creation? He judges men and women to determine the fate of their 'spiritual bodies' – He is in control of our *ultimate* destinies (1 Cor. 15.35–49). But what of the present? To understand God more fully in this respect we need to reflect upon how He interacts with His creation.

It is easy to see how people determine what happens physically in the *material* world. Though our perception of spiritual processes may be poor, the material changes which take place before our eyes in the physical world are clearly visible. One year people in Brazil or the Philippines can see the rainforest around them, the next year they cannot. There is no room for doubt! But what of the underlying spiritual powers at work? God's apparent choice not to preserve the diversity of creation is disconcerting.

This raises questions concerning the extent to which God compels, the extent to which He *determines* that His will must prevail. If God always intervened humans would no longer have free will and the order of creation would have to be substantially different; He chooses instead to offer freedom. Although He has created universal laws of nature to operate, His creation is diverse – full of uniqueness and individuality – because He leaves room for differing responses from species within His creation. There is order, but not *inevitability*.

This suggests that God must, in a sense, be vulnerable. This may seem to conflict with conventional teaching that

He is all-powerful, but there is no necessary contradiction. God *freely* chooses not to exert His authority and power at all times, knowing that if He did so the order of His creation would change and ultimately be predetermined. However, this choice not to coerce inevitably leaves God susceptible to disappointment. If intimately involved in His creation God surely feels pain when humans, whom He created as free agents, make choices against His will.

In the past century a new school of thought, known as process theology, has been developed in response to this question. Influenced by the philosophy of Alfred White-head, process theology focuses on the development of the world, and how God orders and preserves it, rather than on reasons for its existence. Ideas relating to existence or *being* are treated as less vital than those about *becoming*. Process theology does not *equate* God and the world, but it suggests that God has chosen to take the uncertain outcome of the life of created things into His very being. In consequence the world conditions God's activity and may even, perhaps, constrain Him. Moreover, process theology stresses that God seeks to influence His created entities by *persuasion* rather than *compulsion* (see also Chapter Five).

One of the problems with such thinking is that it appears to challenge, if not contradict, the sovereignty of God. Christians like to cling to certainty, the sense of security that ultimately there is someone 'in charge'; however, free will demands a degree of uncertainty in life. The insights of process theology cannot be totally dismissed unless God is understood as wholly separate from His creation. Ultimately God's sovereignty rests in the fact that He retains coercive power *at His disposal*, which He may or may not choose to use. God is neither bound by nature, nor by the human will. He is the source of love, and it is in the nature of love to allow others opportunities to respond freely to that love.

The human ascent

The poet Robert Burns wrote that he was

> truly sorry man's dominion
> Has broken nature's social union.[6]

We destroy our earthly home partly because we distance ourselves and God from nature. Nature is no longer viewed as divine, or even as sacred, and is consequently devalued when, seeing ourselves as separate from nature, we *objectify* it. People look upon nature as the world 'out there', an expansive external area of infinite possibilities to explore, control and dominate. The history of the relationship between humankind and the rest of nature reveals how the biblical doctrine of human dominion has been confused and abused.

According to some historians, people in the early Middle Ages did not feel 'isolated' from nature to the same extent as people do in the modern world. They had a deeper sense of their integration with the external environment and felt a part of nature, aware of vulnerability to extremities of weather. Wesley Granberg-Michaelson cites an analogy comparing the different eras – in the past, people saw themselves in relation to their surroundings as an embryo; in the present, they see themselves as an island.[7] The former is linked to its surrounding environment, while the latter is distinctly separate.

As the modern scientific age unfolded people believed that the world had been created for the sole benefit of humankind, and that humankind had a pivotal place in the created order. The influence of the thirteenth-century theologian Thomas Aquinas was profound. Aquinas stressed the distance between God and His creation, using the long-established theological idea of a 'hierarchy of being'. He wrote that just as "imperfect beings serve the needs of more noble beings", so it followed that "plants draw their nutriment from the earth, animals feed on plants, and these in turn serve man's use."[8] It followed that "lifeless beings exist for living beings, plants for animals, and the latter for man."[9] To Aquinas the whole of nature was subordinate to human needs: "The life of animals and plants is preserved not for themselves but for man."[10]

The pivotal place of humankind continued in the thought of Francis Bacon, who wrote around the turn of the sixteenth century that people "may be regarded as the centre of the world" and if they were taken from the world "the rest would seem to be all astray, without aim or purpose."[11] In *Man and the Natural World*, a fascinating study of attitudes to nature in the Tudor and Stuart periods, historian Keith Thomas describes the 'breathtaking anthropocentric spirit' in which preachers of that era understood their faith. 'Human ascendancy' was considered central to the Divine plan.

Every animal was thought to serve some human purpose, whether practical, moral or aesthetic:

> Savage beasts were necessary instruments of God's wrath, left among us 'to be our schoolmasters' ... they fostered human courage and provided useful training for war. Horseflies ... had been created so 'that men should exercise their wits and industry to guard themselves against them.' Apes and parrots had been ordained 'for man's mirth'. Singing-birds were devised 'on purpose to entertain and delight mankind'. The lobster ... served several purposes in one: it provided men with food, for they could eat its flesh; with exercise, for they had first to crack its legs and claws; and with an object of contemplation, for they could behold its wonderful suit of armour.[12]

As people sought to prove that animals had been carefully designed and distributed to meet human needs, their explanations became so contrived that logic was turned on its head. The louse was thought indispensable "because it provided a powerful incentive to habits of cleanliness."[13] A seventeenth-century preacher explained that savage beasts were designated to live in deserts "where they may do less harm", seeming to discount the possibility that people might choose not to settle close to them![14] Equally unconvincingly George Cheyne, a physician, explained that "the Creator made horse's excrement smell sweet, because he knew that men would often be in its vicinity."[15] And the fact that fish came in shoals to the seashore was considered a sign that they were intended for human use.

The primary justification for this human arrogance was a belief in fundamental differences from other species. Physical attributes and skills considered lacking in other creatures were cited in defence, such as the human capacity to laugh, cook, use tools and own property. Speech was stressed, as was reason – an intellectual superiority from which, it was said, came a superior memory, greater imagination, curiosity, a sense of time, a sharper concept of the future, the use of numbers, a sense of beauty, and the capacity for progress. Others argued that humans were, quite simply, more beautiful and perfectly formed than any other animal. It was pointed out that 'beasts' look down, while humans stand erect, as if looking up to heaven. However, most decisive of all was the belief that people acted through free will rather than from instinct alone, and had consciences, a sense of the religious, and an immortal soul.

This long-standing belief in human supremacy began to change somewhat as interest developed in natural history. Initially animals and plants were analysed and classified in terms of their usefulness to humankind, but increasingly naturalists studied them out of sheer curiosity. In 1691, after a lifetime spent classifying animals and plants, taxonomist John Ray wrote in *The Wisdom of God manifested in the Works of Creation*:

> It is a generally received opinion that all this visible world was created for Man; [and] that Man is the end of the Creation, as if there were no other end of any creature but some way or other to be serviceable to man . . . But though this be vulgarly received, yet wise men nowadays think otherwise.[16]

By the start of the eighteenth century, the belief that the world had been created solely for our benefit was viewed as a sign of human arrogance. It was increasingly accepted that other creatures exist to reflect divine glory as well as to meet human needs. Before long, however, in another significant trend, the foundations of modern secular humanism were laid through the philosophy of the Enlightenment. Enlightenment thinkers not only reinforced belief in the superiority of human beings over the rest of nature; they also had a desire for autonomy from God, which they expressed through deism.

Kings of creation?

In the second half of the nineteenth century, Charles Darwin's books *The Origin of Species* and *The Descent of Man* made a considerable impression as, in support of his theory that humans evolved from apes, he pointed to the similarities between humans and other animals.

One contemporary Christian environmentalist has suggested that to emphasise our link with nature is "to indulge a half-truth". It is precisely *because* of our uniqueness that we have special responsibility for the rest of nature.[17] If humans were not fundamentally different from other species, we would have no more responsibility for the natural environment than has, say, a hedgehog. Acting mainly through instinct, we would have no special moral duty to preserve our future, or that of other species.

It is through the self-reflective consciousness, which (as far as we can tell) God has given uniquely to humans, that we see the morality and wisdom of modifying our present path of development. Thus our special place in creation means that we have a *greater* responsibility to ensure that God's intended purposes for creation are realised. Being made in His image we alone have the capacity to exercise free choice in responding to Him, with the potential to act on God's behalf, as it were, to carry out His will. Our 'mandate' is distinctly different from that given to birds and fish (compare verses 22 and 28 of Genesis 1). In what sense does this mean, however, that we are called to 'rule over' the world?

Christians use the creation story in Genesis as the foundation for defining our proper relationship with the rest of nature. This describes the creational and cultural mandate which has had such a central place in Christian teaching on the use and value of nature. The author of Genesis states that God declared:

> Let us make man in our image, in our likeness, and let them rule over the fish of the sea and the birds of the air, over the livestock, over all the earth, and over all the creatures that move along the ground. (Gen. 1.26)

Then, having created the first humans, God blessed them and said:

> Be fruitful and increase in number; fill the earth and subdue it. Rule over the fish of the sea and the birds of the air and over every living creature that moves on the ground. (Gen. 1.28)

The Bible portrays humankind as very special to God. We have a distinctly different status from the rest of God's creation, between heavenly beings and other living creatures. In this sense humans are 'higher' than other creatures:

> You made him a little lower than the heavenly beings and crowned him with glory and honour. You made him ruler over the works of your hands; you put everything under his feet: all flocks and herds, and the beasts of the field, the birds of the air, and the fish of the sea, all that swim the paths of the seas. (Ps. 8.5–7)

Taking these texts alone, it may not appear surprising that some Christians have tolerated – if not encouraged – environmental abuse by asserting that humankind has *unrestrained* authority over the rest of nature, through this special position in creation. If people are to 'rule over' (the King James Version uses the phrase 'have dominion over') creation they are, it has often been claimed, entitled to assert their will over other species.

The crucial question, though, is whether exploitation which arises from the call to rule over and subdue the Earth is the result of misguided application of Christian teaching, or whether the very force of this instruction is *constitutive* to Christianity, that is to say essential and permanent. Terms such as 'rule over' and 'subdue' need careful definition, and the passage must be interpreted in the context in which it was written and is to be applied, and in the light of the Bible as a whole. The Hebrew word *kabash*, from which 'subdue' is derived, suggests treading down, or conquering. The term *radah* in Hebrew, from which 'rule over' is derived, resembles the verb to trample.[18] However, use of this strong language becomes more understandable when it is recognised that the focus is limited to the *ground*. Thus, suggests Wesley Granberg-Michaelson: "For a people at the dawn of creation, subject to the forces of nature and facing the task of establishing agriculture, instructions to take the ground under control in order to produce food would make sense."[19]

In other words, several thousands of years ago forceful language was appropriate to sanction primitive people to use their power to force nature to meet their needs. Even in the current age the state of the land in the poorest regions makes food difficult to grow and often the land needs treatment before it can be fertile; in these circumstances the strong language of Genesis seems fitting. In the struggle for mere survival, human force against the elements is often necessary. The problems arise when the force used is unwarranted or undisciplined and applied with little foresight.

Appropriate development of the Earth, so that it is kept fertile for future generations, demands that people restrain themselves when 'treading upon it'. The Earth should be given periods of rest, which allow its fertility to be regained through natural processes (for which biblical support is given in the sabbatical laws – see below).

It is significant that immediately prior to this crucial

passage is a proclamation that people are made in the 'image' of God. This phrase suggests that certain attributes of God (such as will-power, speech, observation and judgement) have been passed to humans. It becomes our responsibility to use them wisely to serve and sustain the whole creation for the sake of its Creator-owner. In *Imaging God* Professor Douglas Hall argues that the image of God is not an *endowment*, something that people *have*, but, rather, defines an active relationship to God through which we become more like Him, representative of Him. Hall uses the term 'image' as a verb rather than a noun; people are called *to* image God.

Augustine, considered by many to be the Father of Western theology, did not understand dominion in terms of an 'operational status', a God-given right to reshape the Earth by exercising power over other creatures. He saw it instead as the ability of the human mind to know the ways and the will of God, to perceive 'the things of the Spirit of God' in a way that other creatures cannot. Another insight is that of Gregory of Nyssa, a contemporary of Augustine who wrote from an Eastern theological perspective. Gregory believed that humankind had to *acquire* dominion by personal effort. In this context Paulos Gregorios writes that "we best see the royal stature of man in those who have become really free by learning to control their own wills."[20]

In the Bible kingship is linked with *servanthood*. Jesus Christ, the 'King of kings', said that he "did not come to be served, but to serve" (Matt. 20.28). He "did not consider equality with God something to be grasped, but made himself nothing, taking the very nature of a servant" (Phil. 2.6,7). The imagery used in Genesis reflects the idea of a 'shepherd king' who is totally responsible for the welfare of his subjects. Jesus and David are both identified as 'shepherd kings'. God said to David: "You shall shepherd my people Israel, and you shall become their ruler" (2 Sam. 5.2). Jesus, the 'son' of David, was "the good shepherd", who "lays down his life for the sheep" (John 10.11; cf. Matt. 2.6). The shepherd cares, feeds, protects.

Human dominion does *not*, therefore, involve unrestrained authority. Immediately after the creational mandate certain limits are placed upon this authority – people are told that they may use vegetation alone for food (Gen. 1.29–30). Eating meat was not sanctioned until after the flood (see Chapter Seven). The tree of knowledge in the Garden of Eden may similarly be seen as a symbol of the limits to human sovereignty. The Old Testament rulers were never given autocratic power; with the authority of kingship came the demand to act with justice, obedience and righteousness, which then would lead to peace. Dominion is thus to be seen not as a licence to exploit and kill, but as a calling to recognise with humility the responsibilities which its authority confers upon us.

Caretakers

The myth of unrestrained dominion has persisted despite God's intention, expressed in the second chapter of Genesis, that our responsibility on Earth is "to work it and take care of it" (Gen. 2.15). The Hebrew words used are very revealing; *abad* means to work in the sense of serving (the equivalent noun means servant or slave), and *shamar* suggests a watchful care and preservation.[21] This puts a proper perspective on the earlier text. We are to serve the needs of the Earth and to preserve it.

The Bible calls us to be Earth's caretakers. We are free to use the Earth for our benefit, because the material world is good, but our duty is to use it *responsibly*. It is to be treated with the very special care of a gardener looking after a small plot of land.

There is wisdom in thinking of the fruits of the Spirit as we seek the benefit of the fruits of the soil (cf. Gal. 5.22):

> LOVE God's creation,
> have JOY in it,
> pursue PEACE with it,
> have PATIENCE with natural processes,

be KIND and GOOD towards it,
be FAITHFUL in our stewardship of it,
be GENTLE with it, and
exercise SELF CONTROL in our demands on it.[22]

People often assume power over the natural environment on the basis that it is subject to their control because they *own* it. The very concept of 'owning' nature suggests that it may be treated as a commodity, although, as explained earlier, such a view of nature as an entity, existing without reference to God, is alien to biblical thought. Creation, in the sense of a continuous process in which God is making the world, obviously cannot be owned. The Bible is emphatic that it is God who owns the natural environment:

The earth is the Lord's, and everything in it, the world, and all who live in it. (Ps. 24.1)

The heavens are yours, and yours also the earth; you founded the world and all that is in it. (Ps. 89.11)

Yours, O Lord, is the greatness and the power and the glory and the majesty and the splendour, for everything in heaven and earth is yours. (1 Chron. 29.11)

The term 'stewardship' has come to be used to describe environmental responsibility. The steward is a responsible servant who takes care of something in the 'absence' of its landlord or master, perhaps a king or ruler.[23] Thus, for example, when God instructs the Israelites: "The land must not be sold permanently, because the land is mine and you are but aliens and my tenants" (Lev. 25.23), this reveals a fundamental principle.

In the New Testament the concept of stewardship is broadened in various parables, notably those of the tenants (Matt. 21.33–44), the talents (Matt. 25.14–29) and the ten minas (Luke 19.11–27), and in Jesus's warning of the need for servants to be watchful (Luke 12.35–48). While often there is controversy over the extent to which records of material events *merely* explain

spiritual truths or are literal happenings, to be meaning-
ful these sayings must necessarily affirm an underlying
principle in the material domain.[24]

Luke records in Acts that the early Christians took
the principle of stewardship to mean that their private
property should be shared:

> All the believers were one in heart and mind. No-one claimed
> that any of his possessions was his own, but they shared
> everything they had . . . There were no needy persons among
> them. For from time to time those who owned land or houses
> sold them, brought the money from the sales and put it at the
> apostles' feet, and it was distributed to anyone as he had need.
> (Acts 4.32,34–35)

They thereby integrated the material and the spiritual
aspects of their lives, recognising that for true unity they
had to be 'one' not only in heart and mind, but in their
material possessions. They were also aware of Jesus's
teachings about hoarding wealth and, expecting his return to be very soon, they understandably would not have
regarded ownership of material things as important.

The early Benedictine movement is often cited as a
good example of creative stewardship of the Earth. Rejecting the emphasis placed by Greek scholars upon rational
study and the severe asceticism which was increasingly
common in monastic life, Benedict viewed manual work
positively. He appreciated working in close proximity to
the soil and sought to live in harmony with nature. He
insisted that each monastery was self-sufficient and the
monks thus had to learn to rear livestock and cultivate
land using renewable methods, in order that the fertility
of the soil was maintained.

As noted in Chapter One, the rise of industrialism is
often associated with Protestant reformers, such as John
Calvin, who believed that the Earth was created essentially for use by humankind. However Calvin himself
declared that each person should be regarded as a
'steward', believing that we have only been provided with

the Earth's resources on the condition "that, being content with a frugal and moderate use of them, we should take care of what shall remain."[25] He wrote also that, "If I want to plunder the earth of what God has given it for the nourishment of men . . . I want to bring to nothing the goodness of God."[26] This is not so much to defend Calvinism as to suggest that Calvin's own teachings seem not to have been put into practice by many of his supporters.

In recent times this concept of stewardship is often mistakenly understood solely in the context of financing the Church. The first thought it brings to many people's minds is appeals for church building improvements! It has become too closely identified with raising money for the needs of the Church, instead of using appropriately *all* of the resources which God has entrusted to us – our time, energy and money, and especially the gift of God's creation.

Christians need to understand stewardship in this broader sense. As regards the natural environment, use of the term 'stewardship' is helpful, but not wholly satisfactory. Earlier, the ecological crisis was explained as a crisis of *perception*, relating to how people see the world. The concept of 'stewardship' has attracted criticism because it may be thought to imply that human beings are apart from the rest of nature. Thus, writes Paulos Gregorios:

> Replacing the concept of domination with the concept of stewardship will not lead us very far, for even in the latter there lies the hidden possibility of the objectification and alienation which are the root causes of the sickness of our civilisation . . . We would still be reducing nature to 'nothing but . . .' that is, nothing but an object given into our hands for safe keeping and good management.[27]

In other words, nature is not to be treated as something 'out there'. It must no longer be considered an object, something outside of ourselves. E. F. Schumacher, author of *Small is Beautiful*, wrote of his concern that people do not experience themselves as a part of nature but as an outside force destined to dominate and conquer it. He warned of talk of doing battle with nature which leads us to forget that if we won this battle, we would, paradoxically, "find ourselves on the losing side".[28] Acknowledging that we are *part* of nature is absolutely essential to solving the environmental crises.

Thus, while valuable in pointing to responsibility for the future, the stewardship model for our relationship with nature has certain limitations. Other critics have argued that as well as reinforcing the separation of humans from the rest of nature, it appeals mainly to individual responsibility and so may divert attention from problems rooted in society's economic and political structures. The implication would be that there is no need for political reform so long as individuals try to be good stewards of their personal possessions. Finally, for the many millions of people who are poverty-stricken and own nothing, the concept of stewardship is, of course, largely meaningless.

One alternative is a model of *companionship*, highlighting the significance of empathy and interdependence within nature. This idea was developed for a Church of Scotland project on land use by Ruth Page.[29] Companionship expresses the fact that as people co-exist with other species there is interaction, whilst each species retains its separate identity. True companionship expresses a love for the environment and such a relationship might tend to prevent an adversarial or confrontational attitude. It acknowledges that all living species share this planet, as part of what Jürgen Moltmann has termed the 'community of creation' and Sean McDonagh the 'Earth community'.

Justice, restraint and the land

Timeless principles concerning the proper use of resources may be found in Old Testament laws. These suggest that the accumulation of wealth, the maximisation of output from the land and cruelty towards animals are against the will of God (the latter is discussed in Chapter Seven). Instead, the law demanded justice, restraint and compassion.

Resources, specifically land, were to be allocated fairly. Each Israelite family was entitled to a plot of land, received as an inheritance, which was expected to remain within the family (Num. 26.52–6). From the time when the Israelites settled in Canaan any casual purchase or sale of land was frowned upon (1 Kgs. 21.3). Laws of 'redemption' were intended to ensure that if land ever had to be sold it should remain within the same family – a family would never lose its land permanently, as any land sold had to be returned in the Year of Jubilee (see below). Such laws were founded on a high regard for the family unit and were intended to prevent a gulf in wealth between rich landowners and poor labourers.[30] Any sale of land was supposed to be a temporary arrangement, the land being valued by the number of years of available crops until the next Jubilee (Lev. 25.8–28). Small-scale, family-based production was, it would appear, recognised as the norm; the ideal was for each family to be largely self-reliant, having its own fig tree and vine (Mic. 4.4).

Old Testament writers acknowledge the importance of land being allocated fairly for justice to prevail. Under the kings, beginning with David and Solomon, a new class of wealthy rulers and officials bought up land and accumulated large estates. Differences in wealth became apparent – in the tenth century BC houses tended to be the same size, but by the eighth century BC certain houses were evidently better than others and located together. The powerless were oppressed (Mic. 2.2). Consequently the prophets had to speak out against those "who add house to house and join field to field" (Isa. 5.8).

A further Old Testament principle was to acknowledge the importance of restraint and not to seek to maximise production from the land. The sabbath principle is one of periodical non-intervention in the environment, reflecting God's day of rest after the six days of creation. As theologian Jürgen Moltmann points out, it is the peace of the sabbath which distinguishes the view of the world as *creation* from the view of the world as *nature*. Though nature has seasons and cycles, it is unremittingly fruitful. It is the sabbath, a designated time of non-intervention, of rest, reflection and thanksgiving, which reveals the world to be God's creation.[31]

Work was forbidden on the Sabbath day, which would provide rest for people and their animals (Exod. 20.8–11). The land, too, needed rest and the sabbath principle was applied in cycles every seven years:

> For six years you are to sow your fields and harvest the crops, but during the seventh year let the land lie unploughed and unused. Then the poor among your people may get food from it, and the wild animals may eat what they leave. Do the same with your vineyard and your olive grove. (Exod. 23.10–11)

During this sabbath year the land would recover its fertility and time normally spent farming could be devoted to study.

After seven sabbath years (i.e. forty-nine years) came a very special occasion, the Year of Jubilee, in which liberty was proclaimed throughout the land. This brought together the principles of justice and restraint. Land and property were to be returned to their original owners, and no crops could be sown or reaped, nor vines harvested; the people were to eat what was to be found in the fields. As the Jubilee followed a sabbath year the people were understandably rather concerned as to what they would eat, but God assured them that if they obeyed His laws "the land will yield its fruit, and you will eat your fill and live there in safety" (Lev. 25.19). He promised: "I will send you such a blessing in the sixth year that the land will yield enough for three years" (Lev. 25.21).

Such laws were a sign to the Israelites that the land was not their own and encouraged them to trust in God. Scholars are uncertain as to the extent to which they were kept. Breaches are indeed implied when it is explicitly said that the land enjoyed its sabbath rests during the exile to Babylon (2 Chron. 36.21 and, in the Apocrypha, 1 Macc. 6.48–54; cf. Lev. 26.34–5). But it cannot reasonably be argued that these laws are irrelevant today because they were not always implemented in Old Testament times! The *principles* established relating to restraint and justice in our relationships, were instituted because God knows that they improve the quality of life. These are as valid as ever. Indeed the Year of Jubilee foreshadowed the coming of Christ, the 'year of the Lord's favour' (Isa. 61.1–11; cf. Luke 4.17–21). When Jesus proclaimed that he had come to bring good news to the poor, quoting Isaiah, his message must have been understood to imply actual changes in material relationships (cf. Isa. 49.8).

How we use land is indicative of how we treat the Earth as a whole. People in the modern world view land as a commodity, buying it, selling it, and seeking to maximise its yield. Significantly, the Old Testament laws classified the possession of debts, slaves and land in the same broad category. There seems no self-evident reason why the desirability of ending debt and slavery is accepted today but the issue of land ownership is treated differently. There is grave injustice in many countries because land is concentrated in the hands of very few people. If biblical principles are to be applied in contemporary life improved access to land for the poor must be a priority; it could be redistributed through compulsory purchase, inheritance tax or wealth tax.

Christians should also call for restraint in the use of agricultural land. Pressure to maximise output has resulted in an excessive use of chemicals on the soil and cruel livestock practices. For example, a 'set-aside' policy of encouraging some land to be taken out of production, which may simply lead to other land being farmed more intensively, could be adapted so that a 'sabbath year' for *all* land is encouraged.

Organic farming is desirable because the use of chemicals has led to potentially dangerous residues in food, harmed wildlife and worsened soil quality, threatening erosion. Despite higher prices, consumer demand exceeds domestic supplies of organic food, and lobbyists in Britain are urging that 20 per cent of agricultural production be organic by the year 2000, compared with under 1 per cent at present. The Church of England, as one of Britain's largest landowners, should set an example on its farms. But as individuals perhaps our first need is simply to become more aware of the land around us, including its soil quality and fertility. How is the land cared for in our gardens and in the surrounding countryside? Is the use of it characterised by the knowledge that 'the earth is the Lord's'?

No earthly hope?

How we think of the future affects how we choose to live in the present. If winter is approaching, for example, we may decide to buy a warm coat. If friends are coming to stay at our house, we may buy some extra food. Tomorrow matters.

Sadly, many Christians do not show special care for the Earth and, indeed, have essentially negative attitudes towards it. They see their eventual future in terms of escape from the world and believe in the ultimate destruction of the non-human creation. It is necessary, therefore, to explore how this understanding has arisen and consider alternative interpretations of Scripture.

Most Christians envisage leaving the Earth when they die and going 'up' to heaven. This 'otherworldly' strand in Christian teaching leads many to understand salvation in terms of deliverance from the physical, material, bodily world. The Earth is like a huge airport terminal where we spend what seems to be an unduly lengthy period, overcrowded and a little bored, waiting for the plane to heaven to take us away.

But biblical prophecy points to a transformation of the *whole* creation, through which there will be 'new heavens and a new earth' where God's *shalom* will prevail (Isa. 65.17; 66.22; cf. Rev. 22.1). The inner constitution of creatures will change so that all may live in harmony:

> The wolf will live with the lamb, the leopard will lie down with the goat, the calf and the lion and the yearling together; and a little child will lead them. The cow will feed with the bear, their young will lie down together, and the lion will eat straw like the ox. The infant will play near the hole of the cobra, and the young child put his hand into the viper's nest. They will neither harm nor destroy on all my holy mountain, for the earth will be full of the knowledge of the Lord as the waters cover the sea. (Isa. 11.6–9)

Passages such as this, in which the non-human creation is brought into God's promises, have often not been taken literally (even, paradoxically, by fundamentalists). Instead, people identify clear and distinct realities, the material and the spiritual, the secular and the sacred, the worldly and the otherworldly, and view one negatively and the other positively. The material world is regarded as insignificant and destined for destruction; the human soul lasts for eternity.

The implications of such dualistic thinking are profound. If God is only interested in the salvation of individual souls and is not concerned about other living creatures and inanimate matter, why should *we* think differently? If the world around us is of no ultimate value and destined for destruction why should *we* seek to take care of it? If escape and survival is inevitable, however people treat their surroundings, they will surely be more liable to disregard their responsibility to take proper care of the Earth. And what does a desire to escape from this world say about our belief in the goodness of creation?

An example of the need for new thinking concerns the traditional interpretation of Jesus's teaching about the end times in Matthew 24. Jesus says that no one knows the exact day of the coming of the Son of Man and warns that when He comes two men will be in the field, one of whom will be taken and the other left; similarly, of two women grinding with a hand mill, one will be taken and the other left. Many Christians imagine that it is *they* who will be taken. According to some, an event called the 'rapture' is destined to take place when suddenly they will be lifted physically upwards, leaving chaos behind – cars crashing as Christian drivers are lifted up out of their seats, and so forth.

A more precise study of Jesus's words, however, suggests that it is *Christians* who are left behind. Jesus makes a parallel with Noah's ark and the flood: "As it was in the days of Noah, so it will be at the coming of the Son of Man" (Matt. 24.37). It was the people who disregarded Noah who "knew nothing about what would happen until the flood came and took them all away" (v. 39), and so Jesus seems to be suggesting that it will be *unbelievers* who are taken from the Earth.

An unfortunate weakness of conservative evangelicalism is the tendency to focus virtually *exclusively* on the individual's personal relationship with Christ. Its implied individualism is well suited to Western culture, which helps to explain its continued popularity. However it is something of a paradox that many who (rightly) stress the importance of affirming the bodily resurrection of Christ fail to acknowledge that redemption through Christ also implies physical change to the rest of creation. Although an individual's salvation starts from personal commitment to Christ, the change in his or her life should affect the *whole* created order, for we live in relation to others and to the environment.

Doomed for destruction?

God is not *solely* concerned with the salvation of human souls, desiring to remove them from His creation. He cares about the future of His entire creation. Just as the whole biosphere has been affected by human sin, so it is included within the redemptive work of Christ. Christ established

his own authority over the natural environment by showing his power when he rebuked the winds and waves in a
storm (Matt. 8.26). God has "placed all things under his
feet" (Eph. 1.22).

Paul evidently did not understand Christ's purpose as
merely to redeem human souls. To the Romans he wrote:

> I consider that our present sufferings are not worth compar-
> ing with the glory that will be revealed in us. The creation
> waits in eager expectation for the sons of God to be revealed.
> For the creation was subjected to frustration, not by its own
> choice, but by the will of the one who subjected it, in hope that
> the creation itself will be liberated from its bondage to decay
> and brought into the glorious freedom of the children of God.
>
> We know that the whole creation has been groaning as in
> the pains of childbirth right up to the present time. Not only
> so, but we ourselves, who have the firstfruits of the Spirit,
> groan inwardly as we wait eagerly for our adoption as sons,
> the redemption of our bodies. (Rom. 8.18–23)

The whole creation is to be liberated from its current
'bondage to decay'. It is evident from the reference to
creation waiting for the sons of God to be revealed that
Paul means the *non-human* creation. The term 'creation'
clearly is not equated with the 'sons of God'. Similarly, in
his letter to the Philippians Paul wrote that Jesus Christ
will "bring everything under his control" by the same
power that will "transform our lowly bodies so that they
will be like his glorious body" (Phil. 3.21). 'Everything'
evidently suggests something *in addition to* 'our lowly
bodies'. Moreover, writing to the Ephesians he looks forward to the time when God will put into effect His intention "to bring all things in heaven and on earth together
under one head" (Eph. 1.10).

In another important passage on this theme, in his
letter to the Colossians, Paul explains that everything has
been created by Christ and that all things will finally be
reconciled through him. He is the pivot of creation: "in him
all things hold together" (Col. 1.17). God has chosen "to
reconcile to himself all things, whether things on earth or

things in heaven" through the peace made through the death of Christ (Col. 1.20). The use here of the Greek expression *ta panta*, which means 'all things', again indicates that Paul was not referring to humans alone.

Belief that the Earth is destined for destruction is frequently justified through a passage in the second letter of Peter, in which he writes that "the earth and everything in it will be laid bare ... The elements will melt in the heat." He then refers to God's promise of a "new heaven and a new earth" (2 Pet. 3.10,12–13; cf. Isa. 65.17; Rev. 21.1).

As in the passage in Matthew cited above, a comparison is drawn with the story of Noah (2 Pet. 3.6). The flood did not in fact involve the *total* destruction of the Earth and it is questionable whether Peter is suggesting that at the second coming it is to be completely destroyed. The key phrase 'laid bare' may alternatively be translated as 'found' in the sense of melting and allowing to harden, as in a foundry. This suggests a process of fundamental transformation rather than destruction, which is reinforced by the writer of Hebrews, who refers to the foundations of the Earth being worn out and changed as happens with a garment (Heb. 1.10–12). In *Creation Regained* Albert Wolters foresees a process of *purification* of the Earth and everything in it from the 'filth and perversion' of sin: "the new heaven and the new earth the Lord has promised will be a continuation, purified by fire, of the creation we now know."[32]

Belief that the world is *inevitably* to continue a downward spiral, based on the doctrine of 'premillennialism', remains a potent influence on many Christians, particularly fundamentalists and conservative evangelicals. The quality of life is expected to diminish as the frequency of wars, earthquakes, famines and other disasters increases, until Christ returns to rule on Earth for a thousand years. During this time Satan is bound up, after which comes the final judgement.

The danger inherent in the premillennialist view is that Christians may feel that they have little incentive to improve the quality of life and take care of the natural environment, because its deterioration is predetermined. Indeed evil and suffering is seemingly not only accepted but almost *welcomed*, being a sign that Christ is soon to return! An example of the threatening implications of such thinking concerns nuclear weapons. Some premillennialists would argue from Scripture that a nuclear holocaust is inevitable. It is a short step from this to identifying nuclear disarmament as an attempt to change God's plan for the future. Peace campaigning becomes not merely naive but evil, 'godless communism'. However in a properly balanced view from Scripture it will be noted that while Jesus warned of earthquakes, wars and famines before the end of the age, he also spoke of the kingdom of God unfolding in the present age (Matt. 12.28; 24.6–8; Luke 17.21).

Interpret with care

The scope for varied interpretations of the Bible explains why throughout history Christians have arrived at different conclusions regarding the ultimate fate of the material world. Much depends on the emphasis placed on particular biblical passages and how literally certain of them are taken. Theologian Paul Santmire concludes that it is quite possible to arrive at distinctly different expectations about the future from alternative interpretations. He poses the question:

> Is the final aim of God, in his governance of all things, to bring into being at the very end a glorified kingdom of spirits alone who, thus united with God, may contemplate him in perfect bliss, while as a precondition of their ecstasy all the other creatures of nature must be left by God to fall away into eternal oblivion?
> Or . . . [is it] . . . to communicate his life to another in a way which calls forth at the very end new heavens and a new earth in which righteousness dwells, a transfigured cosmos where

peace is universally established between all creatures at last, in the midst of which is situated a glorious city of resurrected saints who dwell in justice, blessed with all the resplendent fulness of the earth, and who continually call upon all creatures to join with them in their joyful praise of the one who is all in all?[33]

Christians must resign themselves to lacking absolute *certainty* in seeking to identify which image is closer to the truth. The Bible may seem ambiguous. That said, it is important to wrestle with the problem because our response to these different images may affect how we treat God's creation.

Santmire cites a metaphor of experiences on a mountain to describe people's relationship with God and nature. Images of ascent are significant in New Testament writings and have a strong bearing upon how 'at home' we feel on the Earth. The ascent up a mountain may result in a sense of the transcendent, a feeling of being lifted above the mundane things of the Earth as, looking upwards, we experience closeness to the seemingly infinite expanse of the sky. However there is an alternative perspective. The ascent may take us to a vantage point from which we may look down below and gain a new vision of the Earth's fecundity, its vastness and beauty.

In the Bible, the letters to the Romans, Colossians and Ephesians portray Christ as redeeming the whole creation by filling all things in heaven and on earth and thereby holding them together (Rom. 11.36; Col. 1.17; Eph. 1.10; 4.10). But the Gospel of John and the letter to the Hebrews sometimes give a rather different impression. In John, Christ descends to the Earth and ascends carrying with him those he has called away from this world (John 6.44; 12.32). John gives the impression that the new creation consists only of spiritual bodies which are no longer part of the world and that the rest of the earthly world is unaffected by Christ's redeeming work (John 3.31; 15.19). The letter to the Hebrews contains a similar image of Christians being carried away upward to a heavenly city (Heb. 11.16; 12.22). This contrasts with the 'new Jerusalem' coming down out of heaven (Rev. 21.2).

Many theologians have tended to treat John and Hebrews as pivotal and have sought to interpret Romans, Colossians and Ephesians accordingly. However Santmire suggests that it is equally valid instead to regard Romans, Colossians and Ephesians as providing a better basis for interpreting the rest of Scripture. This would result in what he terms an 'ecological reading of biblical faith'.[34]

Finally, different interpretations of the word 'world' in the Bible may account for varying Christian attitudes towards the Earth. It is used in several different senses, on some occasions to refer to all that is created, on others to life apart from God. For example when John writes of the world made through the light, meaning Christ, he is evidently using it in the former sense (e.g. John 1.9–10). Elsewhere, however, biblical writers identify a world characterised by the fall where people live apart from God. Two examples are where Paul calls on Christians not to conform to the pattern of this world and John records Jesus's teaching that his disciples do not belong to the world (John 15.19; Rom. 12.2). Careful use of the Bible is thus important. If the material world is always viewed negatively, where people live apart from God, the full significance of the incarnation may be forgotten – that through Jesus Christ the *whole* creation is redeemed.

Summary

God has given humans a distinct and special place in creation but our dominion is not a licence to exploit other species. We are to be caretakers of the 'Earth community' rather than autocratic rulers. Our authority should be exercised responsibly, with compassion and concern for future generations.

One explanation for the abuse of the planet is that Christians have disregarded the value of nature and looked upon their future as an escape from the Earth. Increasingly, however, many are coming to an awareness that we are redeemed *with* the created order, not from it. This is important, because Christians who see their faith in individualistic, human-centred terms are more liable not to take proper care of God's creation.

It is not only followers of Jesus Christ who look forward to his return; the *whole creation* awaits his coming. At God's appointed time there will be a radical transformation of the present order of things – the Earth will be remade, fashioned into a new creation. In the meantime our duty is to seek to liberate the world from all destructive powers by taking practical steps to live in harmony with nature – conserving endangered species, protecting the Earth's fertility, and avoiding pollution and other forms of abuse.

1 Kallistos Ware, *The Orthodox Way*, p. 57.
2 The Hebrew word for man, *Adam*, sounds like, and may well be related to, the Hebrew for ground, *Adamah*.
3 A distinction is necessary between being made *in* the image of God, and Christ who is *the* image of God, the perfect and full expression of God. Wesley Granberg-Michaelson (ed.), *Tending the Garden*, p. 43. For a fuller discussion see Douglas Hall, *Imaging God*.
4 Paulos Mar Gregorios, *The Human Presence*, pp. 77–8.
5 Douglas Hall, cited in Michael Crowther-Green, *The Steward – A Biblical Steward for Today*, Oxford: Diocesan Church House, 1985, p. 7.
6 Cited in Keith Thomas, *Man and the Natural World*, p. 172.
7 Wesley Granberg-Michaelson, *A Worldly Spirituality*, p. 44.
8 Cited in H. Paul Santmire, *The Travail of Nature*, p. 91.
9 ibid.
10 ibid.
11 Cited in Thomas, p. 18.
12 ibid., pp. 18–19.
13 ibid., p. 20.
14 ibid., p. 19.
15 ibid.
16 ibid., p. 167.
17 Rowland Moss, *The Earth in Our Hands*, p. 35.

18 Loren Wilkinson (ed.), *Earthkeeping*, p. 209.
19 Granberg-Michaelson, *A Worldly Spirituality*, p. 63.
20 Gregorios, p. 70.
21 Granberg-Michaelson (ed.), *Tending the Garden*, p. 54.
22 Andrew Basden, *Ecological Enterprise*, Industrial Christian Fellowship Theme Pamphlet No. 41, July 1989.
23 Although not wholly satisfactory, 'steward' is a better term than 'vicegerent' and 'viceroy', which have an antiquated, colonial air to them.
24 In certain epistles the steward is responsible not just for material things but for the administering of gifts given through God's grace (Eph. 3.2; 1 Pet. 4.10).
25 Cited in Moss, p. 43.
26 Cited in Thomas Sieger Derr, *Ecology and Human Liberation*, p. 20.
27 Gregorios, p. 84.
28 E. F. Schumacher, *Small is Beautiful*, pp. 10–11.
29 Church of Scotland Science, Religion and Technology Project, *While the Earth Endures*, pp. 12–13.
30 Obedience to a range of other economic laws, such as the cancellation of debts and prohibition of charging interest on loans, would likewise have prevented people from accumulating wealth (see Chapter Three).
31 Jürgen Moltmann, *God in Creation*, p. 6.
32 Albert Wolters, *Creation Regained*, pp. 40–41. According to Wolters, just as our resurrected bodies will be changed from their present form, even products of human culture will survive the fire, being transfigured and transformed.
33 Santmire, pp. 217–18.
34 Santmire, pp. 216–18. Keith Innes argues that the Gospel of John and Hebrews are concerned with deliverance through Christ from the sin and imperfection of the present age, rather than the future of the Earth as such. Keith Innes, *Caring for the Earth*, p. 16.

3

MONEY MATTERS:
The cost of affluence

"'Progress' is no longer an expression of hope, as it was in the nineteenth century. It is a fate to which people in the industrial countries feel themselves condemned."[1] These words of theologian Jürgen Moltmann describe the lack of control many people sense over their future. The momentum of industrial expansion seems unstoppable, despite serious environmental destruction and widespread dissatisfaction with the quality of life. Moltmann concludes that unless there is a radical reversal in what he calls the 'fundamental orientation' of industrial societies (by which he means the striving for power and domination), this 'progress' looks set to end in ecological catastrophe.

Protest about the materialism which is responsible has in recent times come not so much from Church leaders as from prominent Greens. Rudolf Bahro, for example, was one of the early influences on the West German Greens. An East German who was thrown into prison for a book which criticised orthodox Marxism, he was eventually released and allowed to move to West Germany where he observed:

> There has never been so much unhappiness as there is today in the rich countries – anxiety, discontent, loneliness either with or without other people, failure and alienation of every kind – not even in the darkest and most impoverished of times.[2]

Bahro's prediction that the global ecological crisis will have a more powerful historical impact than any class struggle seems to be coming true. Behind recent political change in Eastern Europe, for example, the Green movement has had a significant impact. While much of the conflict in the industrial world is related to social class, there is a more critical tension between economic development and the quality of the environment.

This chapter considers the links between ecology and economics and traces how industrial development was criticised even before the rise of the modern Green movement. Economic principles derived from the Bible are considered in the light of the persistence of the 'acquisitive society'.

Managing our surroundings

Economics today conjures up images of management, industry and commerce, but at the start of the modern age the term was used in a rather different sense. Attempts to explain how science could be compatible with religion led to the phrase 'the economy of nature' to describe how nature had been ordered and arranged by the Creator. Eighteenth-century theologians described the divine government of the natural world:

> God's economy was His extraordinary talent for matching means to ends, for so managing the cosmos that each consti-tuent part performed its work with stunning efficiency . . . God was seen both as the Supreme Economist who had designed the earth household and the housekeeper who kept it functioning productively.[3]

In fact, the words 'ecology' and 'economics' share similar roots, ecology being the *study* of our surroundings, while economics is defined as the *management* of those surroundings.[4] As an academic discipline, economics should be expected to follow ecology. E. F. Schumacher, in *Small is Beautiful*, suggested that "a vital part of the methodology of economics has to be derived from a study of nature."[5] Quite obviously study should precede management! Sadly, this has not been the case; while economics has been studied for centuries, ecology is a relatively young subject.

Economies in industrial nations have, in consequence, been managed with very little reference to the natural environment, from which vital resources are ultimately derived. In Britain, as elsewhere, the Government has treated economic and environmental policy almost entirely separately.[6] Any connections hitherto made have typically concerned environmental projects being evaluated for their economic viability. However the reverse of this equation is more vital; the nation's *economic* policies ought to be constantly evaluated for their *environmental* implications. That this has not been done shows an appalling lack of foresight by governments throughout the industrial world. They have chosen to appeal to people's materialistic aspirations and disregarded the environmental impact.

In contrast, people in the Green movement recognise the limits to the Earth's capacity to supply raw materials for production processes, and believe that economics should be subordinate to ecology. The present generation ought not to compromise the ability of future generations to meet their needs; they should have similar opportunities for material comfort as people living today. Green economists recognise that traditional economics makes no real distinction between renewable and non-renewable resources and so fails to take proper account of long-term scarcity. Greens are also critical that the full costs of environmental degradation are not adequately evaluated.

Few books have so far been written on Green economics, the most notable being *The Living Economy*, based on papers from The Other Economic Summit, a series of conferences held in the mid 1980s. Significantly, a recent theological appraisal of this study was overwhelmingly positive; its author urged Christians to encourage its proponents and enter into creative dialogue with them.[7]

The spirit of industrialism

Some people, many of them very affluent by global standards, have an unfortunate tendency to pillory those who
urge resource conservation. Occasionally they suggest
that Green policies would return us to a pre-industrial
age; that, for example, getting rid of nuclear power would
result in power failures and a return to candles. This is
nonsense; Greens *support* industry which combines economic efficiency with environmental responsibility. But,
regrettably, many politicians often seem unable to accept
new ideas because of inflexibility, conservatism or vested
interests.

Although in recent years there have been encouraging
signs of bridge building between industrialists and environmentalists, fear and confusion exist on both sides.
This is not helped when industrialists read Greens such as
Bahro writing of 'industrial disarmament', and environmentalists see the authoritative Brundtland Report
accepting further increases in global industrial output.

Industry would come under much less criticism were
it to be more sensitive to the environment, using the
minimum amount of resources, repairing and recycling
wherever possible, and creating less waste and pollution.
The recent emergence of Green products and services is
welcome, but many industrialists have been exposed for
changing marketing techniques and not production
processes.

It is not always appreciated that Greens have no objections to *industrialisation*, the transformation of a society
from being agricultural to one where appropriate industry
emerges. We are critical, rather, of *industrialism*, values
based on the belief that industrial processes should be the
chief or most characteristic influence shaping society. The
challenge of the Greens is to the extent to which industrial
growth is allowed to determine the nature of our lives, *not*
to the existence of industry.

Jonathon Porritt shares Bahro's belief that similarities
between capitalism and communism are of greater signi-

ficance than their differences. Examples he cites include their materialist ethic and tendency to encourage centralisation, expansion and large-scale developments. There are, he suggests, more fundamental differences between industrialism and ecology: "The logic of ecology stands in direct opposition to the logic of industrialism; for it is clear that in the very process of 'succeeding', industry cannot help but destroy its own material base."[8] He continues:

> From an industrial point of view, it's rational to . . . promote wasteful consumption, to discount social costs, to destroy the environment. From a green point of view, it's totally irrational, simply because we hold true to the most important political reality of all: that all wealth ultimately derives from the finite resources of the planet.[9]

From a Christian perspective, industrialism represents a perversion of what God intends, because a society is wrongly motivated when people's lives are shaped by production processes and revolve around income and possessions.

In their hearts most people know that there is more to life than producing and consuming material goods and indeed throughout the industrial era there have been dissenting voices. This tradition is well documented in Martin Wiener's study *English Culture and the Decline of the Industrial Spirit*, which identifies a deeply-rooted antipathy towards economic expansion extending back to the early nineteenth century. As this helps to explain major influences upon the Green movement and traces traditional Christian objections to industrial capitalism, a short historical detour is appropriate at this juncture.

The earliest critics of industrial society came from the Romantic tradition – philosophers such as Goethe, Thoreau and Emerson, and the British poets Wordsworth, Coleridge and Blake. The 'dark satanic mills' were contrasted with 'England's green and pleasant land'. Romanticism was prompted by a sense of isolation from the natural world which arose as industrialisation and

urbanisation progressed; it expressed people's desire not
to lose their sense of interdependence with nature.

The Romantic tradition ran counter to much Enlightenment thought, with its faith in human reason and
'progress', and drew instead from the philosophy of Jean-
Jacques Rousseau, who sought freedom by learning from
the 'noble savage', rejecting the 'corrupt' influence of
cultural and political life. Denying the high status
accorded to human reason and the detached objectivity of
scientific methodology, the Romantics clung instead to a
belief in the value of learning from the living environment
around them. As William Wordsworth wrote:

> One impulse from a vernal wood
> May teach you more of man,
> Of moral evil and of good,
> Than all the sages can.

The Romantics believed that people's feelings and
passions would release and free their spirit. They sought
inspiration and emotional intensity through contact with
nature and viewed living creatures with wonder. William
Blake's poetry reveals the kind of outrage with which they
reacted to any abuse:

> A robin redbreast in a cage
> Puts all Heaven in a rage . . .
> The wanton boy that kills the fly
> Shall feel the spider's enmity.[10]

As the industrial revolution progressed into the
nineteenth century new protests were voiced by political
philosophers such as John Stuart Mill and William
Morris. Observing the conventional aspirations of his era,
Mill was critical of people's ostentatious displays of wealth
and the quality of their lives. He created a vision of an
economy which took account of the limits of growth, where
there was a 'stationary state' of capital and wealth instead
of expansion. He wrote:

I confess I am not charmed with the ideal of life held out by those who think that the normal state of human beings is that of struggling to get on; that the trampling, crushing, elbowing, and treading on each other's heels which form the existing form of social life, are the most desirable lot of human kind, or anything but the disagreeable symptoms of one of the phases of industrial progress . . . I know not why it should be a matter of congratulation that persons who are already richer than anyone needs to be, should have doubled their means of consuming things which give little or no pleasure except as representative of wealth.[11]

The negative aspects of industrial capitalism also began to attract criticism from Christian thinkers, notably Christian socialists, from around 1870. Wiener's study identifies a tradition of anti-industrial Tory Anglicanism, seen in the writings of W. R. Inge and Arthur Bryant and shared by intellectuals such as C. S. Lewis, Charles Williams and T. S. Eliot. One of their objections to industrialism was its dehumanising impact on people's lives. Thus T. S. Eliot wrote in *The Idea of a Christian Society*, published in 1939, that unregulated industrialism was leading to the 'deformation of humanity' and the exhaustion of natural resources. He warned that "a good deal of our industrial progress is a progress for which succeeding generations may have to pay dearly."[12]

Two years later Archbishop William Temple convened a conference at Malvern at which the industrial order again came under heavy criticism for tending towards 'recklessness' and 'sacrilege' in the use of natural resources, and for reducing working people to "a mere atom in the machinery of production".[13] Some of the participants called for agricultural revival and a return to the land. Shortly afterwards came Temple's book *Christianity and the Social Order*, which helped to popularise social concern among Christians. However, as essential economic reconstruction took place following the Second World War, anti-industrial sentiment waned.

The idol of growth

More recent opposition to industrialism was led by a new generation of critics who emerged in the late 1960s as people began to compare rising personal wealth with the environmental damage incurred. As fears grew, economic growth came under challenge. Objections were voiced to the pressure to consume, and specifically to the manipulation of people's aspirations through direct advertising, the commercialisation of leisure activities (such as artistic and sporting events) and more subtle methods such as payments for displaying 'brand name' products in films and television.

The writings of two Catholics, E. F. Schumacher and Ivan Illich, proved particularly influential and *Enough is Enough* by Anglican Bishop John Taylor was also very popular. It is Schumacher's classic *Small is Beautiful* that has probably been the most powerful influence on the Green movement. His criticism of modern industrial society marked the start of this new wave of anti-industrialism: "In the excitement over the unfolding of his scientific and technical powers, modern man has built a system of production that ravishes nature and a type of society that mutilates man."[14]

Illich, an Austrian philosopher, portrayed industrialism as a disease which depends on people feeling compelled to consume more and more. He wrote that industrial society has become 'infected by growth mania' and that this growth is *addictive*; envy blinds people and makes them 'compete for addiction'.

Other Christian critics of attitudes to wealth in the industrialised world portrayed them as idolatrous. Any idol ultimately assumes extraordinary significance and necessitates that men, women and the natural environment adjust to its demands. Consequently sacrifices are made, such as dehumanising employment practices and the degradation of the planet. Biblical norms and values are discarded. People who appear as obstacles to the goal are portrayed as subversives or enemies.

Identifying two types of needs – 'absolute' needs, which must be met if people are simply to survive, and 'relative' needs, those felt in relation to other people – Herman Daly, Professor of Economics at Louisiana State University, cited the passage in Isaiah in which a carpenter cuts down a tree and uses half as fuel to warm himself and cook food and the other half to make an idol to worship (Isa. 44.14–20). Daly sees this second half as symbolising the use of surplus economic wealth to enslave and coerce others. The 'idol' of wealth takes the form of individual vanity and the desire for power. And so, Daly concludes, nations in the industrial world have become enslaved to wealth as measured by their gross national product (GNP, the statistical measure of how much a nation produces and consumes):

> We no longer speak of worshipping idols. Instead of idols we have an abomination called GNP . . . Instead of worshipping the idol, we maximise it. The idol has become rather more abstract and conceptual and rather less concrete and material, while the mode of adoration has become technical rather than personal. But fundamentally, idolatry remains idolatry, and we cry out to the growing surplus, "Deliver me, for thou art my god!" Instead we should pause and ask with Isaiah, "Is there not a lie in my right hand?"[15]

Another writer who sees idolatry at work is Dutch Christian economist Bob Goudzwaard. Goudzwaard argues that the quest for material progress is idolatrous, in that people in industrial societies have become so obsessed with becoming more affluent that they are motivated more by this than by any relationship with God.

The desire for economic growth provides a similar motivation at company level. Increasingly industrial power is accumulated in the hands of relatively few businesses (notwithstanding Old Testament laws implying that such concentrations of power should be avoided, a point considered later).

Ordinary people see such strong economic forces at work that they believe them to be wholly outside of their control. Through major political reforms they could, in fact, be changed, but governments are reluctant to act, partly because they fear that structural change to reduce the power of industrial giants will cause economic instability. Of course many politicians on the political right may not even *wish* to act, being financially backed by such companies. There is also the problem of huge transnational companies, whose affairs cross national boundaries.

Modern economic forces are so powerful that they threaten to determine (not merely affect) how we live and act and, in the process, mould people's aspirations, and even their very characters. This is the true implication of industrial society being out of control. Illich portrayed ordinary people as victims, whose characters were corrupted to fit the demands of industrialism. He wrote of people's minds being 'industrially distorted', their imaginations 'industrially deformed'.[16] Goudzwaard himself concluded:

> The goal of material prosperity requires us to adjust our behaviour to its means – continuous economic growth. We have become dependent on economic growth, and it has ensnared us. Though initially a relatively innocent tool, it has become established as a power against us. It coerces us and reveals to us what we must do to survive.[17]

Idols betray their makers and never leave them alone. Thus we have to choose either to reject the goal of material prosperity, and make the necessary changes to our life-styles, church-based and other social activity and politics, or resign ourselves to a life of unfulfilled desire.

Growth as traditionally measured is in any case a poor indicator of a nation's development and of the quality of people's lives; statistical measures of the growth of output have serious limitations. As a simple example, if road accidents increase and this results in more new cars being built, then the statistics show a higher output and this suggests that the quality of people's lives has increased, although this is patently untrue.

One of the current weaknesses with economics is that it

lacks the theoretical tools to go beyond what is quantitative; it relies heavily on using *money* as a measure. Major difficulties tend to arise in attempts to measure people's wellbeing by weighing up costs and benefits in non-financial terms. Judging the desirability of economic growth in relation to increased happiness requires ethical criteria and, therefore, the skills of other disciplines such as philosophy and theology.

New, more sophisticated indicators of progress are needed to replace gross national product. However the industrial world remains obsessed with quantitative measurements and international comparisons of income and expenditure. Bringing into this world signs of the presence of the kingdom of God – that would be *true* progress. But it is rather difficult to draw up an international league table of the quality of relationships and the presence of love!

Regardless of whether or not measures of economic growth are ideal, Greens question the motivation for growth. Is it to meet people's *needs* or the demands of the present economic system – demands deliberately stimulated so that industrialists can expand their markets and increase their profits? The fact that demand exists for any particular product or service does *not* provide ethical justification for its provision. Many highly profitable products and services are essentially destructive, military weapons and pornographic materials being two obvious examples. Consider the growth in military expenditure.

Many people in low-income countries would benefit if resources devoted to military purposes were devoted instead to solving malnutrition and disease. In recent decades military expenditure in such countries has risen at 7 per cent annually, twice the rate in affluent nations, and the major arms exporting countries have been more than willing to perpetuate this trend.[18] Poor countries often do, of course, require a certain amount of military equipment, but pressure is put on them to import more. The major arms manufacturers stimulate demand to maximise their sales, not merely to respond to needs, because exports bring down the unit costs of production.

The British Government justifies arms exports to low-income countries on the grounds that if we withdrew from the market these countries would simply turn to other suppliers. This pretence at amorality represents appalling reasoning. By the same logic, should Christian entrepreneurs not run businesses supplying hard core pornography (with biblical texts on page three, perhaps)? If they do not, others will! The idea is, of course, ludicrous. The Government also claims that arms exports provide

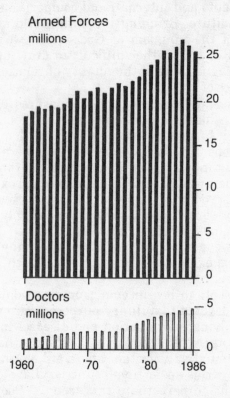

FIG. 4 ARMED FORCES AND DOCTORS – WORLDWIDE TOTALS
Source: Ruth Sivard, *World Military and Social Expenditures 1989*,
(World Priorities Inc., 1989)

jobs. But such reasoning is again flawed – if resources were to be switched from the military to health care, more doctors and nurses could be employed. People who support governments which encourage arms exports or work for electronics firms which supply arms to countries whose populations are starving are indirectly contributing to global hunger.

The trade-off between military expenditure and meeting people's basic needs provides a vivid example of choice between alternative patterns of expenditure. But in the West it is not just a matter of alternative consumption, but the *level* of consumption. The myth of so-called 'Green growth' is that countries in the West need only to consume differently and not less. True Greens reject this, because even 'Greener' products consume energy and other raw materials. Instead, Western nations should no longer seek endless increases in output and consumption.

The true test of a Christian society is not its rate of economic expansion and wealth accumulation, but faithfulness to God and our practical response to the Christian principles by which we are called to live. Green Christians would thus propose an alternative to industrialism (whether capitalist or socialist), which appeals to people's highest qualities instead of accommodating their selfish and materialistic inclinations. Such an alternative would be based on strong family, community and regional loyalties, and on co-operative forms of ownership rather than international conglomerates and large public companies. It would oppose the excess profits and industrial expansion which reflect distorted priorities, by which good stewardship and a sense of sufficiency are lost in the quest for affluence.

The forgotten commandment

Despite the objections to industrial expansion, the negative 'rat race' image of moneymaking which re-emerged in the 1960s and 1970s did not determine the dominant cultural trend of the 1980s. It was, instead, overshadowed by the 'yuppie' syndrome.

Many conservative industrialists defend their activities by claiming a need to 'make money' or 'create wealth'. Certain Christians believe that God wants them to be materially prosperous and equate financial success with divine favour. Right-wing preachers and politicians even suggest that Christian teaching should be amended in the light of society's growing affluence. American 'televangelists' and so-called 'prosperity theologians' seemingly deny Jesus's warnings about putting faith in money, desiring to get rich and displaying wealth. Their occasionally scandalous antics have proved embarrassing to fellow Christians.

Politicians, likewise, are unashamed of profligate wealth. In 1989 a British Government minister, John Patten, pointed to the growing prosperity of large sections of society and called on Church leaders to develop a theology "appropriate for the climate of success that we have in the late 1980s."[19]

But God promises to provide for our need, not our greed. The Bible provides scant comfort for those who strive to accumulate wealth as an end in itself. According to the author of Ecclesiastes, "Whoever loves money never has money enough; whoever loves wealth is never satisfied with his income" (Eccles. 5.10). Jesus taught plainly that people cannot serve both God and money because "No one can serve two masters" (Matt. 6.24). People end up hating one and loving the other, or being devoted to one and despising the other. The apostle Paul warned Timothy that "the love of money is a root of all kinds of evil" (1 Tim. 6.10).

Industrial capitalism, the politically right-wing form of industrialism, is unashamedly based upon the desire to make money. Without this motivation businesses will not perform well on London's Stock Exchange or New York's Wall Street and will find difficulty in attracting finance for the expansion which capitalism requires. It has to be admitted that many Christians seem too often to be compliant in defending activities which promote materialism, individualism and injustice. The problem is that the system of industrial capitalism *demands* a love of money, a desire to maximise profits, and tends to reward highest those who are most selfish.

Indeed it is often argued that capitalism works precisely because people are selfish. The system is said to suit our fallen nature. However, many biblical writers warn that the kind of pressures which capitalism demands are a challenge to faithful obedience to God. Often they result in exploitation, greed, and injustice (Lev. 25.14; Luke 12.15; Jas 5.4).

Too easily people forget the tenth commandment, that we should not eagerly desire, or 'covet', anything that belongs to our neighbours (Exod. 20.17). Covetousness often clouds our vision of the true effects of consumerism. As our wills become distorted we find ourselves enslaved to an idolatry of material progress and confuse the language of *needs* and *wants*. Basic needs cannot be disputed, but people often imagine that virtually *all* of their material desires are needs!

The Bible also discourages Christians from comparing their material wellbeing with others. The commandment to "love your neighbour as yourself" involves meeting their needs (as did the good Samaritan) and recognising that "love does no harm to its neighbour" (Luke 10.25–8; Rom. 13.9–10; cf. Lev. 19.18). When we desire things that belong to our neighbours we are, in effect, harming them, because we are viewing them according to what they *have*, not what they *are*.

People are put under great pressure to covet. Advertising seeks to raise their aspirations by encouraging a particular image, and leads people to feel a dependence on possessions for a sense of security. Advertisements may reflect reality, but they also distort it by appealing to people's basic urge for immediate gratification of their desires. Offering information about products is important, but all too often advertisements encourage people to believe that without more possessions they will be unfulfilled and, in a sense, less than 'whole' people. Wholeness, according to the advertising industry, comes from having the most whole, most full, pay packet and the best-equipped house – a perversion of the true biblical *shalom*. They encourage people not to seek peace with the planet, but with the purse.

Industrialism is propped up by politicians claiming that they can best meet the nation's 'needs'. Voters who are content with their possessions may be liable to reject conventional party politics, and so politicians of the left and right seek to tempt them with more. Thus as one set of needs are fulfilled, new demands grow. Yesterday's wants become today's needs.

Far from encouraging people to maximise their consumption, the Bible teaches a rather relaxed attitude to wealth. Jesus said that "life is more than food" and urged his disciples not to worry about what they would eat or wear (Luke 12.22–3). Old Testament laws on giving generously to those in need without demanding repayment are perpetuated in his teaching (Matt. 5.42; Luke 6.30–5; cf. Deut. 15.7–8). Although it seems that certain private property rights are approved, there is a notable degree of flexibility about private wealth (see, for example, Deut. 23.24–5 and Luke 6.29–30). When Zacchaeus welcomed Jesus to his house, he not only repaid fourfold those whom he had cheated but gave away half of his possessions to the poor (Luke 19.8). God does not want an affluent Church; He wants a just world.

The desire for wealth is perhaps the greatest danger to spiritual life. Affluent Christians often say, rather defensively, that they believe that what is demanded is a 'detached' attitude to wealth. A rich young man came up to Jesus and, having kept all the commandments, asked what he needed to inherit eternal life. The gospels do not record that the rich young man was told by Jesus to adopt a right *attitude* to his wealth. Jesus said that the man should *sell all that he owned*: "Sell everything you have and give to the poor, and you will have treasure in heaven. Then come, follow me" (Luke 18.22). The man went away, sad but unwilling to give up his wealth, and

Jesus observed how hard it is for rich people to enter the kingdom of God. Far from seeking affluence, Christians should consider *selling* what they already own, according to their conscience.

"Anything which transforms the material world so that it can be of greater use to fellow human beings is an act of wealth creation," writes Professor Brian Griffiths, a Christian and one of Mrs Thatcher's key economic policy advisers.[20] But it is often forgotten that the natural environment *itself* is a form of wealth, just as manufactured products are wealth. Industrial activity transforms elements of the natural environment into, first, raw materials, and then material products. Thus it *uses up* wealth as well as *creating* wealth.

Creating wealth can never justify causing permanent damage to the balance of nature (a point acknowledged by Griffiths),[21] though evidently much damage has been caused through the 'wealth' creation during the Conservatives' past decade in power. Energy reserves are rapidly being depleted (especially oil), the hole in the ozone layer represents damage which may never be repaired, the global climate is being changed, and many thousands of animal and plant species are becoming extinct. This is indeed permanent damage. The apologists for industrialism must be exposed for gravely underestimating the damage which those in powerful positions are shortsightedly and sometimes greedily causing.

Traditionally, the main criterion used for decisions on whether to initiate or increase production is whether it will be 'economic'. However, production which is economic in a free market may well damage the environment, while environmentally sensitive production methods, which are in our long term interest, may well not be economic because the rewards come far too late – perhaps not for a generation or more.

For example, recycling is often considered uneconomic because short-term profits are small and problems such as resource depletion and shortages of waste dump facilities may not be immediately apparent. Forestry is another example. Trees can take several decades to grow and there may not be an adequate financial return in the short term. Destroying a rainforest, on the other hand, can be remarkably economic – at least for those who reap the profits.

Economic factors exert a very powerful influence on the environment and the free market often does not take effective account of the future, a fact only just being recognised by government advisers and supporters. Taxes and government regulations are needed to prevent the increased output of environmentally undesirable products or, at least, to make them less economic.

Biblical restraint

There is a story of an African fisherman relaxing in the sun, lying on a beach in Mombasa in Kenya. Clearly enjoying himself, he was suddenly accosted by a white-faced, camera-laden tourist who asked of him why he was idling his time away. He should, said the tourist, be out catching fish. "But," said the African, "I have enough for the day for my wife and family. What need is there for catching more?" The tourist replied that if he were to catch more he would be able to afford better equipment – a better net, for example. "But why do I need a better net?" enquired the African. "Well," replied the tourist, "if you caught even more fish you would be able to buy a boat, then several boats, and then employ people and form your own company. And then when it was running smoothly you would be able to take a holiday – and lie on the beach in the sun, relax and enjoy yourself." "Thanks," said the fisherman, "but I can do that every day already."[22]

The modern industrial world lives by a curious logic. People are said to be better off than ever before and yet seem to need to work harder than ever to gain a satisfactory quality of life. The stresses and strains of life daily take their toll – some suffer mental breakdown, 'burnt out' through overwork, while others become 'workaholics', with only their work to give life meaning.

The Bible teaches us to live with *restraint*: "Do not wear yourself out to get rich; have the wisdom to show restraint" (Prov. 23.4). The sabbath principle established at creation is crucially important to a biblical understanding of work and production. The fourth commandment, to keep the Sabbath day holy, was created not just so that people would remember God, but to stop people from working. Significantly, it applies equally to animals and, elsewhere, the same principle is applied to the land. It is not just tired business people 'at the top' who need rest but *the whole creation*.

The writer of Ecclesiastes saw overwork springing from envy of one's neighbours as meaningless, though he noted also that "the fool folds his hands and ruins himself" (Eccles. 4.5). People should find a balance, neither busy all the time, nor idle: "Better one handful with tranquillity than two handfuls with toil and chasing after the wind" (Eccles. 4.6).

The Bible indicates that modest income or wealth is God's norm for us. People who live below a subsistence level are regarded as unfortunate; those much above it are portrayed as in danger of being diverted from worshipping God. The biblical principle to be neither destitute nor affluent is expressed clearly in Proverbs:

> Give me neither poverty nor riches, but give me only my daily bread. Otherwise, I may have too much and disown you and say, 'Who is the Lord?' Or I may become poor and steal, and so dishonour the name of my God. (Prov. 30.8–9)

Similar sentiments are expressed in the New Testament by Paul: "If we have food and clothing, we will be content with that" (1 Tim. 6.8).

People who are relatively affluent are to share their wealth with the less fortunate (Deut. 15.7–11; Luke 12.33; 18.22; 2 Cor. 9.6–11). Such sharing is for the sake of the *rich* as well as the poor, because wealth distracts us from commitment to God. On the other hand, being close to poverty encourages trust in God to meet our needs. This is a crucial challenge to the idea that money brings fulfilment in life, a recognition that the *rich* will be liberated as much as the *poor*, and is part of Green thinking and true Christianity alike.

The acquisitive society thus stands condemned. Jesus told a parable of a man who, already rich, acquired even greater affluence. To store all of his possessions the man planned to build a bigger barn (just like many today who aspire to a larger house). God threatened the man with death and asked him to consider who then would get what he had gained. "A man's life does not consist in the abundance of his possessions," Jesus warned (Luke 12.15). Acquiring possessions does not give meaning to life. Instead we are called to be "rich towards God" (Luke 12.21). Directly following that parable Jesus called upon his disciples to observe how God meets their material needs just as He feeds ravens and 'dresses' lilies. Instead of acting like unbelievers who strive for wealth, we are to seek "treasure in heaven that will not be exhausted, where no thief comes near and no moth destroys" (Luke 12.33).

In 1944 C. S. Lewis voiced his fear that "man's conquest of Nature, if the dreams of some scientific planners are realized, means the rule of a few hundreds of men over billions upon billions of men."[23] So it has proved. Throughout the world vast power is concentrated in the hands of relatively few landowners, multinationals, financiers and politicians. Industrial expansion has been possible because companies borrow against their assets, allowing them to invest in additional plant and equipment to enable further growth. Giant industrial conglomerates emerge and their huge power is often sufficient to squeeze out smaller competitors. Companies expand and industry becomes highly concentrated. Transnational companies now control over a quarter of total global industrial production and the larger ones have annual sales which exceed the vast majority of low-income countries.

However, the laws in the Old Testament, if kept, would restrict or even prevent economic growth.[24] If Israelite families had been allowed to accumulate large sums of capital this might well have encouraged more rapid economic advance, but various regulations of the market seem designed to hinder this process. As noted in the previous chapter, these laws would have tended to prevent any Israelite from building up large reserves of land or financial capital. Debts between fellow Israelites were to be cancelled every seven years and land returned to its original owners in the Jubilee Year (Deut. 15.1; Lev. 25.8–28). Lending money to fellow Israelites at a profit, known as usury, was forbidden (Exod. 22.25; Lev. 25.36–7).

In addition, there are examples of restraint in relation to farming. People were not allowed to eat from trees in the first four fruiting seasons (Lev. 19.23–5). There was also a tradition of 'gleaning' – crops which were thinly scattered, neglected or overlooked were not supposed to be gathered in, but left for the poor and for 'sojourners', people temporarily passing by. Farmers were expected to avoid reaping close to the edge of fields, which would not only help the poor but also wildlife (Lev. 19.9–10; Deut. 24.19–21). This is in stark contrast with the modern demands for agricultural 'efficiency' which have led to hedgerows around fields being destroyed in order to maximise yields and minimise costs.

Finally, the command not to work on one day each week would obviously have reduced the output of the economy. Although much of industry and commerce today is likewise restrained, a powerful lobby seeks to increase legal trading on Sunday, in order to increase their output. Their success would be a further sign of the power of materialism in contemporary society.

If Old Testament laws had been strictly applied in the West, so that money markets offering speculative gains were forbidden, it is questionable whether capitalism would have emerged. Dr Michael Schluter, Director of the Jubilee Centre, argues that the ban on interest would not have stopped technological development but believes that it might have precluded many contemporary institutional forms, such as the public company, pension funds, bank credit arrangements and government borrowing.[25]

Old Testament economic laws have gained increased attention in recent years as Christians have sought to understand their contemporary significance, particularly because of concern at the growth of consumer credit and the effects of interest rates on those in debt. Nations, companies and individuals alike are inclined to spend beyond their immediate means, the latter particularly with credit cards. For individuals the indebtedness which often follows becomes a form of oppression and it is no exaggeration to suggest that there are similarities with slavery, with credit companies as slave-owners. The 'Mastercard' credit card scheme is more appropriately named than perhaps intended; people's cards have become their masters.

Care is needed to avoid drawing false conclusions from the Bible; for example, in the Old Testament era borrowing tended mainly to take place where a family had suffered a temporary misfortune, not to facilitate expansion. It is surely most significant, however, that usury was forbidden. The primary concern was of further exploitation of those already poor: "the rich rule over the poor, and the borrower is servant to the lender" (Prov. 22.7).

The modern pressure to consume has led to a 'debt epidemic'. In the absence of adequate credit controls, crafty advertising, exploitation by credit financiers, and foolishness by consumers have combined to cause widespread debt-induced misery. People whose desires are easily manipulated are exploited, offered easy credit facilities with often extraordinarily expensive repayment terms. In 1987 outstanding debt on consumer goods (excluding mortgages) amounted to £37,000 million in Britain. Interest rates on outstanding credit card loans were typically around 30 per cent at the turn of the decade. Usury cannot realistically be outlawed in the immediate future, but credit controls such as minimum deposits and maximum legal interest rates could be introduced.[26] This would be in keeping with biblical principles.

Members of the Church of England might reflect on their indirect involvement in the consumer society. The Church Commissioners own shops, offices, housing, industrial property and farmland worth over £1,300 million and, in addition, hold investments worth over £1,000 million on the Stock Exchange. The multi-million pound MetroCentre in Gateshead, a retailing complex with an estimated annual turnover of £350 million, was built in the 1980s on Church land. While the area undoubtedly needed revival, this glorification of consumerism, including Sunday opening, raises a few questions about appropriate Church investments.

Green development

Economic growth may serve as an indicator of affluence, but it can equally be seen as a measure of decay, providing a rough guide to how fast the global environment is being destroyed. Perhaps what most clearly distinguishes the Greens from environmentalists is a belief that economic growth is no longer justifiable because it causes such damage that future generations are bound to suffer.

Defining countries as 'developed' and 'undeveloped' judges them according to their consumption. This is surely misleading. The arrogance of over-industrialised countries has led them to define themselves as 'developed', but what have they developed into? An appropriate Green path of development is needed.

A potentially useful concept is 'sustainable development', defined in a major report by the World Commission on Environment and Development (popularly known after the Commission's chairperson as the Brundtland Report) as "development that meets the needs of the present without compromising the ability of future generations to meet their own needs"[27]. One risk is that such a general term is open to abuse, especially by complacent industrial powers. Moreover if true progress is to take place, growth should only be regarded as acceptable in *poor* countries, whose populations need to escape from absolute poverty. Elsewhere, as a general principle the annual consumption of non-renewable resources (i.e. those in finite supply) must be reduced.

Greens propose changes in taxation as one means of encouraging sustainable development. For example, taxes should be charged on energy, minerals and metals which are in relatively scarce supply. Taxes on income and employment could then be reduced proportionately (although the scale would need to be more progressive because of the regressive impact of 'indirect' taxes, i.e. taxes on products).

Recent debate in international forums on environmental concerns has highlighted a tension between industrialised and low-income countries. The latter fear that as countries address environmental problems the poor will suffer unduly. Growth through industrialisation has brought an end to malnutrition and squalor for millions. When the world's poor hear affluent nations calling for restrictions on consumption (such as refrigerators, which contain ozone-depleting chemicals, in India), many are understandably sceptical. Too easily it appears as if the rich are denying opportunities to those who remain poor.

Nor must it be forgotten that even *within* industrial nations there are pockets of severe poverty. Accusations that environmentalists come from more affluent areas and simply wish to prevent others from disturbing their comfort may be exaggerated, but often have an element of truth. For example, building developments that provide houses for the homeless and jobs for the unemployed may cause disturbance or hide the pretty views of the countryside from houses on the suburban fringe. There is a degree of selfish hypocrisy in those who only ever object to developments in their own 'back yard'.

Justice must be secured in industrialised countries. If, in order to reduce the pace of environmental destruction, consumption is no longer to increase and industrial output is restrained, there should be a redistribution of income to protect people on the margins of poverty from facing an unfair burden. The Bible teaches that "the Lord loves the just" (Ps. 37.28). Our aim must be for justice between rich and poor, and between the present generation and generations to come.

Throughout the world the powerful take advantage of the weak. International agreements almost invariably favour the most affluent; for example, the pickers on tea plantations receive a tiny proportion of the sum which goes to manufacturers and retailers. Similarities may be drawn with the recurring problem in Old Testament times of dishonesty through the use of inaccurate weights and measures (Lev. 19.35–6; Prov. 11.1). The instruction regarding economic matters which God gave to the Israelites provides a timeless principle: "Do not take advantage of each other, but fear your God" (Lev. 25.17). When people do not get a just reward for their work they are effectively dispossessed; it is a form of theft. The prophet Ezekiel told the Israelite princes: "Give up your violence and oppression and do what is just and right. Stop dispossessing my people, declares the Sovereign Lord" (Ezek. 45.9).

A basic income

People's incomes are, of course, closely related to economic development. By tradition they are tied to an individual's employment, and social security systems aim to ensure that no one starves through lack of employment. The linkage between income and employment has, however, increasingly come under challenge, as widespread unemployment has led many to question the justice of a system where some are permanently and substantially better off than others because of favourable employment opportunities. Another criticism of this long-established tradition is the implication that homemakers (or 'housewives') and voluntary workers are not doing a 'proper job' and, because of their (lack of) remuneration, are of less worth than others.

The time has come for rethinking the links between income, consumption and employment. As Oxford economist Donald Hay has pointed out, "Christians should not accept the capitalist assumption that great abilities or ownership of resources entitles a man to a commensurate level of consumption."[28] The relaxed attitude to wealth encouraged in biblical teaching suggests that we should not cling to our earnings and spend it on ourselves. Moreover, our expenditure on consumption should be based not merely on the size of our income, but on an analysis of true need.

In recent years there has been growing interest, stimulated by Greens, in the idea of a 'basic income scheme', through which each citizen would receive a guaranteed minimum income to replace all tax allowances and most social security payments. (In practice, most people would not notice any change; the basic income would merely replace the equivalent tax allowance on their PAYE form.) The income would be roughly equivalent to current social security payments, but paid unconditionally, irrespective of any income received from employment. It would meet people's survival needs, but they would not be able to live comfortably on that sum alone and most would choose to find employment. However, with the security of a small income and a reduced 'poverty trap' effect, people would have greater freedom to choose the exact amount of time to spend doing paid work.

The scheme would increase flexibility in the jobs market, because by reducing the poverty trap it offers a substantial incentive for part-time work to those who prefer it. It would thus encourage a better distribution of employment, which is important if jobs are to be provided for all who seek them without industrial production rising.

Significantly, two Christians are prominent in the campaign to introduce a basic income scheme in Britain, Malcolm Torry and Tony Walter. Torry argues that the scheme fits the Christian insights which should guide social policy. It affirms the preciousness of each individual citizen and "reflects in the social order the character of the God who freely gives the wealth of creation."[29]

The scheme would offer recognition for the value to society of people who do unpaid work, including homemakers and voluntary workers, which is a general application of the biblical principle that each part of the 'body' is valuable to the functioning of the whole (1 Cor. 12.21–6). It also would recognise interdependence in society: "the whole of society would provide for the whole of society".[30] This contrasts with our present divisive system, in which those who have incomes, the 'haves', are divided from, and forced to give to, the 'have nots'.

Several criticisms are made of the scheme. Some see it as representing a move towards equality of income and, as such, a form of communism. Certainly it would involve a considerable redistribution of income and wealth to poorer people, but this is in any case essential if nations are to consume less without the poorest having to cut back and suffer injustice. The scheme could be funded partly by raising revenue from people on relatively high incomes and also from a reallocation of public spending priorities – the Green Party, for example, would use revenue which other parties might spend on nuclear weapons, new motorways and other roads, airport expansion and other environmentally dubious programmes.

Other critics point out that as a government scheme it contrasts with the voluntary sharing of possessions among the early Christians. However, for society to pledge collectively to share its wealth and not just rely on individual acts of charity is surely an acceptable principle. Tithing in order to help the Levites, foreigners and lone-parent families was expected of all Israelites (Lev. 27.30; Deut. 14.22–9). The Israelites' 'basic income' was provided by the right of each family to a plot of land, which was an effective means of providing their economic security. Being a small sum it need not encourage 'state dependence'. Indeed the Green Party advocates major decentralisation to strengthen regional loyalties, and would administer the scheme on a regional basis. Finally, some critics point to the biblical teaching that "if a man will not work, he shall not eat" (2 Thess. 3.10). However the scheme would actually *reduce* the number of jobless people by encouraging a trend towards sharing out available employment.

Green purchasing

Good stewardship, managing well that which ultimately belongs to God, involves accepting *sufficiency* and *sharing*. This is difficult enough, as it is much easier simply to frown upon the materialism of modern society than to escape from its straitjacket. But it demands that we consider not only how much we consume and the price and quality of products which we purchase, but how they are produced.

During the 1980s a sudden, remarkable shift took place away from highly processed foods and those with unnecessary additives. What began as a relatively minor trend towards more 'natural' food, met largely by specialist health food shops, became a revolution in dietary habits. Meat and food with 'E' numbers were increasingly frowned upon, while wholefoods and low-fat, less-sweetened foods were encouraged.

This was a mere foretaste of a much more widespread change in consumer behaviour heralded by Green Consumer Week in 1988 (backed by, among others, Christian Ecology Link) and the publication of the immensely popular *The Green Consumer Guide*. By the turn of the decade, as research revealed the willingness of consumers to spend slightly more on products for ethical reasons, ever-shrewd marketing agencies capitalised upon this and a 'Green' image was increasingly used to advertise products. Consumer-led change has thus become one of the most effective means towards influencing industrial production. What does life as a Green consumer entail?

Firstly, checking our *energy use*. Reducing the consumption of fossil fuels is essential if the problems such as global warming and acid rain are to be solved. Countless opportunities exist for lower energy use in the home. As an example, we should be motivated to avoid unnecessary lighting and heating not simply out of concern at the bills but to conserve finite non-renewable energy resources! All too many households have gadgets which are unnecessarily powered by electricity, including carving knives, tin openers and even toothbrushes! And what transport do we use? A significant proportion of energy consumed goes on transport, for which much blame rests with car users. Cars are essential to some people, particularly the infirm and those in rural areas. But how often are they used unnecessarily – out of habit – on very short journeys, or where public transport is readily available? It's never too late to learn to ride a bicycle (I began, belatedly, at thirty-one!).

Secondly, the Green consumer seeks to *reduce pollution*. If a car is absolutely essential, as distinct from desirable, does it run on lead-free petrol and is it fitted with a catalytic converter? Certain detergents and other cleaning materials are more environmentally friendly than others and buying organic food helps to reduce damage caused by agrochemicals. Aerosols are mostly unnecessary, and any which damage the ozone layer should certainly be avoided. Often opportunities exist to prevent our workplaces from polluting the environment, perhaps through trade union initiatives.

Thirdly, industrial societies tolerate far too much *waste*. Frequently people unnecessarily use attractively designed, brand new paper for telephone notes, shopping lists and the like! Disposable goods such as teaspoons, cups, nappies, razors, handkerchiefs and even cameras add to the problem. And how easy it is to accept new plastic shopping bags on every visit to a supermarket! A truly Green consumer intervenes and objects when shop assistants mindlessly wrap products into a multitude of bags. The three Rs for Greens are recycling, repair and re-use. Many items which are thrown away have some value – newspapers, clothes, cans, oil, metals, glass and rags can all be recycled. There are few things of absolutely *no* value.

Finally, the Green consumer seeks to *avoid cruelty* to other creatures. Anyone who buys eggs which are not 'free range' is contributing to the perpetuation of factory farming – if fewer consumers buy factory-farmed eggs, fewer chickens have to suffer cruel conditions in battery cages. Much suffering is involved in producing meat and consequently many Greens avoid eating meat (see Chapter Seven). If you *do* eat meat, to take the trouble to buy from cruelty-free suppliers is important.

There are many obstacles to being a Green consumer. Few people can easily switch habits of a lifetime. Changing one's diet, in particular, may be a gradual process. Public transport is often inadequate and for some people a car may be essential, but it should perhaps be used with a degree of reluctance. Recycling facilities are often hard to find, though local collection schemes may be organised by voluntary groups. Wherever such problems exist the government and local authorities should be lobbied for more facilities.

Another problem is that products such as free-range eggs, cruelty-free meat, and organic fruit and vegetables are often expensive and local supplies may be poor. It might, perhaps, be possible to cut back on other consumption to enable such purchases. Costs may be high because production is currently small-scale, reflecting economic forces at work which politicians could influence. Because supplies are low, retailers may be exploiting the consumer and making large profits. Governments should be asked why they are so reluctant to encourage cruelty-free and organic farming.

Many campaigning organisations would welcome help from people aiming for Greener lifestyles; our protests need not be isolated or uninfluential. Christians have a special calling to lifestyles which reflect integrity. Jesus taught: "Let your light shine before men, that they may see your good deeds and praise your Father in heaven" (Matt. 5.16). We are 'the light of the world'; if we do not live according to our Green principles the light seen by others will expose a hollow, hypocritical faith.

Summary

Greens form part of a long tradition of poets, philosophers and politicians who have sought to expose the corrupting influence of industrialism. No one denies the need for efficient industry, but its influence on our culture should not be excessively dominant. Its current scale and power exerts too great an impact on people's aspirations.

A new, Green economics is slowly emerging which embraces many Old Testament principles concerning economic life, such as the need to restrain the accumulation of wealth, to achieve justice through a 'bias to the poor' in public policy, and to focus upon stewardship rather than ownership.

Not enough resources exist for all the world's population to live according to the present demands of the most affluent, and we have failed to use our affluence to attack injustice. To bring about an end to this over-consumption and injustice, a major redistribution of economic power, nationally and internationally, is required. The Bible commands us not to seek after the possessions of others but calls instead for restraint. In the light of the environmental crises, to be faithful stewards of God's creation it is necessary to say 'enough is enough'.

Progress and development are too often defined simply by trends in economic growth. A Christian society should be measured not by the size of its gross national product, but by the quality of people's relationships with the Creator and with each other. Change is needed and this must be achieved politically and through people purchasing goods responsibly as Green consumers.

1 Jürgen Moltmann, *God in Creation*, p. 28.
2 Rudolf Bahro, *Socialism and Survival*, p. 75.
3 Donald Worster, *Nature's Economy*, p. 37.
4 Both terms share the Greek root *oikos*, meaning surroundings (or, strictly, house or household). The other root of ecology is *logos*, meaning discourse or study, while that of economics is *nomos*, meaning law or management.
5 E. F. Schumacher, *Small is Beautiful*, p. 39.
6 Tim Cooper, 'Twinning Economics and Ecology', *Financial Times*, 18th April 1989.
7 David Welbourn, 'The New Economics – A theological appraisal', *Industrial Christian Fellowship Quarterly*, Autumn 1989, p. 26.
8 Jonathon Porritt, *Seeing Green*, p. 47.
9 ibid., p. 48.
10 Cited in Andrew Linzey and Tom Regan (eds), *Compassion for Animals*, pp. 45–6.
11 Cited in Herman E. Daly (ed.), *Economics, Ecology, Ethics*, p. 15.
12 Cited in Martin Wiener, *English Culture and the Decline of the Industrial Spirit 1850–1980*, p. 115.
13 Wiener, pp. 117–118.
14 Schumacher, p. 246.
15 Daly, p. 28.
16 Ivan Illich, *Tools for Conviviality*, pp. 14–15.
17 Bob Goudzwaard, *Idols of Our Time*, p. 51.
18 World Commission on Environment and Development, *Our Common Future*, p. 307.
19 *The Independent*, 14th February 1989.
20 Brian Griffiths, 'The Background to Jesus's Teaching', *Industrial Christian Fellowship Quarterly*, Spring 1985.
21 Brian Griffiths, *Morality and the Market Place*, p. 92.
22 I am indebted for this story to Patrick Peacey.
23 Cited in Daly, pp. 178–9.
24 This is even accepted by Brian Griffiths, *Morality and the Market Place*, p. 83.
25 Michael Schluter, 'The Old Testament Ban on Interest: its relevance for reform of Britain's industrial structure in the 1980s', Jubilee Centre Working Paper, 1984.
26 Roy McCloughry and Andrew Hartropp, *Debt*, p. 24.
27 World Commission on Environment and Development, p. 43.
28 Donald A. Hay, *A Christian Critique of Capitalism*, p. 21.
29 Malcolm Torry, *Basic Income for All*, p. 21.
30 ibid., p. 21.

4

THE RISE OF THE GREENS:
Secular prophets?

The Green movement offers the world a sign of hope in an age of despair. Its emergence represents a growing appreciation of the Earth, a recognition of its vulnerability to abuse, and a desire for the kind of development which will protect its richness and beauty for future generations. What principles and beliefs are held by its supporters? In what ways are Christians and Greens working together throughout the world?

International awareness of the Greens rose gradually during the early 1980s. Environmentalism in the 1970s had tended to take the form of community-based lobbying and projects. However, environmentalists began to recognise a need to confront the powerful political and industrial interests which appeared to be generating environmental problems, and increasingly campaigners became better organised and more bold. Greenpeace, supported by millions worldwide, gained widespread publicity for numerous inspiring acts of civil disobedience which highlighted the most serious threats, and the evident need for legislative action resulted in the emergence of Green political parties. Politically, the Greens hit the international headlines after twenty-seven MPs were elected from *Die Grünen*, the West German Green Party, in 1983, although the first Green MP was in fact elected in Switzerland in 1979. By 1990 there were Green MPs in eleven countries and thirty MEPs in the Green group in the European Parliament.

The term 'Green', though often misused, properly refers to a set of ideas based upon ecology. It identifies political parties, although within the Green movement some choose not to join or become active in a party. The Green philosophy has not been formulated by any single philosopher, politician or preacher, but has arisen out of 'grass roots' development. There have been some key thinkers and exponents, such as Illich, Schumacher, Bahro and Porritt, but its strength is in people working together through communities and networks, with a common sense of identity and purpose.

As ecology lies at the heart of Green thinking and there exists much public confusion between Green ideas and environmentalism, it is vital to distinguish the *ecological* from the *environmental*. 'Environment' is essentially a neutral term meaning surroundings, and environmentalism merely indicates an active interest in these surroundings. Politically, therefore, it is a rather vague term, which communicates little about underlying values and proposals.

Strictly speaking, it is inappropriate to speak of an 'environmental' crisis, as if a single problem exists with the environment. There is, more accurately, an *ecological* crisis, a crisis of how people see their relationship with the rest of nature and how they value it. This crisis of ecology is one of people's perceptions and search for meaning. It results in a whole multitude of environmental *crises*, many of them interrelated. These cannot be solved unless the root causes of the ecological crisis are addressed and individuals and governments accept the need for a new perception of their relationship with the world and new values. A few superficial changes will not suffice.

Green principles

The basic principles of the Greens may be summarised as follows. First, Green thinking is not centred upon humankind but on the entire biosphere, the sphere where life is found (i.e. the Earth and its atmosphere). In other words, it tends to be *biocentric*. The whole creation is considered to be intrinsically valuable. We therefore recognise and respect the needs of other species, and do not care for them merely because this is in our interest.

Second, as a general rule, all of life is seen as interconnected. Thus the methodology used by Greens is *holistic*. Wherever possible and appropriate the aim is to understand different aspects of life as integrated into a whole, rather than as essentially separate, autonomous units. Environmental problems are not easily solved in isolation from one another and a range of responses, across all disciplines (philosophy, health, economics, education and so on), is often required. Frequently they are linked to questions of peace and justice.

Third, Greens regard *sustainability* as imperative. This may be described as a desire for development which does not cause such damage to the environment that fewer opportunities exist for future generations to enjoy an adequate quality of life.

Greens are, fourthly, advocates of radical *decentralism*, believing that change should start in individuals and communities at local level rather than be imposed by central government. A general principle which Greens apply to schools, firms, hospitals and other institutions is 'small is beautiful'.

Finally, the Green approach to all issues is characterised by unequivocal *radicalism* (meaning, literally, 'proceeding from the root'). Consider two examples. Our planet is simultaneously facing global warming and global thawing! The warming of the Earth's atmosphere through the greenhouse effect demands that we lower our energy consumption. And the thawing in relations between East and West 'superpowers' makes a nonsense of the $1,000 billion spent annually worldwide on military weapons. On a planet threatened by profligate materialism and thousands of potentially life-destroying nuclear weapons these threats must be removed by courageous and thoroughgoing reform.

The essentials of Green politics are summarised well in Jonathon Porritt's influential book *Seeing Green*.

Sketching the wide parameters of Green thinking, Porritt describes his 'minimum criteria for being green' as:

- a reverence for the Earth and for all its creatures;
- a willingness to share the world's wealth among *all* its people;
- prosperity to be achieved through sustainable alternatives to the rat race of economic growth;
- lasting security to be achieved through non-nuclear defence strategies and considerably reduced arms spending;
- a rejection of materialism and the destructive values of industrialism;
- a recognition of the rights of future generations in our use of all resources;
- an emphasis on socially useful, personally rewarding work, enhanced by human-scale technology;
- protection of the environment as a precondition of a healthy society;
- an emphasis on personal growth and spiritual development;
- respect for the gentler side of human nature;
- open, participatory democracy at every level of society;
- recognition of the crucial importance of significant reductions in population levels;
- harmony between people of every race, colour and creed;
- a non-nuclear, low-energy strategy based on conservation, greater efficiency and renewable sources;
- an emphasis on self-reliance and decentralised communities.[1]

These form only one person's vision, but it is representative of the thinking of Greens even though differences may exist on exact priorities and proposals. A recent study, *The Coming of the Greens*, points out that people with concern for the environment have been variously described as light Greens, dark Greens, shallow environmentalists, deep ecologists, Green socialists and Green capitalists! Greens clearly share with Christians the same tendency to what may be described either as a healthy diversity of opinion or a destructive factionalism! Reformist environmentalism, the belief that only minor changes are needed to bring about environmental sustainability, is viewed as a sham. 'Dark greens' like Porritt see such an approach as unduly conservative, offering inadequate, superficial treatment.

Spiritual roots

The set of Green ideas outlined above forms the basis for a philosophy, but is not in itself a religion. A person's religion is dependent on *faith*, an 'ultimate commitment' based on assumptions made about the nature of reality and the meaning of life. Such a commitment could be to the Earth, the human species, a personal God or another deity. Green ideas are provided in a framework of reasoned *thought* (hence it is a philosophy), but the underlying faith is a religion, Christianity or otherwise.

A consensus exists among most Greens that the ecological crisis has a religious dimension. Their motivation to act goes beyond prudence and self-interest and tends to be based on a deeply felt respect for the Earth and its Creator. This draws people to reflect upon that to which they are strongly bound or devoted – their ultimate commitment.

Greens are consequently inclined to believe that for true change people must develop spiritually through their chosen faith. This is revealed by the notice boards found in wholefood shops frequented by Greens, which often advertise opportunities to explore different forms of spirituality, although it is surprisingly rare to find notices about Christianity displayed.

Historian Arnold Toynbee once wrote: "The present threat to mankind's survival can be removed only by a revolutionary change of heart in individual human beings. This change of heart must be inspired by religion in order to generate the will power needed for putting arduous new ideals into practice."[2] Greens similarly see the challenge which now faces the industrialised world as a need for no less than a cultural transformation motivated by spiritual change. As Porritt writes, "We have lost our way by disregarding the planet and by disregarding the spirit ... Some kind of spiritual commitment, or religion in its true meaning (namely, the reconnection between each of us and the source of all life), is a fundamental part of the transformation that ecologists are talking about."[3]

This need for *fundamental personal change* has long been recognised. In the early 1970s leading environmentalist Max Nicholson called for "an intensive spell of environmental repentance" and Michael Allaby wrote that what was required, as never before, was "a change of heart" because "no less than such a conversion will avert the series of catastrophes that are beginning to happen already."[4] Schumacher spoke of the need for 'metaphysical reconstruction', and concluded *Small is Beautiful* by urging readers to make their first step to put their 'inner house' in order.[5]

More recently Rudolf Bahro has said that only the 'needs of heart and spirit' will provide sufficient motivation for the necessary change to a sustainable society, and has urged Christians to work together with the Greens. In Britain successive Green Party manifestos have explicitly acknowledged the importance of recognising and giving value to spiritual needs as well as physical ones, stating that to talk of the future without reference to the spirit is 'absurd'.

Significantly, the Green critique of Western culture has similarities with that of several recent Christian writings.[6] Ronald Sider, author of *Rich Christians in an Age of Hunger*, has noted how evangelical Christians have used arguments much the same as those of influential Green thinker Fritjof Capra.[7] In *The Turning Point* Capra denounces various aspects of modern Western culture, "the belief in the scientific method as the only valid approach to knowledge; the view of the universe as a mechanical system composed of elementary material building blocks; the view of life in society as a competitive struggle for existence; and the belief in unlimited material progress to be achieved through economic and technological growth."[8]

Christians and Greens may share objections to secular humanism and hold in common a belief that the *entire* biosphere is of significance and value and that there is a spiritual dimension to *all* of life. They may advocate the same policy prescriptions – Sider, for example, reacts sympathetically to Green proposals on economics, energy, peace and decentralisation. But underlying foundations may differ. For example, the complex web of relationships between humankind and the rest of nature may be seen by Christians in the context of a belief that humans were created by God from the dust of the Earth and that all things are held together through Him. Others, however, may understand it as a sign that 'all is one', a monist belief that the entire universe, including humankind, is divine. Indeed Capra's own faith is essentially a form of monism.

The starting point of Green thinking is not *necessarily* Christ but observation of our surroundings; it is biocentric, not Christocentric. Neither God nor Christ are necessarily embraced within it. Yet a vital belief of Christians is that Jesus Christ is "the radiance of God's glory and the exact representation of his being, sustaining all things by his powerful word" (Heb. 1.3). This promises access to a spirituality which offers us the potential, if we model ourselves on Christ, to reflect the glory of God. Those who do so should seek, through Christ's power, to sustain all things, to preserve and encourage life.

Any philosophy, whether capitalism, existentialism, liberalism, socialism or another school of thought, may allow people different starting points or ultimate commitments. It is the faith upon which it is based which is finally important, because faith defines our loyalties and reveals assumptions about life which affect our actions. We thus need to discern carefully the underlying assumptions of *any* philosophy. As an example, consider these words of David Brower, founder of Friends of the Earth:

> I owe an allegiance to the planet that has made me possible, and to all the life on that planet, whether friendly or not. I also owe an allegiance to the three and a half billion years of life that made it possible for me to be here, and all the rest of you too.[9]

This loyalty to the planet and to evolution seems to come close to forming the basis of a faith. A fundamental allegiance to the Earth and its evolution, however, implies an inclination towards paganism, a faith in the Earth as a self-regulating entity. Appreciation of the planet and a process of evolution is not in itself, of course, incompatible with Christianity. The Earth may be respected and even revered, without being *worshipped*.

Ideals and vision

Awareness of Christ enables many Christians to escape from self-centredness and be motivated to work according to his ideals. Jesus Christ taught his disciples to be *perfect*, just "as your heavenly Father is perfect" (Matt. 5.48) and Paul wrote to the Romans: "Do not be overcome by evil, but overcome evil with good" (Rom. 12.21). God does not wish our deeds to be "neither cold nor hot" (Rev. 3.15).

One attraction of Green thinking is that it is essentially idealistic. Some people may regard this as criticism, but idealism should be viewed positively in that it offers vision and a sense of hope. It does not have to be based on a blind belief that utopia can be built on Earth. Christians will want to temper any such idealism to take account of sin, but there is surely much to commend in aspiring to ideals rather than being content with imperfection. Christians acknowledge the nature of sin and the significance of the second coming and should have a 'realistic idealism', aiming high but accepting the possibility of not fully realising our goal.

The Greens' vision of peace and environmental harmony bears a resemblance to that of the Old Testament prophets. Isaiah envisaged the time when disputes would no longer be settled by warfare and people would "beat their swords into ploughshares and their spears into pruning hooks" (Isa. 2.4), and Ezekiel's vision was that the time would come when people would say that "this land that was laid waste has become like the garden of Eden" (Ezek. 36.35).

People who share these ideals need to use their imagination, intuition, and senses. For those of us brought up in this scientific age, where all mystery and mysticism is viewed sceptically, this may be a difficult task. Some people point to the dominating masculine influence in society to explain this scepticism. Yet as Schumacher put it, "we jolly well have to have the courage to dream if we want to survive and give our children the chance of survival."[10] The essence of hope is that change is indeed possible. It might help if we try to conceive images of the future, to project in our minds the ideal future as it *ought* to be, and then to imagine moving towards it, working out practical steps towards our *real* future in the light of these images. Through this we engage in a prophetic task.

Greens have often been more visible than Christians in creating such appropriate images. Because Christians have focused so much upon images of the past and have not looked confidently to future life on Earth, perhaps God has decided to speak through the Greens, in which case they might be thought of as 'secular prophets'. God does not only act through His chosen people and sometimes the vehicle He chooses for communication can be quite surprising (Num. 22.28; Isa. 45.4).

Deep or social?

When ecology forms the basis of philosophical study various assumptions are made relating to human behaviour which are significant. An example is the contrast between 'deep ecology' and 'social ecology'.

The former has arisen out of attempts to articulate a comprehensive religious and philosophical world view based upon observation of nature. According to advocates of deep ecology the problem with much contemporary thought is that it treats humans as isolated beings, fundamentally separate from the rest of nature. They are critical also of the materialistic view of reality. In contrast they view people as part of the total biosphere, part of a total organic whole, and do not treat spiritual and material aspects of reality as isolated or separated. Norwegian philosopher Arne Naess, whose article in 1973 first popularised the concept, identified two 'ultimate norms' which provide the foundation of deep ecology, *self-realisation* and *biocentric equality*.

Deep ecology is regarded as a challenge to the conventional Western idea of the self as an 'isolated ego' which strives for hedonistic gratification or for "a narrow sense of individual salvation in this life or the next".[11] Spiritual growth will only begin once people stop seeing themselves as isolated, competing 'egos' and instead seek to identify with others – not just family and friends, but the entire human species and non-human world. Thus in deep ecology 'self-realisation' becomes in practice concern not only for oneself but for what Naess calls "the realisation of the potentialities of life".[12]

On the surface this does not seem so far from the apostle Paul's idea of creation being liberated from its bondage to decay. But in Naess's philosophy Christ is not imperative. Naess believes that the principles of deep ecology may be applied to *any* religious tradition. Such universalism rests uneasily with traditional Christian belief in Christ's uniqueness.

Serious problems also exist with the principle of biocentric equality, that all organisms in the biosphere, being parts of an interrelated whole, are of equal intrinsic worth. The biosphere is considered a community in which humans are 'plain citizens'. However, as Naess indeed recognises, mutual predation is a biological fact of life. *All* species use other species for food, shelter and the means for survival. Thus although the implications of biocentric equality for, say, eating meat may at first sight appear significant, in reality the concept calls into question our right to eat *any* species, plant or animal!

Advocates of deep ecology thus tone down this principle and propose that humans should seek to have 'minimum impact' on other species. This is vague enough to be uncontentious but because it is imprecise it is liable to lack consequence. In short, deep ecology faces problems when, in taking Green ideas to extremes and turning a valid principle into an absolute truth, it attempts to make a religion out of a philosophy.

Bill Devall and George Sessions, who have done much to popularise the concept, cite St Francis of Assisi and the Italian philosopher Giordano Bruno as early advocates of deep ecology. However, although there may be some connections with Christianity, deep ecology has more important influences, including so-called 'ancient wisdom', the Romantic tradition, the teaching of 'native' peoples, such as American Indians, and the 'new physics'.

Social ecology draws from the utopian socialist and anarchist tradition of Peter Kropotkin and William Morris and might be a helpful corrective to any deep ecologists who believe that a cockroach is of equal intrinsic worth as a human being. Its advocates, led by Murray Bookchin, argue that the primary root cause of ecological problems is not individual behaviour, but the fact that the social order is based on free-market, expansionary capitalism.

However the implication that it may be necessary for political change to be implemented *before* individuals adopt an ecological perspective threatens the same kind of coercion which has bedevilled socialism. In a free society, change to the social order should take place only once individuals change, and ought to be influenced by their new ideas and values.

What makes social ecology unappealing to many Greens and especially from a Christian perspective is its evident distaste for the spiritual. Bookchin apparently believes that ecology is 'avowedly rational' and a form of naturalism that "looks to evolution and biosphere, not to deities in the sky or under the earth", to explain natural phenomena.[13]

Any inclination towards naturalism represents a step away from Christianity as, according to naturalism, the existence of living creatures is merely the product of natural causes; there is no God. Moreover nothing *transcends* nature, nothing (and nobody) can change the course of nature. Thus humans are, in effect, no more than mere animals. There is no free will, and nothing external to us which has moral authority over us which may constrain us. Life may be directed purposefully by 'evolution', or may have no particular purpose or direction at all.

This reduces humankind to being no more than products of our environment, moulded, shaped and enslaved by changes to our surroundings. Far from offering liberation it is, in fact, a disturbing form of environmental determinism. In effect it means that the global situation is out of our control, because it is clear that ecological balance demands certain forms of self-willed, *modified* human behaviour. If nothing transcends nature and ordinary people are thus spiritually powerless, unable to change course, they are susceptible to fatalism. All that remains to motivate us is a vague sense of loyalty to nature on the basis that we belong to it. Indeed if humans do not have any special role it leaves open to doubt what the purpose is of striving for sustainability. We could not survive without a healthy living environment, but the Earth could certainly survive without us!

If Jesus Christ is not acknowledged to be the 'exact representation' of God there is a danger that naturalism will prevail. It should be noted that most Greens do not go as far as naturalism, however, and many stop short at a form of natural theology, which stresses that God is manifest through His creation. He is accessible to all because of what may be experienced through nature.

This focus on God as Creator as distinct from Redeemer provides for only a limited understanding of God's character and activity. It may explain the existence and amazing *structure* of nature, but it has little to say about the *direction* of nature, its purpose or goal. Its primary failing stems from the starting point, namely ourselves. Natural theology seeks a way from ourselves to God. While this is necessary, it is also inadequate, as God also takes the initiative, choosing to reveal Himself to us in Jesus Christ. That said, many Christians have not taken God's revelation through nature seriously enough.

Towards a New Age?

It has been noted earlier that attempts by Christians to improve the human relationship with the rest of nature have followed and not led the upsurge of interest in Green ideas. In the recent past a more significant religious influence among Greens has been the New Age movement. This is an intellectual, cultural and spiritual grouping which has long been influential in America and is attracting growing interest in Britain, West Germany and elsewhere. Green Christians therefore need to unravel similarities and differences between their faith and the assumptions and underlying commitments in the New Age movement and a brief digression here is necessary.

Unfortunately some rather unintelligent nonsense has been written about the New Age by a number of Christian fundamentalists, which has spread fear and near-hysteria rather than true understanding. Consequently some Christians are very wary of the risk of being associated in some way with New Age thinking. According to Russell Chandler, author of a helpfully well-balanced study *Understanding the New Age*, leading critics such as Constance Cumbey and Dave Hunt mishandle facts and do not document their claims, and their logic is flawed at vital points.[14] Chandler himself addresses the New Age

challenge in a manner which is more credible and yet far
from uncritical.

What is the New Age movement? Most observers agree
on at least one thing; it is not easy to define. Lacking any
set creed, the movement takes the form of a prevalent flow
of ideas, and although several books have been particularly influential (among them Marilyn Ferguson's *The
Aquarian Conspiracy* and Fritjof Capra's *The Turning
Point*) none are regarded as sacred. Its ideas are eclectic,
drawing from a range of traditions, which include
Buddhism, Taoism, Gnosticism and native American
Indian religion. It operates not through any central
unifying organisation, but through various networks of
contacts, which often extend worldwide.

Its central conviction is that the world is on the
threshold of a new era which will see change as sweeping
as that of the Renaissance and Reformation. Many regard
this as a global spiritual reawakening. They arrive at this
conclusion in the belief that it is becoming apparent that
more and more people are questioning traditional
assumptions about the future of life on the planet. There is
a shift in people's perceptions, a deeper consciousness of
how they relate to their environment in the face of the
threat of destruction. As people modify their thinking and
adopt new values, their world view (or 'paradigm')
changes.

Underlying the idea of a New Age is the belief that life is
influenced by the orbit of the sun through the signs of the
Zodiac. It takes around 2,100 years to pass through each
age; currently we are on the cusp between the Piscean
Age and the Aquarian Age. Christians will obviously be
concerned at this connection with astrology, which is
condemned in the Bible (Isa. 47.13–15).

The real hope for the planet, New Age followers believe,
is for people to gain an appreciation of the interdependence between mind, body and spirit, between one
another, and between humankind and the rest of creation.
Much New Age thought tends to incline towards monism,
belief that the entire cosmos is undifferentiated, universal

energy. The perception of universal 'oneness' follows logically from belief that all things within nature are intricately interconnected. However monism is not the *only* possible conclusion; Christians would say that these interconnections simply provide evidence that God created a universe characterised by harmony and interrelated structures.

The movement has arisen in part out of people's search for an 'experiential' religion and an important aspect is a quest for personal transformation, or consciousness-changing, through certain behaviour aimed at triggering changes to the body, mind and spirit.

Many followers take to an extreme the simple desire for occasional life-enhancing experiences such as rejuvenation felt through walking in the countryside. Romantic poets and philosophers went beyond this and sought spiritual transcendence in close proximity to nature through the sense of awe gained on mountain tops or in isolated wilderness. New Age followers go still further, through special meditation techniques, mood-altering music, special diets, chanting mantras, seeking to balance and align 'energies', psychotherapeutic programmes, and perhaps even using mind-expanding drugs.

A false premise?

Although there are obviously some fundamental differences, there are also similarities in certain aspects of Christianity and New Age thought. Both reject the destructive, materialistic and utilitarian aspects of modern culture. Both believe in the need for radical transformation by individuals through a new world view. Many Christians agree with New Age followers that there is a need to think holistically rather than dualistically, to protect creation from exploitation, and to live in peaceful coexistence with others.

How, then, should Christians react to New Age thought? Its growth reveals that many people are searching spiritually and yet reject mainstream churches. The Church needs to ask why they are attracted elsewhere. Evidently the movement is addressing questions about threats to modern life and the search for inner and outer peace which Christians have not treated satisfactorily.

Donald Reeves is Rector of St James's Church, Piccadilly, one of relatively few churches in Britain where dialogue between Christians and New Age followers is encouraged. Reeves wisely advises Christians to avoid arrogance with New Age followers and instead to approach them in penitence, grateful for dialogue and humbly acknowledging many people's negative experience of church:

> Many of the New Age movement are people who are disenchanted by institutional religion . . . It is largely the result of our decaying, life-denying institutions, where the Spirit has been firmly squashed, that the New Age movement exists.[15]

It is relatively easy to share goals, however, and explanations of the source of problems and the means of overcoming them are significant. There is, for example, a considerable difference between rejecting dualism and accepting monism. Christians aspire to *communion*, not *union*, with God. We anticipate new spiritual bodies and being wholly reconciled with God, not fused into becoming part of Him. While Christians may reject dualistic thinking, we still believe in the existence of *separate* powers of good and evil. In contrast, one of the dangers of New Age thinking is its moral relativism.

In the New Age view of reality no absolutes exist. However if everything is God and there are no absolutes, how are the parameters for what is morally permissible drawn? The fact of evil and the source of suffering tends to be by-passed, transcended or simply ignored in New Age thought. There is no adequate explanation for the existence of evil and suffering – the only sin appears to be ignorance of wholeness and unity. It is less than satisfactory to define sin as 'unawakened consciousness' or 'ignorance of wholeness and unity' – sin is essentially idolatry, giving undue status to something other than the true God.

The inadequate explanation of evil and suffering in New Age thought leads to further weaknesses. Because of belief in the possibility of *unlimited* human potential in this life, there is neither *grace* nor *atonement* in the New Age world view. There is without doubt much to commend in holistic thinking and improving our 'inner ecology' – the relationship between our mind, body and spirit. But even this is ultimately inadequate because without Christ there is no redemption of our *whole* selves, and therefore no sense of liberation gained through the certain knowledge of forgiveness through God's grace.

The New Age movement has also been criticised for a near-obsession with 'self', its emphasis on self-discovery, self-healing, self-development. Objectors criticise this as narcissism and some regard it as suspiciously close to the individualism of the political right. The Christian understanding of the coming of the kingdom of God, the true new age, involves not only the individual's self-improvement but collective change and the renewing of the whole creation. Self-fulfilment for Christians is a by-product of faith, not a goal in itself.

Much New Age thought is rooted in a belief in 'self-actualisation' and makes an existentialist assumption that we create our own reality. There are links here with Abraham Maslow's idea of a 'hierarchy of needs', which extends from the basic demands of self-interest, food and shelter, to the highest point, which is self-actualisation, a sense of becoming at one with all reality. People are understood to have virtually unlimited potential which for some (largely unexplained) reason is not fully 'realised'.

This exposes a basic contradiction with Christianity. People are elevated to divine status through 'personal transformation', a process of gaining a 'planetary (or global) consciousness'. Ultimately they are themselves said to become 'God'; there is no other, autonomous being.

'God' is both the agent and the recipient of people's acts. Thus American actress Shirley MacLaine has proclaimed 'I am God', while David Spangler, one of the originators of the Findhorn Community in Scotland, a major New Age centre, has suggested that we are each our own Christ. The New Age understanding of God is of an impersonal, universal power which they speak of as 'Christ-consciousness' or 'Christ-energy'. This contrasts markedly with Christian belief in a personal, trinitarian God revealed through Jesus Christ.

The term 'New Age' is not directly used in the Bible, although the idea of a new era is apparent in references to the immediate presence of the kingdom of God (e.g. Luke 17.20–21) and the inauguration of the kingdom in its fulness (Rev. 21.1–22.6). Matthew records the disciples asking Jesus for "the sign of your coming and of the end of the age" (Matt. 24.3), and refers to a harvest at "the end of the age" in Jesus's explanation of the parable of the seeds (Matt. 13.39). Such sayings gave people a sense of urgency and accountability.

New Age followers fall into a similar trap as those Christians who adopt a 'postmillennialist' interpretation of the end times, believing that the thousand-year reign of Christ foretold in the Bible begins on Earth as we know it (the New England settlers in America being an obvious example). This suggests that there is no radical break with the past when the present age comes to an end, even though this is clearly suggested in the Bible (2 Pet. 3.10). Some New Age followers believe that Jesus gave a sign foretelling the coming of the Age of Aquarius when he told his disciples to look for a man carrying a jar of water who would lead them to the room to be used for the Last Supper (Mark 14.13). The symbol of the Age of Aquarius is a man bearing a pitcher of water. This use of Scripture appears extremely contrived.

That said, Christians can learn from some aspects of New Age thought. Many New Age supporters were Greens long before Christians woke up to the environmental crises and are in a position to communicate valuable insights. Secondly they recognise, in a way that many Christians do not, that to enable people to be healthy the whole self – body, mind and spirit – must be involved.

Certain practices which have attracted the 'New Age' label are quite wrongly dismissed by some Christians. Certain techniques used to advance human wellbeing, such as healthy dieting and listening to inspirational music, may well be beneficial. Although some complementary health therapies are dubious from a Christian perspective others, such as osteopathy and homeopathy, can be perfectly acceptable. Even natural foods are critically associated by some with the New Age, although there are examples of wholefood companies which are run explicitly as Christian businesses, such as Community Wholefoods and the Daily Bread Co-operative.

Dialogue will inevitably expose some of the conflicts. Christians must be wary of any prolonged involvement in New Age activities because of the link with astrology and the fact that certain practices are connected with the occult. Russell Chandler's study urges particular caution if a therapy, course or teaching: (1) is explained in terms of manipulating, balancing or polarising energies; (2) deprecates the value of the mind or critical thinking; (3) is supported only by testimonial anecdotes of the committed rather than by solid evidence and outside evaluation; or (4) is based on 'secret' esoteric knowledge revealed only to an inner elite.[16] This is sound advice.

In conclusion, the New Age is, as Chandler suggests, "neither the hellish conspiracy that fundamentalist critics charge, nor the utopian bliss its fondest supporters imagine."[17] There are certain ideas within New Age thinking which are helpful, although Christians will reject others, which conflict with basic biblical truths and expose its false foundation. Even so, by challenging Christians to examine their own world view more rigorously at a crucial time in history, the New Age movement is at least encouraging one valuable, overdue task.

Global Greening

Although Christians have been slow to grasp the urgency of responding to environmental problems and few have grasped the relevance of ecology to their faith, a learning process is now taking place. Two international initiatives in particular have helped to raise awareness among Christians, the World Council of Churches' 'Justice, Peace and the Integrity of Creation' (JPIC) initiative and the World Wide Fund for Nature's 'Network on Conservation and Religion'.[18]

At its 1975 Nairobi Assembly the World Council of Churches expressed its vision of the future in terms of a 'Just, Participatory and Sustainable Society'. Its Advisory Committee wrote: "Christians believe that the whole world is God's creation, continuously being renewed by the power of redemption and living under the promise of God's kingdom, the reign of peace and justice. Christians believe that all human beings are part of a dynamic pointing towards the messianic kingdom."

During the next eight years many worrying global developments occurred – the introduction of a new generation of nuclear weapons in Europe, new evidence of serious environmental threats, and an increasingly volatile world economy, with many people suffering unemployment and several nations in serious debt. The current, slightly amended theme of 'Justice, Peace and the Integrity of Creation' was chosen at the 1983 WCC Assembly to signify that these areas of concern are to be seen as interrelated. The concept of 'integrity of creation' was intended to go beyond that of 'sustainability' in taking account of the *wholeness* of life created by God. It was described as a plea to recognise that we live in an interdependent world, 'a world of relationships and delicate balances'. A series of meetings took place throughout the world, including a major ecumenical gathering in Basel in Switzerland, and a World Convocation for Justice, Peace and the Integrity of Creation was held in Seoul, Korea in 1990 as a key part of the ongoing 'conciliar process'.

Links between economic justice and environmental sustainability have been increasingly evident to aid workers in low-income nations, and organisations such as Christian Aid, CAFOD (Catholic Fund for Overseas Development), TEAR Fund and Oxfam have begun to take account of this. It is now accepted that poverty is both a cause and a result of environmental degradation. There is a deadly cycle. In consequence many aid agencies are looking more carefully at their work to ensure that their projects offer a means of support to local people which is environmentally sustainable. Peace and justice concerns have often been linked; environmental issues are related to each.

There are countless examples of these links; consider the situation in the Dominican Republic. Rich landowners and international consortia extract wealth from forestry, farming, and mining. The poor farmers have been forced on to marginal land where, with little option but to maximise yields in order to survive, they inevitably damage the soil. Marine resources around the island are threatened by over-fishing, and industrial pollution causes problems both on land and at sea. But the biggest threat of all is from deforestation. The land is only really suitable for trees, and excessive tree-felling has led to serious soil erosion. Without tree cover even a single rainstorm can carry away precious topsoil. The damage caused results in crop failure and farmers are forced to clear further land, continuing the process of decline.

Similarly environmental damage is inevitably caused in any military exchange. The environment in Vietnam, as well as its people, still bears the scars of bombing during the war when American planes dropped deadly chemicals to defoliate the landscape. The situation in Central America similarly reveals the problem. In El Salvador and Guatemala cropland and forest have been destroyed by bombing aimed at overcoming guerrillas, and in Nicaragua the American-backed Contra rebels have deliberately targeted agricultural and environmental projects for damage. Practical problems relating to peace, justice and the integrity of creation are often clearly related.

Links between Christianity and ecology are being forged from both directions. The World Wide Fund for Nature (WWF) has played a valuable part in awakening interest among Christians. The organisation's first major initiative on religion coincided with its twenty-fifth anniversary in 1986. At the suggestion of HRH the Prince Philip, Duke of Edinburgh, who is the President of WWF International, it was decided to hold an event to bring together leaders of the world's major faiths to discuss conservation. Prince Philip's reasoning was that because religion has a major influence upon cultures throughout the world, only with the active involvement of religious leaders can the global environment be protected from abuse. Moreover, as most of the Earth's inhabitants do not live in Christian cultures, all of the world's major faiths have to be involved if the environment is to be protected from irreversible damage.

Multi-faith dialogue raises many problems, but in the context of protecting the global environment it makes much sense. If, for example, Christians were in danger of drowning in a sinking ship they would look to anyone in a position to help, irrespective of their religious faith, as well as to God. In such circumstances co-operation is obviously more beneficial than confrontation.

The initial gathering took the form of a pilgrimage and consultation at Assisi in Italy, birthplace of St Francis, attended by around eight hundred people. Prince Philip declared during the ceremony that the event signified that "a new and powerful alliance has been forged between the forces of religion and the forces of conservation."[19] Welcoming those present, Father Lanfranco Serrini, Minister General of the Franciscan Order, one of the five representatives of the world's major faiths, said:

> No-one pretends that our respective beliefs are or can be held in common; but we do believe that religious concern for the conservation and ecological harmony of the natural world is

our common heritage, our birthright and our duty ... Let us now, each according to the wealth of our own religious traditions, share our common concern for the future of the world.[20]

Thus rather than seeking to prepare a joint statement, which it was thought might represent a 'superficial unity', the leaders of each faith issued a 'Declaration' outlining its distinctive insights concerning nature. The WWF consequently formally established a 'Network on Conservation and Religion'.

This Assisi event was followed up in Britain with a three-year programme initiated in 1987 which aimed to turn Harvest Festival back to a proper consideration of Christian responsibility for creation. According to the WWF many people love the Harvest Festival but feel that in recent years it has lost a sense of direction. It therefore produced a 'Creation and Harvest' liturgy for a major celebratory service in 1987 at Winchester Cathedral. During the service people were invited to make a 'Rainbow Covenant' with all the creatures of the Earth, tying to each other's wrists an interwoven thread of different colours as a reminder of God's covenant to Noah after the Flood. According to the WWF the service was subsequently repeated at three thousand other churches throughout the country.

The following year a second 'Creation Festival' was held at a Harvest service at Coventry Cathedral, and liturgies were developed and distributed for Easter and Advent. Controversy arose in 1989, however, when the WWF programme culminated with a major celebration entitled 'Faith and the Environment', which included pilgrimages, a service at Canterbury Cathedral and a conference on 'Theology and Ecology' held in conjunction with the British Council of Churches.

A group of fundamentalist Christians led by Action for Biblical Witness to our Nation (ABWON) vociferously condemned the event, apparently under the misapprehension that the Archbishop of Canterbury and the

Pope had attended the earlier Assisi event and that there was to be multi-faith worship in the Cathedral. The objectors were, in fact, wrong on both counts. Neither the Archbishop nor the Pope had been at Assisi and the Cathedral service was a very orthodox celebration of Holy Communion. The situation was not made any easier by the fact that there was an unintended clash in scheduling with a nationwide day of 'Marches for Jesus'. The misinformation spread by ABWON was regrettable and embarrassing to environmentally concerned evangelicals who appreciated how the attack could be perceived as criticism of involvement in any environmental activity.

In his sermon, which gained widespread publicity, the Archbishop of Canterbury described the source of the crisis as people's demand for more than the planet can give, and called on Christians to engage in penitence and prayer. He spoke of the 'sheer preciousness' of life and how the intimacy of God's care shows that His creation should not be treated as a 'cheap universe' or a 'throwaway world'.

In the meantime another initiative sparked off by the WWF's new interest in religion was a series of consultations held at St George's House at Windsor Castle on the theme 'The Christian Attitude to Nature'. These brought together many specialists and culminated in a book, *Survival or Extinction*, co-written by HRH the Duke of Edinburgh and Michael Mann, outlining the factors influencing environmental trends and a biblical approach to creation.

Networking

One of the earliest initiatives by people wishing to explore the connections between ecological beliefs and Christian faith was Christian Ecology Link, formed (as the Christian Ecology Group) in 1981 when a small number of people decided to meet informally for prayer at a Green Party conference.[21] I convened a meeting in the following spring which formally established the group, and those present decided to organise an autumn conference at Ammerdown, near Bath. Out of this came a booklet, *God's Green World*, the first attempt to bring together the ideas of the newly-emerging Green movement and Christianity.

In its formative stage Christian Ecology Link decided to broaden its appeal by loosening its ties with the Green Party. It also established two aims, 'to spread ecological insights among Christian people and churches' and 'to spread Christian insights throughout the Green movement', and decided upon a brief theological basis which reflected its desire to embrace Christians of all traditions while affirming a loyalty to mainstream Christian teaching.[22] By the late 1980s local groups were forming throughout the country, setting up community-based initiatives and providing speakers for meetings.

Thus for almost a decade Christian Ecology Link has spearheaded interest in Christianity and ecology in Britain with its magazine *Green Christians* and conferences on themes such as 'Animals in Creation', 'People, Technology and the Environment', 'Growing Awareness' (on food, farming and health), and 'Consuming Issues' (which followed 'Green Consumer Week'). It has responded to initiatives such as the Church of England's reports on nuclear weapons and the environment and that of the World Commission on Environment and Development, *Our Common Future*; it has also contributed to the WWF's Network on Conservation and Religion.

Initiatives are also taking place in several other countries to bring together Christians and Greens. One of the most significant has arisen out of the 'North American Conference on Christianity and Ecology', which took place in August 1987 in Indiana and was attended by some five hundred participants. This brought together prominent figures from a wide range of traditions and backgrounds, including theologians from various traditions, poets, native Indians, and Amish farmers. The event became a focus for exchanging information and has spawned a permanent secretariat, many regional activities and an occasional magazine, *Firmament*.

In West Germany a group called *Christen Bei Den Grünen* has worked closely with the Green Party. A major study of the religious beliefs among West German Greens appeared in 1988.[23] In predominantly Catholic Austria, where Green MPs were first elected in 1986, seminars have been held on the theme of people, the environment and creation and resulted in a pamphlet.[24] A 'Working Group' of Christians and Greens (*Arbeitskreis 'Christen Und Grüne'*) has organised discussions about liberation theology and the challenge of St Francis, and has voiced concern at recent conservative trends in the Austrian Church, distributing leaflets when the Pope visited Vienna in June 1988.

Links are also being made in New Zealand, where a successful conference held in 1989 called 'Repainting the Rainbow' attracted over two hundred participants. The conference title referred to the sign of God's covenant, but also to the *Rainbow Warrior*, the Greenpeace protest boat which was bombed by the French while docked in New Zealand. The success of the conference led its organisers to form a permanent Christian Ecology Group to organise further events.

Spreading Green awareness

One of the vital tasks of Green Christians is to inform and encourage other Christians. The 1988 Lambeth Conference of Anglican Bishops from throughout the world referred to stewardship of the Earth as "a necessary part of Christian discipleship". At present far too few Christians have grasped the relevance of ecology to their faith, although a learning process is beginning to take place and there are more and more examples of projects through which Christians are showing proper care for the Earth.

In Britain the work of Christian Ecology Link has assumed particular importance because until very recently the response of churches to the ecological crisis has been woefully weak. The Church of England produced a timely report in 1970 called *Man in His Living Environment* which, though focusing primarily on practical problems rather than theological analysis, concluded with stark clarity:

> We are all seeking a cultural revolution in which it is affirmed that *despoiling the earth is a blasphemy* and not just an error of judgement, a mistake; in which a proper concern for all living creatures, including man, becomes righteousness and not mere sentimental kindliness.[25] [my emphasis]

The report attracted much attention. It sold over four thousand copies and was discussed in numerous church groups, diocesan synods and educational establishments. Copies were submitted in evidence to the World Council of Churches' Consultation on 'Technology, Faith and the Future of Man' and to the major United Nations conference in Stockholm in 1972. In a review two years later, Christians were encouraged to take up practical conservation work through the British Trust for Nature Conservation.

The next step taken was by the then Archbishop of Canterbury, Michael Ramsey, who established a small committee to work with the Church's Doctrine Commission on the implications of Christian belief for attitudes to the environment. The result, published in 1975 as *Man and Nature*, was a valuable amplification of the biblical and theological material of *Man In His Living Environment*. For the next ten years, however, while a few bishops and other Church leaders occasionally spoke out (notably John Taylor, Bishop of Winchester, in *Enough is Enough*), the institutional Church remained largely silent.

Such apparent apathy may be attributed to several factors. Between the mid 1970s and mid 1980s Britain's economic problems distracted attention away from the environment and interest was also overshadowed by the problems of mass unemployment and nuclear arms escalation. There was little interest at parish level. Many Christians were inclined to express their beliefs in a form of individualism, in keeping with the prevailing political climate, sometimes under influence from the American 'religious Right'.

The Church of England's next statement on the environment, produced in 1986, when public concern was reaching new heights, met with considerable criticism. The report, *Our Responsibility for the Living Environment*, was to many people a huge disappointment. Several critics in the General Synod debate on the report criticised its bland tone and inadequate sense of urgency, and its failure (apparently deliberate) to provide virtually any concrete proposals. Though duly commended by Synod for study, its fate seems to have been to gather dust on ministers' bookshelves. In the light of this, the report of the Archbishop's Commission on Rural Areas has gained a special significance.

The recent record of the Church of Scotland is rather more impressive and through the Science, Technology and Religion Project it has a long-established study programme. In addition to a video exploring problems of nuclear waste disposal, lead in petrol and acid rain (*Not in My Backyard*) the Science, Religion and Technology Project has produced reports on theological and ethical issues in land-use (*While the Earth Endures*), and the greenhouse effect (*Scorching Heat and Drought . . . ?*) These constitute rare and valuable examples of Christian consideration of practical environmental issues set in a theological context.

Elsewhere in Europe the most significant developments, including theological work and practical action, are in West Germany. Jürgen Moltmann, Professor of Systematic Theology at the University of Tübingen, is responsible for important theological developments in recent years, notably in *The Future of Creation* and *God in Creation*. These have been particularly significant coming from West Germany, where natural theology, linked with social Darwinism, has suffered an association with Nazism. The Lutheran Church has for some years employed an official ecological adviser and several regions have part-time advisers working to an 'environmental mandate', who may themselves have a dozen specialist advisers.

Swiss theologians, too, have been rethinking Christian attitudes to creation. Discussions which followed an ecumenical conference in 1980 led to the publication five years later of a manifesto entitled *La place de l'homme dans la création* (*On Being Human in the Whole of Creation*). This urged Christians not to abuse their power over nature but to use it carefully, and offered suggestions for action. An ecumenical organisation in Switzerland was subsequently formed to promote understanding of the need to care for the environment and provide practical advice to individual parishes (*Communauté Oecuménique de Travail Église et Environnement* (COTE)).

The impact of St Francis is sometimes evident in Christians' response to the environmental crisis. In the Netherlands there is an ecumenical 'Church and Environment' group which is part of the National Council of Churches. Among the participants is an organisation which in 1987 set up a project called 'Honour the Earth' backed by forty-three Franciscan orders and congregations. This collects liturgical material, study resources and exhibition material, and organises celebrations which focus on creation and vigils of silence and prayer at places where the Earth is under threat. Several series of study days are being held, the first of which resulted in a book *Als de Schepping zucht* (*When Creation Sighs*). Encouragement is given to appropriate lifestyles, informing people through visits to Franciscan communities where they participate in practical work and spiritual reflection. In addition, links are being made with like-minded people overseas, including Franciscans in Germany, Poland, Belgium and Uruguay. In Uruguay a Franciscan Ecology Centre has been established to develop a programme to study the social implications of ecology within an ethical framework. Franciscans have also been vocal in Switzerland, where alongside members of the Protestant Church they protested against Government inaction on air pollution with a candlelit procession in Zurich in 1986.

People at an event in Italy in 1982 marking the 800th anniversary of the birth of St Francis called upon bishops, pastors and local churches, in a report named *The Gubbio Document*, to "make the faithful aware of their responsibility to be active participants in the development of a different quality of life and in the protection of nature and the environment". The authors of the report, named after the city in which they met, included representatives of the Club of Rome (who a decade earlier had produced *The Limits to Growth*), the Italian WWF and other leading organisations concerned with environment and development issues. Five years later they produced a further document, *Towards the Third Millennium – What Progress?*, which questioned 'indiscriminate' economic and technological development.

Several organisations in North America are dedicated to studying Christianity and the environment, including the Michigan-based Au Sable Institute for Environmental Studies and, in California, the Eleventh Commandment Fellowship and the Institute in Culture and Creation Spirituality (the New Creation Institute, established in Montana, is now based on Switzerland). The Institute of Christian Studies in Toronto, Canada, aims to encourage Christians to develop an integrated world view, in which all of life is influenced by their faith. It has, in the process, encouraged the development of a theological basis for belief in the redemption of the whole creation. Inspired by the Reformed tradition (in particular the Dutch thinkers Kuyper and Dooyeweerd) it produces much valuable material challenging the dualism of modern Western culture.

Calvin College in Michigan took a major step forward in 1977 in instigating a programme of study on 'Christian Stewardship of Natural Resources', which led to the influential book, *Earthkeeping*. In 1980 the Au Sable Institute began holding a yearly forum to discuss specific themes concerning biblical stewardship of the environment, bringing together Church leaders, educators, experts in the environmental sciences, theologians, activists and others. Meanwhile members of the United Church of Christ, whose Ecological Task Force of the early 1970s had disbanded, were prompted to establish a Network for Environmental and Economic Responsibility by an ecumenical conference in 1986 held in New York, 'For the Love of Earth and People' (sponsored by the National Council of Churches).[26]

The North American Conference on Christianity and Ecology, referred to earlier, gained international coverage and was significant in highlighting the rich variety of opinions held by Christians concerned for the environment. The theological controversy was raised in particular by a vocal minority led by Thomas Berry, a Catholic priest strongly influenced by the writings of Teilhard de Chardin. Berry sought to sway the conference participants behind 'creation-centred spirituality', an interpretation of Christianity popularised in recent years through the writings of Dominican priest Matthew Fox, notably *Original Blessing*. Berry's ideas attracted criticism from many participants who saw them as contrary to orthodox Christian doctrine; some even described them as a form of neo-paganism (see Chapter Eight).[27]

The Catholic Church has in recent years been particularly prominent in spreading awareness about environmental responsibility, especially in low-income countries. In 1979, in his first encyclical, Pope John Paul II said that "it was our Creator's will for man to relate to nature as intelligent and unselfish 'master' and 'steward' and not as unconcerned 'exploiter' and 'destroyer'," and in the 1987 encyclical *Sollicitudo Rei Socialis*, he urged Catholics not to 'transgress' towards nature. Early in the following year, the Vatican opened the first ever Pontifical Faculty of Christian Ecology, to train priests in environmental awareness. Following this lead, a group of bishops of the Italian Episcopal Conference formulated a set of ecological criteria as spiritual guidelines for defending the environment, which observers dubbed the 'green gospel'.

Criticism was targeted at urban planners and the bishops called for moderation in resource consumption through appropriate, simple lifestyles. The Christian faith, they said, demanded 'ecological conversion'.[28] Then as the decade closed the Pope chose his World Day of Peace message to be on the theme 'Peace with God the Creator – Peace with All of Creation' as an invitation for reflection on the moral implications of ecological crisis. The Earth, he said, was a common heritage for humankind.

During the 1980s a succession of Pastoral Letters from Catholic bishops throughout the world have expressed growing concern at environmental destruction. For example, such letters have been issued by the bishops in the Philippines pointing out that "the attack on the natural world which benefits very few Filipinos is rapidly whittling away at the base of our living world and endangering its fruitfulness for future generations."[29] In one gesture of sincerity two bishops proceeded to donate 270 hectares of Church land for distribution by the Government through the land reform programme. The need for land reform has also been highlighted in letters from bishops in Guatemala and Paraguay. In the former the bishops called for a redistribution of unused and little-used land to the poor, and for taxes on large landholdings.

The bishops in the Philippines recognised that Christians have themselves been to blame and a Pastoral Letter read out in all Catholic pulpits in 1988 urged them to "develop a deep appreciation for the fragility of our island's life systems" and to take steps to defend the environment. It continued: "Be aware of what is happening in your area. Do not remain silent when you see your environment being destroyed. Use your influence within your family and community to develop this awareness." The letter ended by recommending the setting up of a 'Care of the Earth' ministry at every level of Church organisation, from the smallest local Christian community to national level. The *Far Eastern Economic Review* referred to it as a 'highly unusual document' which was without precedent in Roman Catholic Church history.

A further example is the Dominican Republic. When a new government took office in 1982, Catholic bishops called for a 'well planned and stringent' policy on deforestation and warned: "We cannot go on being indifferent to the preservation and improvement of the environment in which we live. No ecological imbalance can go unpunished. Man's sin against nature always turns back on man himself." Since then the problems have far from disappeared and the bishops continue to speak out, calling for an end to wasteful consumption, injustice to the poor, and exploitation of nature. In 1987, in a further Pastoral Letter called 'The Protection of Nature is a Condition of Survival', they urged responsible action to their followers and did not mince their words: "Parish priests, assembly leaders, lay ministers and all the pastoral agents must insist on the duties of human beings towards nature . . . There has been negligence, complicity and rapacity on the part of many to whom vigilance was entrusted."

A final example is the Pacific region, where people on many islands have suffered at the hands of the global superpowers and other industrial nations, resulting in the international Campaign for a Nuclear Free and Independent Pacific. Nuclear tests have been undertaken over many years in Pacific atolls and waters, threatening people's health and that of other species. In some areas local people have been forced to move home; in others the native culture is threatened by tourism. Issues of justice, peace and the integrity of creation are clearly revealed to be interconnected.

The churches in the region often play an influential role in community life and host meetings on social issues. The concern of Church leaders was highlighted in 'The Pacific and Peace', the bishops' 1986 Pastoral Letter, which addressed the suffering caused by the military programmes of the superpowers and fear of the continuing nuclear pollution of the ocean, and questioned whether the kind of development taking place would truly lead to peace. The letter also invited local Christians to consider the implications if they aspired to the lifestyle of richer countries. Such development, the bishops warned, would make them more dependent on foreign resources rather than those available locally, might lead them to abandon traditional forms of sharing among family and community, and posed further risks to the environment.

One way in which interest has been aroused is special days or weeks during which concern for the environment is underlined. In Britain Harvest Sunday has, of course, been established for over a century. The 'One World Week' theme in 1988, 'Making Peace with the Planet' proved highly successful and brought many Christians and Greens together, working alongside anti-poverty campaigners, for the first time. For many years there has been a Conservation Sunday in churches in Zimbabwe, and recently the Lutheran Church in Sweden instituted an annual World Nature Day on Midsummer's Day, when member churches have sermons on an appropriate theme. In Finland the Lutheran Church has in recent years held special weeks on the theme 'So Beautiful is the Earth – Our Responsibility for Creation', with special publications and activities. Finally, in Greece the Orthodox Church has announced a conservation 'feast day' as a focal point in the Orthodox calendar for encouraging environmental awareness and education.

Projects and protest

Once better informed of the need for environmental responsibility, Christians are often inspired to initiate practical projects or to protest against the destruction being caused. In several countries they have helped to establish conservation projects. In Britain one example is the Community Recycling Opportunities Programme (CROP), run by Baptist minister Robert Brown, which was set up in 1983. This involves the reclamation of some two thousand tonnes of waste material each year, including glass, paper and plastic, which is then recycled and sold back to industry.

Two other Britons, Les Batty and Peter Harris, have set up a Christian Field Study Centre and Bird Observatory, 'A Rocha' (Portuguese for 'the Rock') in south-west Portugal. This was planned over four years and opened in 1986. The Centre aims to act as a Christian witness and so help local churches, to study bird life in the area and encourage nature conservation, and to provide opportunities to visitors for field studies. Hunting and shooting are widespread in the region and tourism developments pose a serious threat.

Sadness at the lost beauty of the Lebanese environment when he returned after an eighteen-year absence led Father Étienne Sacre to involvement in conservation work. Having helped to form the Lebanese Federation for the Protection of Nature, he then had the idea of creating a nature reserve. His work and enthusiasm led to Lebanon's first National Park, which opened in 1987 in one of the country's few remaining oak and pine forests, an important site for birds. Faced with questions about the warfare in his country, Father Sacre responded: "We must redirect the energy wasted on destroying people in this war towards saving man and his environment." He added, *My work in ecology is a duty.* In my work as a priest, a believer, it is my duty to save life and nature."

Such a duty invariably leads to conflict. An example is East Germany, where until recently the Church was the only institution where people could assemble freely, discuss political issues and publish material. Consequently it became an important vehicle for environmental protest during the 1980s. The East German Church is itself an important landowner, possessing 500,000 acres, and has actively worked with environmentalists, providing land for organic farms and ecological houses and workshops. This connection inevitably led to clashes with state authorities and in 1987 three Church-funded workers were arrested in a raid on an East Berlin parsonage known to house a Church-sponsored environmental library. As the conflict began to escalate state authorities attacked the Church for maintaining an interest in the environment.

Christians have been active in several countries in responding to another problem, deforestation. In Honduras a Christian body called MOPAWI is working to support the indigenous Indians, who are struggling to protect the remaining Mosquitia rainforest from destruction, assisted by a team from TEAR fund. The rainforest is being destroyed by ranchers who raise cattle to provide beef for North American hamburger chains. The team aims to help the Indians improve their lobbying and use other means to defend the rainforest, such as identifying and claiming their land rights.[30]

In Brazil, where the Amazon rainforest is being destroyed so rapidly, there is frequent and sometimes violent conflict between the local rubber-tappers and small-scale farmers and the landowners and cattle ranchers. In a notorious murder in 1988 Chico Mendez, leader of a rubber-tappers' union in the western Amazon, was shot dead by a landowner's gunman. Christian Aid is helping the union to establish a co-operative to market their produce. It is also assisting the Paxato Indians in north-eastern Brazil who are in danger of being expelled from their forest and have had eight of their leaders shot dead. Meanwhile in the western state of Acre so-called 'feet-on-the ground' theologians have pressurised officials into establishing areas where deforestation is prohibited by state law and the land is set aside for the extraction of forest products such as rubber and Brazil nuts.[31]

In the Dominican Republic where, as indicated earlier, the threat is particularly serious, an organisation called *Floresta* has been created with the aim of demonstrating Christ's love and salvation to the poor. Recognising that deforestation has to be reversed if the poor are to become self-sufficient, it operates by helping rural farmers to convert to tree cropping.

Another example is the Philippines, where around 80 per cent of the forest has been destroyed since the Second

World War. The equivalent of 100,000 hectares of soil one metre deep is washed into the sea each year, and all the waterways and rivers in Metro-Manila are biologically dead. Many Christians have joined the struggle to save the environment and secure justice for the poor. In South Catabato, where a series of dams are planned which would wipe out the tribal T'boli homelands, church workers have forged links with the local people and taken non-violent protest, including lying down in front of the machines brought in to clear the forest and land. Catholic bishops have been prominent and in the Malaybalay area Bishop Gaucencio Rosales has helped to lead opposition to massive logging operations.

In Ethiopia the drought crisis has worsened as a result of extensive deforestation caused by wood gathering and land clearance for settlement in the highland areas. Since 1985, however, the Ethiopian Orthodox Church has embarked on extensive schemes of afforestation in an effort to reverse this destruction. It has established over twenty nursery centres and raised more than 2.6 million seedlings, which have been distributed mainly in the northern highlands where pressure on the environment is most severe. In addition more than three hundred small plantations have been created, often situated near church grounds and tended by the clergy.

Ecological protest is not simply confined to environmentally destructive developments. Christian animal welfare campaigners in Britain have organised prayer vigils outside the offices of companies involved in animal experimentation and at the Institute of Psychiatry. Christian peace campaigners throughout the world have been involved in protests far too numerous to detail here; many of them have consequently suffered imprisonment.

Church leaders in Italy and Austria have somewhat chequered records concerning the environment. In late 1979 Pope John Paul II declared St Francis as the patron saint of ecology (as called for by Lynn White in 1967) but ironically, on Mount Subasio, where St Francis is said to have preached to the birds, shooting by hunters had by this time killed all the birds. However a three-year campaign to bring birds back to the mountain has resulted in the Italian authorities declaring the area a sanctuary. In their ecological creed mentioned above the Italian bishops urged people to choose appropriate lifestyles, as required by the gospel. Greens were thus somewhat aggrieved when the *Karin B*, a ship carrying toxic waste, arrived at an Italian port, causing a local controversy, and the bishops criticised Greens for 'exploiting' the conservation issue.

In Austria questions relating to nuclear power and weapons have raised controversy in the Church. The Austrian Bishops' Conference issued a Peace Appeal in 1983 calling for the abolition of all weapons of mass destruction by a step-by-step process of disarmament, beginning with the abandonment of all medium-range missiles. In 1986 its President, Archbishop Karl Berg of Salzburg, condemned the nuclear reprocessor at Wackersdorf (in contrast to Bavarian bishops, who spoke out in favour of the plant). However Green Christians in Austria report that recent trends in the Church have been less encouraging to Greens, as the Vatican has encouraged the appointment of right-wing, fundamentalist bishops. This has given rise to contrasting expressions of faith. While suffragan Bishop Florian Kuntner said an anti-nuclear mass for environmental groups during an International Atomic Energy Authority conference in 1986 in Vienna, his newly appointed superior, Archbishop Hans-Hermann Groer, was saying mass for the pro-nuclear IAEA lobby!

Other countries where Church leaders have spoken out against nuclear power include Mexico, the Philippines, Canada and West Germany. In Mexico in 1986 the six bishops of Veracruz publicly endorsed the arguments of Greens who called for a halt to the construction of a nuclear power station on the Gulf of Mexico at Laguna Verde (the aptly named 'green lagoon').[32] In the Philippines Catholic bishops who warned in their 1988 Pastoral Letter that the "assault on the earth is sinful" applauded protest action which blocked construction of a nuclear power station near Manila. They urged their people to avoid a 'fatalistic' attitude and instead to organise themselves around local ecological issues and become involved in concrete action. Meanwhile in Canada the Presbyterian Church and the United Church of Canada have urged a moratorium on further development of nuclear facilities and in West Germany ten of the twelve regional synods of the EKU have voted to oppose nuclear power as appropriate technology.

Another environmental problem which churches in Canada have faced is acid rain. In 1984 they began working together with churches in the United States to reduce acid-rain-causing emissions in North America. By this time the United Church of Canada had published *All Nature is Groaning*, a study on environmental stewardship in the context of acid rain, which itself built upon a 1977 Task Force Report on the Environment. Canadian Church leaders wrote to Ronald Reagan, then President of the United States, expressing concern at American inaction on acid rain. They received no response, so in 1987 the five major Church leaders in Canada wrote an Open Letter, addressed jointly to both the US President and the Prime Minister of Canada, to register further their concern about acid rain, which said:

> We believe that God's creation is being destroyed. Acid rain is one of the most serious causes. We believe that the mystery and magnificence of God's creation demands from humanity a response of respect and stewardship. Instead, the earth continues to be damaged, perhaps irrevocably. Future generations will blame us. In the final analysis, we are accountable to God.

Since then the United Church of Canada has passed resolutions on two other global problems, the depletion of the ozone layer and the greenhouse effect. Early in 1988 its General Council Executive passed a motion requesting its congregations not to use brands of polystyrene products known to damage the ozone layer and urging the Government to extend legislation on ozone-destroying products.

Like the Church of Scotland, the Canadian Church has spoken out on global warming – in 1988 it decided to launch an educational programme on the nature, causes and consequences of the greenhouse effect. The programme affirmed that the most appropriate response to the problem was energy conservation and using renewable sources, not expanding nuclear power facilities.

Summary

The Green movement is now firmly established throughout the world and looks certain to have a major impact on Western culture in the years ahead. It represents a philosophy, as distinct from a religion, and a range of different religious commitments are found among Greens.

Many Greens have an awareness of a spiritual dimension to life, but relatively few have been attracted to Christianity. Some have taken more interest in the New Age movement which, though in several important respects flawed, merits careful study and analysis.

There are many hopeful signs worldwide that Christians are showing increased interest in protecting the environment. In some countries Christians and Greens are beginning to co-operate together. Examples reveal how justice and peace issues are often linked with environmental concerns, and campaigners must expect conflict with governments and vested interests. There are powerful forces to overcome in achieving the radical changes which are so urgently needed.

1 Jonathon Porritt, *Seeing Green*, pp. 10–11.
2 Cited in Porritt, p. 211.
3 ibid., pp. 110, 211.
4 Max Nicholson, *The Environmental Revolution*, p. 264; Michael Allaby, *The Eco-Activists*, p. 45.
5 E. F. Schumacher, *Small is Beautiful*, p. 250.

6 See, for example, Philip Joranson and Ken Butigan (eds), *Cry of the Environment*; Lesslie Newbigin, *The Other Side of 1984*; Brian Walsh and Richard Middleton, *The Transforming Vision*.

7 Ronald Sider, 'Green Politics: Biblical or Buddhist?', *Spiritual Counterfeits Project Newsletter*, Fall 1985, p. 11.

8 Fritjof Capra, *The Turning Point*, p. 12.

9 Cited in Norman Myers (ed.), *The Gaia Atlas of Planet Management*, p. 158.

10 Schumacher, p. 127.

11 Bill Devall and George Sessions, *Deep Ecology*, p. 67.

12 Cited in Devall and Sessions, p. 76.

13 Cited in Jonathon Porritt and David Winner, *The Coming of the Greens*, p. 239.

14 Russell Chandler, *Understanding the New Age*, p. 229. See also Loren Wilkinson's essay 'New Age, New Consciousness, and the New Creation' in Wesley Granberg-Michaelson (ed.), *Tending the Garden*.

15 Sermon given on 20th October 1985, reproduced in *Piccadilly Press*, St James's Church, London, April 1986.

16 Chandler, p. 261.

17 ibid., p. 18.

18 Much of the following material originates from magazines of the World Wide Fund for Nature (*The New Road*); the World Council of Churches (*Forum*); and Christian Ecology Link (*Green Christians*).

19 Martin Palmer, Anne Nash, Ivan Hattingh (eds), *Faith and Nature*, p. 56.

20 ibid., p. 77.

21 The party was then called the Ecology Party.

22 The basis is: "We affirm our belief in God as Creator and in Jesus Christ as Lord, looking to the Holy Spirit for guidance through the Scriptures and seeking to hear Him in the challenges of the present time."

23 Gunther Hesse and Hans-Hermann Wiebe, *Die Grünen und die Religion*, Frankfurt-am-Main: Athenäum-Verlag, 1988.

24 *Katholische Aktion Österreichs, Mensch – Unwelt – Schöpfung*, Vienna, 1985.

25 Church of England Board for Social Responsibility, *Man In His Living Environment*, p. 61.

26 North American Conference on Christianity and Ecology, *Firmament*, Spring 1989, p. 17.

27 Stephen Muratore, 'The New "Teilhard" at the NACCE', *Epiphany Journal*, Winter 1988, p. 6.

28 *Catholic Herald*, 25th November 1988.

29 'The Cry of Our Land', A Pastoral Letter by the Catholic bishops of the Philippines, January 1988.

30 Jill Worth, 'How Green is the Church?', *Today*, August 1989, p. 9.
31 Ghillean T. Prance and Anne E. Prance, paper entitled 'The Environmental Crisis: A Challenge to the Judeo-Christian Faith'.
32 Edward Echlin, 'Not Only Avocados are Green', *Christian*, July/August 1987, p. 27.

BRINGING GOD DOWN TO EARTH:
His revelation through nature

The early Christians not only preached about Christ's resurrection, but spoke of "the living God, who made heaven and earth and sea and everything in them" (Acts 14.15). Even though people disobeyed God, He maintained the testimony of His provision through nature: "He has shown kindness by giving you rain from heaven and crops in their seasons" (Acts 14.17). The Christians acknowledged that God reveals Himself supremely through Jesus Christ, but also through nature.

Paul wrote of God's anger when, despite this, people failed to glorify Him or give Him thanks. He told the Romans that anyone who does not believe in Him is without excuse, because "since the creation of the world God's invisible qualities – his eternal power and divine nature – have been clearly seen, being understood from what has been made" (Rom. 1.20).

Many Old Testament Psalms convey a sense of wonder at what God has made, an awe at its sheer beauty. An example is Psalm 95:

The Lord is the great God, the great King above all gods.

In his hand are the depths of the earth, and the mountain peaks belong to him.

The sea is his, for he made it, and his hands formed the dry land.

Come, let us bow down in worship, let us kneel before the Lord our Maker. (Ps. 95.3–5)

True praise such as this can only flow from direct personal experience. People need to learn to *sense* the beauty of nature in order to truly appreciate God's love of creation. Then, perhaps, we will be more motivated to take care of it.

In seeking proper attitudes to the Earth, the form of God's presence in the world becomes a crucial issue. Certain tensions between different ideas quickly become evident. How do we reconcile the fact that God works through nature and sustains it with the fact that He lives without limits, beyond this world in heaven, which is beyond the horizon of our senses? What is the right approach to nature if treating it as sacred is an affront to God, who alone is divine, while to regard it as profane leads to its misuse?

Recognising the danger of seeing God as wholly separate from His creation, this chapter explores some recent attempts by Christians and others to find an understanding of God in which He is not unduly distanced from the Earth. These are analysed in the light of pantheistic and pagan alternatives to Christianity. A biblical basis is provided for understanding how God expresses Himself in nature through His 'Word' and an explanation is sought for the ugliness and suffering in nature, that negative side which is, in the famous words of Tennyson, 'red in tooth and claw'. To conclude, the value of spending time contemplating upon nature is considered.

Up there or down here?

How often in modern times when we observe nature are we overcome by a desire to worship its Creator? If the answer is rarely, perhaps this is because so much of the natural world bears the scars of human abuse. Instead of beauty, the images before us are often negative – a polluted river, bare land where once there was rainforest, a shed of factory-farmed chickens. Many people have lost – or never even developed – a real sense of nature's glory.

But perhaps the most significant explanation for our failure to appreciate God's revelation through nature is that much Christian teaching has effectively pushed God away from the Earth and up in the heavens. As our understanding of the nature of the Divine has diminished, so has our grasp of the divinely inspired workings of nature. People only see the material where once they perceived the hand of God.

The varied influences upon Western culture have led to a confused array of beliefs about the material world, where a love of nature is combined with a readiness to exploit it. Christianity is essentially positive about this world and yet, aware that it is not perfect, expectant of a radical transformation. Christian understanding of God is in turn different from that held by others such as pagans, who regard the world as the external reality of God, and Greek philosophers, who stressed God's transcendence.

In rejecting the idea that nature is itself divine, Christians have too often translated this into a need to create a gulf between God and nature. As noted in Chapter One, when nature was no longer treated as divine this allowed for humankind to utilise nature without fear of upsetting spirits in trees, rivers or elsewhere. In fact, Christianity long ago absorbed many pagan practices and 'Christianised' them so that people would not have to lose long-established customs which were important to them. Thus, for example, the worship of wells, trees and stones was transformed by changing pagan sites into Christian ones and associating them with a Christian saint instead of a heathen deity. Similarly Christian festivals often took the place of former pagan celebrations. Over the course of time the separation between God and nature became ever more evident.

This separation has also been encouraged by the influence upon Christianity of a belief prevalent in Greek philosophy that, because God belonged to a realm of *being* as distinct from *becoming*, He could not have any direct contact with this world, which is subject to change. Ultimate reality in Greek thought was a realm of eternal, unchanging being; hence it was essentially negative about the material world. From the earliest times Christianity has continually faced a need to counter the influence of such thinking in order to affirm the Hebrew principle of the goodness of God's creation. As an example, many Greeks believed that the Earth was created out of matter which was eternally in existence alongside God. The doctrine of 'creation out of nothing' was actually formulated, without truly explicit biblical support (cf. Gen. 1.1; Heb. 11.3), as an attempt to overcome the dualism within Greek thought by suggesting that matter must be good because it was created by God.

Another factor is that for centuries people believed in a God dwelling, quite literally, 'above' the sky. Scientific awareness eventually led theologians to modify this belief to an understanding of a God 'out there'. In the present century there has developed a further trend, towards the God 'within', influenced by theologians who have considered that the symbolism of height should be replaced by that of depth. God thus became the 'ground of our being'.

This idea was popularised by Bishop John Robinson in the controversial book *Honest to God*, in which he wrote that God should not be understood as a projection 'out there', a Being existing in its own right to whom the world is related in the sort of way the Earth is to the sun. Robinson believed that God can best be understood through an analysis of the depths of our relationships and our experience of love. What counts is "*whether this depth of being is a reality or an illusion*, not whether *a* Being exists beyond the bright blue sky, or anywhere else. Belief in God is a matter of 'what you take seriously without any reservation', of what for you is *ultimate* reality."[1]

At its extreme, this theological trend threatened to reduce God from a personal Being to little more than a yardstick of the quality of relationships. However, in so far as it was a step away from God as a Being wholly separate from the world, it was not entirely unhelpful. It challenged the belief that God's existence is subject to proof and has to be demonstrated. "God is, by definition, ultimate reality," argued Robinson, "and one cannot argue whether ultimate reality *exists*."[2]

It thus offered hope to people who found difficulty believing in God when He seemed so distant, looking down from a 'heaven' located somewhere up in the sky. They found such a God rather inaccessible, like a rather distant architect or strategic planner – remote, indifferent, even tyrannical.

However this understanding of God still left a vacuum and instead of responding, "O Lord, our Lord, how majestic is your name in all the earth! You have set your glory above the heavens" (Ps. 8.1), all too often people cried out, "Where is your God?" (Ps. 42.3). As the environmental crises became more apparent, questions about how the Earth functions became ever more urgent. This stimulated new ideas from scientists and philosophers, two of which merit special attention as they have attracted much interest, notably among Greens. They are James Lovelock's 'Gaia hypothesis' and Peter Russell's idea of an 'awakening Earth'.

Life in the Earth?

Recent interest in 'Gaia', named after the Greek goddess of the Earth, has arisen largely as a result of work carried out during the 1970s by British scientist James Lovelock. Lovelock, who regards himself as an agnostic, questioned why certain planetary conditions exist, such as why the proportion of oxygen in the atmosphere remains at 21 per cent, exactly the right level for life. A little more and the threat of fire to the Earth's vegetation would be much greater, a little less and larger animals would lack the energy to survive. Was the right proportion a mere coincidence?

Lovelock's conclusion was that the physical and chemical conditions of the surface of the Earth, its oceans and atmosphere, appear to be regulated by the presence of life *itself*, and result from the very fact that there is a single, complex system of life. The Earth may, in other words, be seen as a self-regulating, living organism, an idea he called the 'Gaia hypothesis'.

His beliefs contrasted with the conventional understanding that life adapts to planetary conditions as each evolves in their separate ways, and attracted interest not only from scientists but from the Church. Some of this was by no means unsympathetic. Questioned about the Gaia hypothesis, the former Bishop of Birmingham, Hugh Montefiore, replied:

I fail to see how this whole system could sort of happen by chance, by hazard. How can those 'inexplicable' balances of the environment be maintained in any kind of random way? The fundamental theological truth for a Christian is that the world is indeed a living thing: the whole of the spirit of God is at work within it, and everything has intrinsic value of itself.[3]

Indeed Christians have in past centuries identified with such thinking, even though this has brought them into conflict with the Church. They include the sixteenth-century Italian philosopher Giordano Bruno, once a Dominican friar, who was burned at the stake by Church authorities, and the nineteenth-century Russian Orthodox writer Vladimir Solovyev, who believed that "we should treat our social and cosmic environment as an actual living being with which we are in the closest and most complete interaction, without ever being merged in it."[4]

Lovelock's ideas were extended and further popularised by Peter Russell in *The Awakening Earth*, which proposed two alternative descriptions of humankind's relationship to the Earth. One was that humans operate collectively like a vast nervous system, a 'global brain' in which we are like individual nerve cells that communicate, raise consciousness and ensure that the body develops. Russell drew a parallel with humankind as the 'cortex' of the planet, as people's higher mental functions are associated with the cortex of the brain (a thin outer layer of nerve cells). In the alternative, rather less positive view, humans are seen as a kind of planetary cancer, eating away indiscriminately at the surface of the planet.

Russell's conclusion was that ours may be the most significant, dramatic and crucial period of human history, one which offers the potential for "the progressive integration of human minds into a single living system."[5]

We are, in other words, on the threshold of a New Age. However, to achieve the necessary change a 'spiritual renewal' is needed which will only come about if people adopt a new world view through a profound change in attitudes, or, as he puts it, a "widespread shift in consciousness". This demands awareness of our connection to the planet, "the *realization* that the individual is an integral part of Nature, no more isolated from the environment than a cell in the body is isolated from the human organism."[6] The word 'realization' is crucial, Russell stresses, because it involves recognising "our essential oneness with Nature, not just with our intellect and reason, but with our feelings and with our souls".[7] He points to the fact that the Latin root of the word 'religion' means 'to bind', defining that which connects us to our common source.

Balance or heresy?

These ideas challenge the idea of a God who is remote or absent from His creation and reflect objections to the kind of Christianity which stresses God's transcendence and ignores His revelation through nature. But they come rather too close to pantheism or paganism to be consistent with Christianity.

The Gaia hypothesis might be described as 'scientific paganism'. It implies that the Earth regulates *itself* and thereby, in effect, dispenses with a God who has a degree of autonomy from His creation. According to the logic in Christianity, that which makes and that which is made must be two, not one. Lovelock's proposal is not only contrary to Christian claims, but raises questions for Greens. If nature is indeed self-regulating, exactly how has an evident need arisen for an extraordinary human effort to modify the 'natural' course of events? Why is 'Gaia' leaving a correction to the crises so late?

From a Christian perspective the Gaia hypothesis shares with Russell's 'awakening Earth' thesis a fundamental problem in that no supreme significance is attached to Christ. There is an essential difference between Russell's idea of gaining access to the divine through a pantheistic belief in recognising our 'oneness' with nature and traditional Christian faith in the incarnation, belief that the Word of God became flesh in Jesus Christ.

In Christianity God is not equated either with the Earth, as in paganism, or with the universe, as in pantheism. As Professor John Polkinghorne has pointed out in a timely study of God's interaction with the world, *Science and Providence*:

> There are distinctions between God and the world that Christian theology cannot afford to blur. They lie at the root of the religious claim that meeting with God involves personal encounter, not just a communing with the cosmos.[8]

In fact, Russell's view of Christianity and other world faiths is that they are all, essentially, the same – the central core of each is an experience of oneness with creation. The fact that this does not appear to be self-evident is, he argues, because the original teachings have been distorted over time, though he provides no supporting argument to substantiate this provocative claim. Christians would dispute this; the Christ in whom we believe is not merely a good teacher or some kind of mediating, unifying 'principle', but the unique Son of God.

We should be wary, however, of impulsively condemning those who are exploring new and different ways of making sense of the world. It is far less easy than some may suppose to identify poetical passages in the Bible from those which are literal, and quite proper to explore what to make of, say, the idea of the Earth having feelings as it awaits judgement (Ps. 96.11–13; Rom. 8.22).

Christian alternatives

In a sense God is utterly transcendent, without limitations. To many Christians it is this very distinctiveness of God from the world, combined with a sense of our finitude and dependence upon Him, that makes Him worthy of adoration and leads them to worship Him. However although belief in a God who is almighty and omnipotent is often comforting and provides a sense of security, it represents a *partial* understanding of God. To some Christians it does not seem to convey much about God's loving interaction with creation.

Moreover, there is a danger that those who stress that God is *omnipotent* may thereby regard themselves as effectively *impotent*. While in theory believing that people have free will and are responsible for exercising choice, many suffer from fatalism and apathy. Often underlying this belief is a sense of assurance that everything is in the power of God and a false conclusion that there is no need to protect His creation. When this leads to complacency such thinking becomes positively dangerous.

Christians need to express a recognition that God is, in one sense, beyond our reach and yet, at the same time, accessible to us. This must be done in a way which does not suggest that He is wholly separate from the Earth, wholly contained within the Earth, or which equates Him with the universe. In order to correct past damage done through over-emphasis on the fact that God is transcendent, the fact that He is immanent needs to be stressed, the fact that He penetrates, dwells within, and is diffused throughout creation.

One of the Psalms says: "Where can I go from your

Spirit? Where can I flee from your presence? If I go up to the heavens, you are there; if I make my bed in the depths, you are there" (Ps. 139.7–8). But to say that God is immanent goes beyond expressing His 'omnipresence', belief that He is everywhere. It speaks of His Spirit's *continuing presence* within the whole of creation. God does not set Himself over against the world but, as He creates, He enters into the world through the Holy Spirit. Jürgen Moltmann writes: "Through the energies and potentialities of the Spirit, the Creator is himself present in his creation. He does not merely confront it in his transcendence; entering into it, he is also immanent in it."[9]

The Eastern Orthodox tradition has provided an enlightening insight into God in terms of His 'energies' and His 'essence'. God's *essence* is His transcendence, an 'otherness' which is an incomprehensible mystery to us. Thus John's Gospel says that nobody has ever seen God, and He is made known to us through His Son (John 1.18). God's *being* is inaccessible; no-one may see His face and live (Exod. 33.20; cf. 1 Cor. 13.12).

At the same time, the world is penetrated by God's *energy*, by which is meant His activity and operation in the universe. Everything that exists is sustained only because of the unceasing flow of energies with which God enlivens it, and through this He is revealed. "We know the essence through the energy," wrote Basil the Great in the fourth century. "No-one has ever seen the essence of God, but we believe in the essence because we experience the energy."[10] According to a seventh-century Greek Father, Maximus the Confessor: "We do not know God in his essence. We know him rather from the grandeur of his creation and from his providential care for all creatures. For by this means, as if using a mirror, we attain insight into his infinite goodness, wisdom and power."[11]

It may be helpful to consider the environment around us in the light of such thinking and to attempt to see in it a dynamic movement of God's will and energy. Viewing it in this way, we might treat it more respectfully. Thus the modern Orthodox scholar Paulos Gregorios, in a profound passage, defines the very constitution of matter in these terms:

> The creative energy of God is the true being of all that is; matter is that spirit or energy in physical form. Therefore, we should regard our human environment as the energy of God in a form that is accessible to our senses.[12]

In such an understanding we are continually in direct contact with the power of God. Changes which take place in our environment every fraction of every second confirm His living presence.

A rather more recent attempt at reconciling the closeness of God with His otherness is 'panentheism', belief that God is in everything and that everything is 'in' God. This understanding has been popularised through process theology. The biblical basis for such thinking is rooted in Paul's teaching:

> From one man he made every nation of men, that they should inhabit the whole earth; and he determined the times set for them and the exact places where they should live. God did this so that men would seek him and perhaps reach out for him and find him, though he is not far from each one of us. 'For in him we live and move and have our being.' (Acts 17.26–8)

In fact, it is not so very different from the thought several centuries ago of the Protestant reformer Martin Luther:

> God is substantially present everywhere, in and through all creatures, in all their parts and places, so that the world is full of God and He fills all, *but without His being encompassed and surrounded* by it. He is at the same time outside and above all creatures.[13] [my emphasis]

There is, in other words, continual interaction between God and His universe, but each retains a *separate identity*.

One of the implications of panentheism is that if everything is *in* God then, because He offers free will, He has taken the uncertainties of life into His own being. It

follows that He must feel deeply for His creation. Panen-
theist thought thus implies that having created the universe out of love, God is not a dispassionate spectator but
continues to interact with it. It suggests also that God
persuades and *influences* created beings rather than
compelling them. He experiences our joy and suffering,
but is vulnerable – perhaps, even, in a sense, dependent.

The world as God's body

In a new attempt to counter the past over-emphasis given
to God's transcendence, Christian theologian Sallie
McFague has explored the idea of divine embodiment by
using the metaphor 'the world as God's body'. Writing
from a liberal perspective, McFague argues in *Models of
God* that Christians need to introduce images and concepts in their faith which are appropriate for the present
age of ecological and nuclear threats. God should be
thought of in a new way. McFague is critical of the
language often used, of imperialism and triumphalism,
and regards the commonly used metaphor of 'the world
as king's realm' as potentially oppressive and life-
threatening. Thus she asks how we would feel and act differently in a world that we perceived as 'the body of God'.

The language of the world as God's 'body' is, it should be
emphasised, strictly *metaphorical*. It is used not to *define*
God but to invite people to apply their imagination to
describe an experience of relating to God. McFague explains that "what a metaphor expresses cannot be said
directly or apart from it, for if it could be, one would have
said it directly."[14] Jesus often used metaphors, of course,
such as when he described the kingdom in terms of being
'like' something as distinct from 'the same as'.

McFague suggests that her idea might have a very
positive impact on how people see God:

What if God's promise of permanent presence to all space and
time were imagined as a worldly reality, a palpable, bodily

presence? What if, then, we did not have to go to somewhere special (church) or somewhere else (another world) to be in the presence of God but could feel ourselves in that presence at all times and in all places?[15]

This may help to overcome the kind of dualistic thinking which, she argues, is encouraged by the frequently used metaphorical descriptions of God as king, ruler, lord, master and governor. These appear hierarchical and imperialistic, stressing the distance between God and the world and the total reliance of the world on God. Through them God tends to be seen as absolutely transcendent and omnipotent, and this permits little sense of mutuality, shared responsibility, reciprocity and love. As a result, with little or no sense of intimacy and interaction between God and the world, people's understanding of God verges on deism.

That said, for all its provocative value, 'the world as God's body' cannot be the determining metaphor for Christianity because it is the identity of God in *Christ's* body which in Christianity is the foundational model for God's presence in the world. In true Christianity God is not present in the Earth in *essence* but by mediated action, and His presence is not through *necessity* but by His own initiative.

A subtle balance

Some Christians are sceptical of the idea of divine embodiment. John Polkinghorne, for example, points to the need to avoid the extremes of 'divine impassibility', in which God asserts a 'divine tyranny' over the world, and 'divine vulnerability', in which the world imposes itself upon God. The idea of divine embodiment will, he suggests, "force God to destroy the liberty of creation if he seeks to safeguard his own independence."[16]

Polkinghorne is right in concluding that a subtle balance is required. This may be found in Moltmann's suggestion that God, though omnipresent and omnipotent, deliberately withdraws His presence and restricts His power. This allows the creation the freedom to 'be itself': "In order to create a world 'outside' himself, the infinite God must have made room beforehand for finitude in himself. It is only a withdrawal by God into himself that can free the space into which God can act creatively."[17] Thus the Maker and what is made can be different without being wholly separate.

A further problem is the fact that the model most readily drawn out from the Bible is not 'the world as God's body' but 'the world as king's realm'. One explanation for this may lie in the cultural context, especially the apparent need to differentiate clearly God and the living environment.

The Canaanite people who inhabited the Promised Land practised a religion which involved the worship of gods and goddesses personifying the powers of nature. In their religion, the divine was revealed in the rhythms of the natural world, encouraged through fertility rituals. This was not the God of Israel. The Israelites first came to belief in God through the evidence of historical events, as their liberator from the injustice and oppression of slavery in Egypt.

God chose to reveal Himself to the Israelites in ways which would show a clear distinction from the Canaanite gods and goddesses. It is simply inconceivable that He would speak through metaphorical imagery such as 'the world as God's body'. The God of Israel is no mere fertility deity. He is separate enough from the world to change its course by acting *upon* it. This distinctiveness of God from the Earth enabled an alternative to fatalism, by allowing for the possibility of divine intervention to secure the release of the Israelites from injustice and oppression.

Thus God specifically instructed the Israelites to destroy everything to do with the Canaanite religion and told them not to worship Him "in their way" (Deut. 7.5; 12.2–4). He warned them not to worship any idols and, specifically, not to make any images of a man, woman, animal, bird or fish, or to worship the sun, moon or stars (Exod. 20.4; Deut. 4.15–19). In fact, even before the Israelites invaded the land they ignored this warning and began to worship Baal, the weather-god who the Canaanites believed controlled rains, mist and dew, and thus the harvests.[18] Ultimately Jeremiah had to remind the Israelites of the true God (Jer. 10.1–11).

A second explanation why such a metaphor was inappropriate for the Israelites is that the Middle East provided a barren, inhospitable environment. Even in the Fertile Crescent it was necessary to terrace hillsides, drain swamps, and dig irrigation canals in order to grow food. The Israelites' experience of the natural environment was that it was harsh and needed much effort if wilderness was to be kept in check. It would therefore more easily be seen as ground cursed by God than as God's 'body' (Gen. 3.17).

God's creative expression

Having explored a range of recent ideas from Christian and other perspectives, what biblical insights provide the basis for Christian understanding? Two are particularly significant, the Word as God's expression through creation and the presence of Christ in the world.

God is not only the original creator of the heavens and the Earth, but is *continually* creating; He *sustains* creation. Each part of creation is portrayed in the beautiful Psalm 104 as fed, nourished, and cared for by Him – rivers, grass, trees, creatures of every kind:

> How many are your works, O Lord! In wisdom you made them all; the earth is full of your creatures.

> There is the sea, vast and spacious, teeming with creatures beyond number – living things both large and small.

> There the ships go to and fro, and the leviathan, which you formed to frolic there.

These all look to you to give them their food at the proper time.

When you give it to them, they gather it up; when you open your hand they are satisfied with good things.

When you hide your face, they are terrified; when you take away their breath, they die and return to dust.

When you send your Spirit, they are created, and you renew the face of the earth. (Ps. 104.24–30)

God thus expresses Himself through the creative processes of nature. It is now known that each individual life form bears its own special hallmark through DNA, which defines its genetic composition. Nothing is duplicated in nature; every creature is special. As scientific discovery has progressed and explained life in greater detail, this has not made the idea of a Creator redundant but adds to the wonder of His creation.

Indeed, observation of nature has led many people to a belief in God. As the study of nature became more common, from the late seventeenth century onward, writers such as Sir Kenhelm Digby, John Ray and Carl Linnaeus pointed to its order and harmony which, they believed, provided evidence of an intelligent, wise and benevolent Creator. It was Linnaeus, the outstanding figure in natural history in the eighteenth century, who considered the underlying purpose of ecological thought to be "to find the hand of God in nature".[19]

Such thinking became widespread after the publication in 1802 of William Paley's *Natural Theology*. This popularised 'argument from design', belief in God through the evidence of a benevolent creator provided by the perfectly arranged structures in nature. Building upon the thinking of his contemporary, Robert Boyle, Paley drew an analogy of a person on a desert island who finds a watch, the parts of which fit together to achieve a particular purpose. From this the person would assume the existence of a watchmaker. By the same reasoning the presence of design in living organisms is considered to provide evidence of an intelligent designer of the world.[20]

Many theologians, especially Protestants, have stressed the inadequacy of natural theology and pointed to the necessity of God's revelation through historical acts – law-giving, the teachings of the prophets and, supremely, Jesus Christ. This 'revealed theology' is needed as a basis for moral judgements and to understand atonement between God and humankind. Moreover, not everyone seems to have the same capacity to perceive God through His creation. Though its beauty and intricacy may lead some to belief in God, the ugly, unattractive side to nature demands an explanation. Thus critics such as Albert Wolters conclude that God reveals Himself most unambiguously and personally through events in history recorded in the Bible, which is "like a verbal commentary on the dimly perceived sign language of creation".[21]

The Bible is often spoken of as the 'Word of God' which, though true, is an inadequate interpretation of the full meaning of God's 'Word'. Indeed, the idea of a collection of books, the Bible, being the Word is not found within the biblical text itself; to its authors, God's Word meant His *creative expression*, or *sovereign command*. As God speaks His will is revealed and His Word releases a power which sustains creation, shapes people's lives and affects the course of history.

This understanding is arrived at through a comparison of the first chapters of Genesis and the Gospel of John. In Genesis creation is called into being by God's Word; each of His creative acts is preceded by the phrase 'and God said'. The Psalms echo this:

He sends his command to the earth; his word runs swiftly.

He spreads the snow like wool and scatters the frost like ashes.

He hurls down hail like pebbles. Who can withstand his icy blast?

He sends his word and melts them; he stirs up his breezes, and
the waters flow. (Ps. 147.15–18)

The Word is God's expression not just to humankind but to
the whole creation. As God calls creation into being, what
was at first "formless and empty" (Gen. 1.2) begins to take
the shape of the Earth. God *structures* it and *fills* it. In the
process, His Word is reflected back; the whole creation is
given a voice and expresses itself by praising God (Ps.
19.1–4; 148.1–14; 150.6). A tree growing upwards, a rose
petal unfolding or sunshine pouring out may each be seen
as examples of the creative expression of God.

Similarly the apostle John describes how it is through
the Word of God that all things are made:

> In the beginning was the Word, and the Word was with God,
> and the Word was God. He was with God in the beginning.
> Through him all things were made; without him nothing was
> made that has been made . . . The Word became flesh and
> made his dwelling among us. (John 1.1–3,14)

God's *supreme* expression is therefore as a man – 'the
Word became flesh'. Thus is a mystery revealed, that
Jesus Christ, the Son of God, is intimately involved in
creation.

The presence of Christ

Some Christians like to use neat and tidy time periods
when describing the Trinity. In Sunday Schools (and,
indeed, elsewhere) the impression is sometimes given that
God the Father created the universe, His Son later lived
on Earth and, then, after Christ's death, the Holy Spirit
came. A more careful understanding, however, suggests
that God *as a Trinity* is involved in creation. The Father
creates through His Word (the second person) and His
Breath (the third person) (Ps. 33.6), and just as the Spirit
of God was "hovering over the waters" at the dawn of

creation (Gen. 1.2), so Christ was "with God in the beginning" (John 1.2).

Jesus Christ is God's supreme expression, the "exact representation of his being" who is "sustaining all things by his powerful word" (Heb. 1.3). Far from being confined in time and space, he has an *eternal* and *cosmic* presence which is identified by Paul: "There is but one Lord, Jesus Christ, through whom all things came and through whom we live" (1 Cor. 8.6).

Some Christians tend to view Christ as *totally* distinct from the created order. An alternative is to explore how he is present throughout all time and space, and the possibility of our becoming part of his body. Paulos Gregorios writes: "As Christians we are united with him in an especially intimate way. By baptism and by faith, he has incorporated us as members of his body. By participation in his body and blood, we grow to be integral parts of him."[22]

This is understood in the Eastern Orthodox tradition through the idea of *mediation* between God and His creation. Since the beginning of time our task as humans has been to manifest the spiritual in and through the material and so harmonise the spiritual and material realms. We were intended to be mediators between God and His creation, but have been disobedient. In our failure, God, in human form, fulfils this task by uniting Himself to His creation in the closest possible way, taking the form of that which He created. Christ is 'one of us' because he took a material body and thereby became part of the created order.

Gregorios explains that the full significance of the incarnation is that, in some mystical sense, by entering humanity Christ enters *all* things:

Christ the Incarnate One assumed flesh – organic, human flesh; he was nurtured by air and water, vegetables and meat, like the rest of us. He took matter into himself, so matter is not alien to him now. His body is a *material* body – transformed, of course, but transformed *matter*. Thus he shares his being with the whole created order: animals and birds, snakes and worms, flowers and seeds. All parts of creation are now reconciled to Christ.[23]

Thus the nineteenth-century theologian F. D. Maurice preached in a sermon:

> If you have heard the singing of the birds or the running of the stream, or the voices of children as you came to church, then reflect it was Christ who caused you to hear them. He fills the earth and the air with all melodies, and He gives to men the power of taking them in.[24]

Christ's earthly presence provides the ultimate affirmation of the value of the material world and offers the basis for a 'sacramental' understanding of the universe. Through the sacraments is perceived 'the divine in the ordinary'. For example, in the sacraments of baptism and Holy Communion the water, bread and wine are regarded as vehicles of God's grace. These products of nature have an *instrumental* function, fulfilling God's purpose, and also a *symbolic* function, revealing God's presence in His creation.

The sacramental principle may thus be extended to the whole creation, which is seen as the outward, visible sign of an inward, spiritual grace. This should lead to God's gifts in nature being used in a more reverential manner, in recognition that nature is precious and ours only by God's grace.

Creation not only has its origin in Christ, but owes its settled state to him. Paul answered a key cosmological question regarding the source of harmony in a world characterised by diversity and freedom by teaching that Christ *unites* all things, which was an important concept at the time because people in cities such as Colossae and Ephesus were "aware of a cosmic fault, a kind of catastrophe in the universe, a gulf between the higher (heavenly) and lower (earthly) world".[25] Paul responded by describing Christ as bridging the fault by filling all things with his power: "In him all things hold together . . .

God was pleased to have all his fulness dwell in him, and through him to reconcile to himself all things" (Col. 1.17,19–20). "And he made known to us the mystery of his will . . . to bring all things in heaven and on earth together under one head, even Christ" (Eph. 1.9–10).

This reconciliation was made only through Christ's sacrifice and suffering. The ultimate abuse of parts of God's creation was at the death of Christ, the Lord of Creation, when wood was used for a cross, iron for the nails, jute for the whip, and thorns for a crown.

In the present age those who are committed to work with Christ in 'sustaining all things', should recognise the certainty of sacrifice and the likelihood of suffering. It may, for example, involve sacrifice by forgoing consumption for the sake of future generations, or risking suffering by acts of civil disobedience in response to environmental abuse.

Red in tooth and claw?

There is a certain less attractive side to nature, a menacing aspect or 'dark' side, manifest in the occurrence of earthquakes, hurricanes, epidemics, storms and droughts, which may cause people fear and pain. For example, co-existing with the most beautiful of creatures is the parasitic organism which causes malaria, designed with the potential to cause much suffering and with no evident good purpose.

If God is indeed the creative power within the natural world, the suffering of many creatures and the seemingly frustrating and wasteful processes in evolution demand an explanation. In some philosophies such tensions are resolved by defining the entire material world as evil (although this then raises questions about our *positive* experience of nature!). In Christianity, however, which affirms the inherent goodness of creation, material things are not *themselves* evil.

Taking the Genesis story at face value, it appears that

the natural environment was somehow affected by the fall. Originally in the Garden of Eden all creatures were vegetarians (Gen. 1.30), there is no explicit evidence of death, pollution or suffering, and the whole creation was declared 'very good' (Gen. 1.31). However the perfect creation which God finished on the sixth day has become the flawed world which we experience today.

Historically, many Christians have found the idea of a change in the constitution of creatures after the fall hard to believe. Augustine rejected the idea of a cosmic fall and Aquinas, too, was convinced that the nature of animals "was not changed by man's sin, as if those whose nature it now is to devour the flesh of others, would have lived on herbs, as the lion and the falcon."[26] After all, Adam must have had *some* understanding of death to make sense of God's warning not to eat from the tree: "When you eat of it you will surely die" (Gen. 2.17). Moreover, as the Earth has always been a biological entity, with food chains and flows of energy and minerals, it was surely dependent, as today, on cycles of life and death.

On the other hand, if nature was unaffected when God cursed the ground after the fall, why did Adam have to exert himself in "painful toil" to produce food (Gen. 3.17)? There is no definitive answer to whether the actual constitution of beings changed as a result of the fall. The most likely explanation is that there were the same processes of life and death prior to the fall but that no suffering was actually *felt* by any creature.

The existence of an apparent negative aspect to nature raises parallel questions to those raised by the problem of human suffering, and these similarly have to be seen in the context of free will. The whole of God's creation has within it an element of freedom. According to John Polkinghorne our earthly home is:

A world of orderliness but not of clockwork regularity, of potentiality without predictability, endowed with an assurance of development but with a certain openness as to its actual form. It is inevitably a world with ragged edges, where order and disorder interlace each other and where the exploration of possibility by chance will lead not only to the evolution of systems of increasing complexity, but also to the evolution of systems imperfectly formed and malfunctioning.[27]

Just as God has given people free will, so He allows the physical world to 'be itself', granted that independence and freedom which is the mark of an act of love.

Paul wrote that the whole creation is frustrated while it "waits in eager expectation for the sons of God to be revealed" (Rom. 8.19). In other words, it awaits those who are led by the Spirit of God to live accordingly, as only then will it be "liberated from its bondage to decay" (Rom. 8.21). God gives free will in the knowledge that, despite the problems of the present era, when creation "groans as in the pains of childbirth", in due course all things will be well (Rom. 8.22). These groans include the suffering within nature 'red in tooth and claw'.

A distinction is thus necessary between what is *initially* possible and what is *eventually* possible in God's creation. In the fulness of time all things will be reconciled in Christ, but our experience of life in the meantime provides educational and developmental opportunities from which to gain. Suffering the dark side of nature is a part of that process. It is significant, perhaps, that Jesus was sent by the Spirit into a desert for the temptation which prepared him for his ministry (Matt. 4.1).

Martin Luther offered the explanation that even the less attractive side to nature may reveal God:

> Our body bears the traces of God's wrath, which our sin has deserved. God's wrath also appears on the earth in all creatures ... And what of thorns, thistles, water, fire, caterpillars, flies, fleas, and bedbugs? Collectively and individually, are not all of them messengers who preach to us concerning sin and God's wrath?[28]

A further explanation for the apparently negative aspect to nature is that "the aesthetic panorama of the whole justifies the sacrifice of some of the parts."[29] What is good and necessary for some species, and for the whole, may be bad for others. To use a musical analogy, apparent discords of instruments heard on their own, in isolation from others, may be part of a greater harmony played by a whole orchestra.

Some people ask why an omnipotent God could not have created a world in which all created beings are wholly free but always choose correctly! This judges God by *human* standards and in such cases the Bible points to divine independence and sovereignty, as in the case of Job. It is a difficult and humbling truth that it is not *our* place to challenge the Creator. Thus when Job asserted himself in this way God responded: "Where were you when I laid the earth's foundation?" (Job 38.4). God's great creative power and wisdom are then described in detail and Job is left totally humbled: "Surely I spoke of things I did not understand, things too wonderful for me to know" (Job 42.3). The prophet Isaiah similarly reminded the people that God's thought and purpose transcend ours (Isa. 55.8 –11). Suffering is a mystery which cannot be explained adequately by human reasoning.

This temporary suffering should not be confused with evil. Athanasius, a Greek Father, taught that evil is lapsing into nothing, or ceasing to be. It is, in other words, the reversal or defeat of a creative process. Each part of God's creation may achieve its potential or may, alternatively, decay into nothingness. When the threat is of a *wholesale* destruction of God's creation, through a nuclear winter, the depletion of rainforest or another such global catastrophe, this is utterly blasphemous, as it represents *a negation of the main thrust of the creative process.*

Sensing God's presence

A Christian's redemption should have a real effect on his or her perception of the world. This was the case with Luther:

If I believe in God's Son and bear in mind that He became man, all creatures will appear a hundred times more beautiful to me than before. Then I will properly appreciate the sun, the moon, the stars, trees, apples, pears, as I reflect that he is Lord over and the centre of all things.[30]

Is that our experience? As Christians do we know God's living presence in our world merely by rational judgement, or as a personal encounter? Many of us need to rethink our relationship to the natural environment and ask ourselves how the planet has been brought to the brink of destruction. We need to ask why *we* do not burst into praise to God like the Psalmists, or repent like Job in awe and humility, or gain great wisdom, like Solomon. What obstacles are inhibiting us from sensing God in the natural world?

Most people do not live in beautiful rural areas and, though there is now a trend to 'green the cities', the urban landscape has suffered because often the few remaining pockets of wildlife have disappeared under building developments. People have often thought that God's presence is less easy to sense in urban environments; there is a traditional saying that 'God made the country, man made the town'. Just as the Romantic poets and philosophers believed that close communion with nature offered spiritual and moral value, people living today in urban areas in industrial society 'escape' to the countryside, believing that it somehow reaches to their hearts and rejuvenates them.

Even so, a human-centred world view has led many to find it easier to praise the products of industry than the direct handiwork of God. For example, people are more inclined to admire a new manufactured product or technological development than the fresh image of seasonal change. The British may be renowned for commenting on the weather but our attitudes are often negative. We equate 'sun' with 'beautiful' and 'damp' with 'miserable', failing to relish the value of pouring rain and the moody, mysterious fog.

Another problem is that people's education and experience in society tend to teach them not to credit their intuition and emotions, but to think in terms of 'hard facts'. Viewing nature with wonder and awe is less instinctive to those whose sensitivities are hardened and whose minds tend to focus on how nature can be *used* and on what particular species are *for*, rather than nature's intrinsic worth. We interpret God's creation as a world made for humans. Forgetting that the world is *God's* creation and that God is not *solely* concerned for us, we look at the world and recognise only its instrumental value.

If nature is to be valued properly we need to relearn the importance of actively contemplating the world around us. In *Wind and Sea Obey Him* Roman Catholic priest Robert Faricy describes many ways of finding God in nature. One necessary step is to learn to *experience* direct contact with nature with such intensity of feeling that praise for the wonder, beauty and power revealed in nature becomes instinctive – even its harsh side, of bitter winds and teeming rain. Faricy distinguishes thanksgiving, gratitude for God's gifts to us, from praise, a response not for His gifts, but for being Himself. Praise reflects the fact that the Creator of the universe is worthy of adoration irrespective of the 'instrumental' value of the natural environment to ourselves.

Bishop Kallistos Ware suggests a need to steady ourselves in this busy world:

I cannot contemplate either nature or God without learning to be present where I am, gathered together at this present moment, in this present place. Stop, look and listen. Such is the first beginning of contemplation. The contemplation of nature commences when I open my eyes, literally and spiritually, and start to notice the world around myself – to notice the *real* world, that is to say *God's* world. The contemplative is the one who, like Moses before the Burning Bush (Exod. 3.5), takes off his shoes – that is, strips himself of the deadness of familiarity and boredom – and who then recognizes that the place where he is standing is holy ground.[31]

This process of contemplation leads to greater awareness of the material world, so that each moment becomes in some sense special. He adds: "Becoming sensitive to God's world around myself, I grow more conscious also of God's world *within* myself."[32]

One technique which could be used to encourage sensitivity to God's presence is to pray in different directions – west, north, east, and south – acknowledging that at the centre of all things is God.[33] Think of the state of the global environment, taking each compass point in turn, and consider what it really means to pray "Your kingdom come, your will be done on earth as it is in heaven" (Matt. 6.10).

Why is this encounter with God through nature so important? Firstly, nature communicates something of the character and purpose of God. It provides examples of God's sustaining power. He gives the power to seedlings which grow in the spring each year, sometimes with such strength that they burst through the tarmac of a tree-lined path. Some years ago I saw a tree in California over two thousand years old; it had been cut horizontally so that the ring which grew the very year that Christ was born could be identified!

The Bible speaks of the greatness of God and His strength and ability compared to ours, which is manifest in nature (Isa. 40.12–31). The sheer power of God which is reflected in nature is seen in the thunder, lightning and earthquakes which accompany His acts (Ps. 77.16–19).

Nature is responsive to God. Several Psalms portray images of the whole creation singing, shouting and praising God. The writer of Psalm 148, for example, calls upon the sun, moon and stars to praise God, "for he commanded and they were created. He set them in place for ever and ever; he gave a decree that will never pass away." He addresses the mountains, trees, living creatures of all kinds, and even the elements of weather, saying "Praise the Lord . . . for his name alone is exalted" (Ps. 148.5–13). Perhaps we in turn should occasionally take our church congregations into the deepest and most unspoilt countryside and sing psalms to the Creator from the depths of our hearts!

Nature also offers a means of gaining wisdom. Solomon's wisdom and breadth of understanding was recognised through his knowledge of the natural environment, specifically the life of plants, animals and birds, reptiles and fish, as well as his many proverbs and songs (1 Kgs 4.29–34). The Bible teaches that God creates through 'wisdom' (Ps. 104.24; Prov. 3.19) – wisdom is personified as a creative force which calls out: "The Lord brought me forth as the first of his works" (Prov. 8.22). The wisdom reflected in God's craftsmanship – putting the mountains in their place, establishing the clouds above, giving the sea its boundary, and appraising the weather to confirm its suitability – is accessible to us through His Spirit (Prov. 8.23–31; Job 28.25–7).

Jesus withdrew into isolated areas on special occasions, such as to the desert for the temptation and the garden of Gethsemane prior to the crucifixion. He often chose to preach in the open countryside and used images from nature as metaphors, such as in referring to himself as the 'true vine'. Frequently he drew upon observation of nature, teaching his disciples to learn by looking at the 'birds of the air' and the 'lilies of the field' and using an example of the growth of seeds in his parables (Matt. 6.26–8; 13.1–43; Mark 4.26–9; John 15.1).

As we contemplate nature we may wish to imagine Jesus's presence around us, as in the famous poem by Joseph Mary Plunkett:

> I see his blood upon the rose
> and in the stars the glory of his eyes,
> His body gleams amid eternal snows,
> His tears fall from the skies.

> I see his face in every flower;
> The thunder and the singing of the birds
> Are but his voice – and carven by his power
> Rocks are his written words.

> All pathways by his feet are worn,
> His strong heart stirs the ever-beating sea,
> His crown of thorns is twined with every thorn,
> His cross is every tree.[34]

Just as Christ chose to heal our relationship with God by entering into the weakness and wounds of the world, if we become more sensitive to the workings in nature we may gain more compassion for creatures we cause to suffer. It is possible to identify with other living creatures because we share with them a dependence on the breath of God for life (Gen. 6.17; 7.15,22; Eccles. 3.19–21). We should learn to 'make friends with nature', just as St Francis thought of animals and birds as his relatives. Our concern for chickens in factory farms should not be merely intellectual; we need to feel for them and even cry for them. Only through such an experience of *feeling* will many people lose their complacency and be motivated to act to stop such cruelty.

Part of the purpose of seeking to sense God's presence in creation is thus to gain a greater sense of responsibility. In the eighteenth century William Cowper, in contrasting our lack of compassion for animals with that of God, wrote:

> I would not enter on my list of friends
> (Though graced with polish'd manners and fine sense,
> Yet wanting sensibility) the man
> Who needlessly sets foot upon a worm.
> An inadvertent step may crush the snail,
> That crawls at evening in the public path;
> But he that has humanity, forewarn'd,
> Will tread aside, and let the reptile live.[35]

We need a 'new sensibility', a feeling in the depths of our being that we are part of nature and a recognition that our *power* to extinguish life is matched by a *responsibility* to avert this. Sallie McFague suggests comparing the metaphor of 'the world as God's body' with images of the end of the Earth or its desecration, and using our imagination to "call up concrete images of events, people, plants and animals, objects, places, whatever – as long as they are particular, cherished aspects of our world – and dwell upon their special quality, their distinctiveness, their value, until the pain of contemplating their permanent loss, not just to you or me, but to all for all time, becomes unbearable."[36]

More positively, we will benefit by refreshing our awareness of the value of nature, its intrinsic goodness and the greatness of the Creator. Time spent in reflection, the wisdom gained, and the praise offered to God ought to bring a sense of *peace* with nature. We should feel a part of the interdependent web of life and sense a deep compassion for all creatures, even those species which we may choose to 'use'. Our love of God will grow as we appreciate more His wonderful creation, and by reflecting upon our surroundings and sensing His presence, we may be inspired to take proper care of it. We will aim to adopt lifestyles in which we achieve a balance between frugality and feasts, and in which the seasonal cycles of God's creation are acknowledged and celebrated.

Summary

The past separation of God from the world has been a contributory factor to the abuse of the environment. An alternative Christian understanding is of God continually present in the world, calling it into being by breathing life into it, and expressing Himself through it. God fills the Earth but He is not encompassed within it.

New ideas such as the Gaia hypothesis and the 'awakening Earth' offer different and provocative means of exploring the operation of nature. However, from a Christian perspective a careful distinction must be made from pantheism and paganism. The Earth is not self-regulating but sustained by the Creator and He cannot be equated with the universe but is a personal Being.

The presence of Christ in the material world is the ultimate affirmation of its value. He acts as the supreme mediator between God and the world, reconciling all things by harmonising the spiritual and material realms, and showed that we can learn about God by observing the world around us. Spending time contemplating nature, reflecting on its value and becoming more sensitive to its needs may encourage us to participate in his redemptive work.

1 John Robinson, *Honest to God*, p. 55.
2 ibid., p. 29.
3 Cited in Jonathon Porritt and David Winner, *The Coming of the Greens*, p. 250.
4 Cited in Paulos Mar Gregorios, *The Human Presence*, p. 79.
5 Peter Russell, *The Awakening Earth*, p. 130.
6 ibid., p. 131.
7 ibid., p. 95.
8 John Polkinghorne, *Science and Providence*, p. 16.
9 Jürgen Moltmann, *God in Creation*, p. 9.
10 Cited in Kallistos Ware, *The Orthodox Way*, p. 27.
11 ibid., p. 31.
12 Wesley Granberg-Michaelson (ed.), *Tending the Garden*, p. 90.
13 Cited in H. Paul Santmire, *The Travail of Nature*, p. 129.
14 Sallie McFague, *Models of God*, p. 33.
15 ibid., p. 70.
16 Polkinghorne, p. 21.
17 Moltmann, p. 86.
18 See Judg. 2.11; 8.33; 1 Kgs 16.31; 22.53; 2 Kgs 17.16.
19 Cited in Donald Worster, *Nature's Economy*, p. 33.
20 Paley drew from Robert Boyle's earlier analogy of the world as a clock and God as divine clockmaker, made after Boyle observed the famous clock at Strasbourg.
21 Albert Wolters, *Creation Regained*, p. 33.
22 Granberg-Michaelson (ed.), *Tending the Garden*, p. 88.
23 ibid., p. 89.
24 Cited in Andrew Linzey and Tom Regan (eds), *Compassion for Animals*, p. 12.
25 Edward Schillebeeckx, cited in Santmire, p. 204.
26 Cited in Santmire, p. 89.
27 Polkinghorne, p. 49.
28 Cited in Santmire, p. 125.
29 McFague, p. 141.

30 Santmire, p. 131.
31 Kallistos Ware, pp. 157–8.
32 ibid., p. 158.
33 This is derived from the practice of American Indians. See Wesley Granberg-Michaelson, *A Worldly Spirituality*, p. 28.
34 Cited in Granberg-Michaelson, *Tending the Garden*, p. 96.
35 Cited in Linzey and Regan, p. 66.
36 McFague, p. 187.

6

THE VALUE OF LIFE:
Promises and threats

As the Green Party began to emerge as a significant force in the 1980s the slogan which it often used was 'Politics for Life'. The threat to life provides the primary motivation for the Green movement, a concern for "the process of life itself and everything that nurtures and sustains that process".[1]

Publicising the 1989 mission tour in England of evangelist Billy Graham, the posters proclaimed: 'Life. Come and hear one man who can make sense of it'. Christianity, too, is essentially about life. God declared that the living world which He created, of animals, birds, fish, trees and plants, is fundamentally 'good' and in Christ took the form of flesh so that we "may have life, and have it to the full" (John 10.10). Throughout the Bible longevity of life is considered a sign of God's blessing.[2] People are created with a desire to live *for ever* and have an instinctive fear of death (Heb. 2.15). God has "set eternity in the hearts of men" (Eccles. 3.11).

Christians thus share with the Greens an affirmation that life is essentially good and, more specifically, that *biological life* is good. Similarly, irrespective of any differences in belief about life after death, Christians and Greens have in common a desire to sustain life and to improve the quality of people's lives.

This chapter explores how people value the rest of creation. The most profound questions which scientists now face relate not to the *origin* of life, but the *continuation* of life. All life is valuable – all species, all people around the globe and all generations to come. But people continually face some risk in life, whether crossing a road or climbing a mountain and so it is necessary to ask at what point life is *unduly* threatened. Should any activity involving high risk be avoided, or does this represent undue caution? More specifically, what is an appropriate response to the imposition of risk by some upon others? Such questions will be considered here in the context of the power acquired through nuclear technology and genetic engineering.

Is all of life valuable?

If there is value in the continuation of life and people are not to live in selfish hedonism, a reference point is needed beyond ourselves. We may be motivated by belief in a divine purpose for the whole creation, or by a selfless desire to enhance the prospects and opportunities for future generations. Consequently Christian faith and parenthood often provide stimulus for involvement in the Green movement. Were life to have *no* purpose it would have no value.

Life on Earth is held together in an immensely complex structure of food, mineral and energy chains. God has deemed the whole creation good, blessing it in its *entirety*, the wild and the ragged as much as the colourful and tidily structured, manure as much as fruit and vegetables. Animals which may be dangerous to humans are still of value to God. He knows every star by name and is aware of each single sparrow (Isa. 40.26; Luke 12.6). He is concerned for cattle as well as humans (Jonah 4.11). He is active even in areas where no people live, and covers the grass in fields with lilies more splendid than Solomon's clothes (Job 38.25–7; Matt. 6.28–9).

In Christianity the supreme affirmation of the value of biological life is the incarnation: "The Word became flesh and made his dwelling among us" (John 1.14). God saw fit to identify Himself in human flesh. Through this act we are able to gain insights into the *origin* and *purpose* of all life. Christ is "the author of life" (Acts 3.15) and God's expression, "the Word of life" (1 John 1.1). He gives us direction: "I am the way and the truth and the life" (John 14.6). And through commitment to him rests our promise of eternal life: "My Father's will is that everyone who looks to the Son and believes in him shall have eternal life, and I will raise him up at the last day" (John 6.40). One of the greatest joys as a Christian is to lose any fear of death.

Built into the structure of creation are cycles of birth, life and death, and over the course of time certain forms of life are sacrificed for the benefit of others. Many people react negatively to these biological cycles. But Eugene Heideman has explored what he terms a 'theology of manure' and, in affirming the essential goodness of biological existence as a *whole*, he suggests that in the eyes of God not only food but even manure is good (cf. Luke 13.8). Perceptively, if perhaps tongue-in-cheek, he concludes:

> It would seem that our attitude toward manure can serve as a gauge of how 'good' we really believe it is that God created a biological world. It is easy enough to thank him for a glorious sunset or the marvellous flavour of an apple. But our gratitude develops a new dimension when in the midst of our technology and our economic systems we can sincerely thank him even for the excrement that feeds the trees, the flowers, the grass.[3]

The living environment has intrinsic value because the world of matter is essentially *good*. As Augustine wrote: "All nature's substances are good, because they exist and have their own mode and kind of being, and, in their fashion, a peace and harmony among themselves."[4] He argued that "evil is not a substance; it is the perversion of a nature that is essentially good."[5]

However, although all of life has intrinsic value, human existence inevitably demands the use of other species. Thus we have to evaluate the worth of its different parts, making decisions concerning, for example, the mining of minerals, developing wilderness territory and eating meat. We discriminate in our treatment of other species and this reflects the fact that we have to evaluate the *degree* of goodness in different parts of nature. It is not practical to live as if, in the words of William Blake, "every thing that lives is Holy."[6] The problems arise when other forms of life are only attributed any value if they can be used by humans.

As already indicated, some Greens believe that nature is not simply valuable but *sacred*. This brings a new dimension into the debate. To claim that nature is sacred either means that it is divine, or that it is to be 'set apart' for God.

The former belief is animist or pagan and those who truly seek to act as if nature is divine would surely have considerable difficulty in making use of it. Christianity challenged such paganism and in the process removed the 'spirit beings' in nature, who although seen by some as guardians, were equally often terrifyingly capricious. Critics argue that nature was stripped not just of its divinity or holiness but also of its value, and thereby became vulnerable to exploitation. There is a degree of truth in this, although it is often overstated. But while nature cannot be considered by Christians as divine, perhaps we should consider 'setting apart' land, in the name of God, for regeneration. Such land might be regarded as sacred.

Bridging national boundaries

The value of life has to be considered beyond a single dimension of space and time. The scale of the ecological crisis forces us to go further than the immediate, local situation, to take account of people on other continents and in generations to come.

Politicians are fond of economic and social comparisons in attempting to reveal national superiority. They appeal to a sense of national pride. However, too often nationalism brings prejudice, intolerance, greed and conflict.

Paul's teaching that "there is neither Jew nor Greek . . . for you are all one in Christ Jesus" (Gal. 3.28) breaks down the barriers of race or region. We must discard our national pride. We live in one world and our 'neighbours' in other continents have equal value in the eyes of God to those living next door. Many life-related issues are international in character. Food, energy and raw materials frequently cross national boundaries, and likewise pollution of air and sea invariably affects more than one country.

Any solution to the ecological crisis will necessarily address the massive gulf between rich and poor which persists throughout the world. In the past, people saw a conflict between helping the poor and saving the environment. Even recently a leading development agency's entrance into environmental campaigning was marred by a leaflet which opened: "No matter how important the threat to plants and animals highlighted by ecologists, [our] prime concern must be to improve the living standards of poor people."[7] This was unfortunate because it gave the impression that people's needs can be met irrespective of the quality of their environment. Such agencies are now much better informed about links between the environment and development. The Brundtland Report communicated very effectively the connections:

It is impossible to separate economic development issues from environment issues; many forms of development erode the environmental resources upon which they must be based, and environmental degradation can undermine economic development. Poverty is a major cause and effect of global environmental problems.[8]

Recent statistics show that out of the world's population of just over 5 billion people, 1.7 billion lack access to clean water, 1.2 billion are without adequate sanitation and the diet of 730 million is insufficient to enable them to work properly.[9] Future prospects are not encouraging. The proportion of the world's population in poverty may fall, but the actual number of people suffering is not expected to decline.

The fragile bodies of the starving, with their emaciated limbs resembling skin-covered sticks, surely causes much grief to God. Linking global poverty with the misuse and squandering of resources in the affluent West, Sean McDonagh has written: "The world economic situation today is particularly embarrassing for Christians. The 1.5 billion followers of Jesus, 'who had no place to lay his head', now control two-thirds of the Earth's resources and,

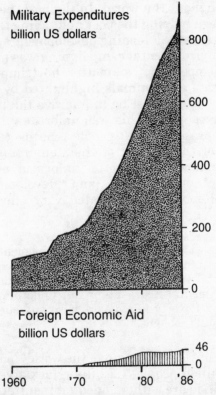

FIG. 5 MILITARY EXPENDITURE AND ECONOMIC AID – WORLDWIDE TOTAL
Source: Ruth Sivard, *World Military and Social Expenditures 1989*, (World Priorities Inc., 1989)

on average, are three times better off than their non-Christian neighbours."[10] Christians bear particular responsibility because "from everyone who has been given much, much will be demanded; and from the one who has been entrusted with much, much more will be asked" (Luke 12.48).

Global injustice is, in fact, increasing. According to World Bank data, between the mid 1960s and the mid 1980s incomes of the world's poorest people (the 611 million people in 'low-income economies', with an average income of $190 per annum) grew by an average 0.9 per cent per annum. In contrast, the richest people (733 million in 'industrial economies', where the average income is $11,430 per annum) experienced an average increase of 2.4 per cent per annum.[11] Moreover, the debts of the poor and their trade imbalances are so high that these actually *exceed incoming aid*, resulting in a net flow of capital from the poor to the rich. This is an absolute scandal and yet nations such as Britain, despite rising affluence, have in recent years *reduced* the proportion of their national income offered to help the poor.

An increase in overseas aid is much needed and long overdue (during the 1980s Britain's aid budget actually *fell*). However the Green approach to international injustice is to recognise that in the long run the poor may be helped most if we also learn to *take less* from them and enable them to become more self-reliant. Affluent nations have turned a huge acreage of farming land in poor nations into, in effect, their own out-of-season vegetable plot. It may bring the latter foreign exchange, but often prevents indigenous people from being able to grow *their own* food. In many regions in Africa and Asia, for example, local people suffer inadequate diets even though their countries have been net exporters of agricultural produce. In any case the foreign exchange is often squandered on arms or other potentially harmful imports from the West, such as pesticides, cigarettes, drugs, refined foods and powdered milk.

Affluent countries should be willing to pay fairer,

higher prices for commodities imported from low-income countries – cash crops such as coffee, cocoa and sugar actually declined in value between the mid 1970s and mid 1980s. In addition, the exporting countries should be encouraged to reap the financial benefit of processing goods prior to export. The West should also write off most of the debts accrued by the poorest countries, because the borrowing terms laid down by their bankers and governments were harsh and unrealistic. All these issues are, of course, highly complex, but it is imperative that alternative models of progress are quickly found to those of the over-industrialised world.

As indicated in Chapter Three, we should reject the kind of language that pompously proclaims that rich industrialised countries are 'developed' and those which are not are 'under-developed'. The latter may well be living in a more sustainable manner! Native tribal people sometimes appear to have a far greater respect for the Creator than people from the affluent West, and their sustainable methods of using the environment often reflect this. There is a *two-way* learning process in links between industrialised and low-income countries.

Historically Christians have travelled widely to communicate their faith, and in the Victorian era, in particular, there was a great upsurge in overseas missionary activity. Missionaries have throughout this time been active as naturalists and many have done valuable work to improve the lives of the poor. Many of them have unique opportunities to help solve environmental problems as they work in tropical forest regions.[12] However in Britain in the 1980s it was not missionaries who proved the most effective communicators to the nation about environmental disasters, but pop singers such as Bob Geldof and Sting. Billy Graham's 'Mission 89' filled Wembley Stadium with the aim of enabling people to make sense of life. Bob Geldof's 'Live Aid' filled Wembley Stadium to enable the starving to live. What will it take to fill Wembley Stadium with people whose Christian faith motivates care for the whole creation? How many Christians are working overseas to save the rainforest, or develop organic farming?

Isaiah prophesied that Christ will establish his kingdom and uphold it with justice and righteousness (Isa. 9.6–7). He comes as God's Spirit-filled servant to "bring justice to the nations" (Isa. 42.1). Christians thus have a special responsibility for justice and righteousness as we are part of his 'body'. Our actions to achieve justice for others are done as if to Christ himself (Matt. 25.31–46; 1 Cor. 12.27).

One of the first sayings in Christ's ministry was that he was fulfilling Isaiah's prophecy:

> The Spirit of the Lord is on me, because he has anointed me to preach good news to the poor. He has sent me to proclaim freedom for the prisoners and recovery of sight for the blind, to release the oppressed, to proclaim the year of the Lord's favour. (Luke 4.18–19; cf. Isa. 61.1–2)

The good news for the poor is *not* simply a message of *spiritual* salvation, as often taught in the past. It includes a promise of *economic redistribution*. This is evident from Isaiah 49, which suggests that, at the time of God's 'favour', the land, the main source of an unjust distribution of wealth, is to be restored to Israel and reassigned according to the Jubilee laws (Lev. 25.10; cf. Num. 34.13).

> This is what the Lord says: 'In the time of my favour I will answer you, and in the day of salvation I will help you; I will keep you and will make you to be a covenant for the people, to restore the land and to reassign its desolate inheritances, to say to the captives, 'Come out,' and to those in darkness, 'Be free!' They will feed beside the roads and find pasture on every barren hill. They will neither hunger nor thirst, nor will the desert heat or the sun beat upon them. (Isa. 49.8–10)

This is a message for Christians *today*. In many churches, however, much more time is spent at church meetings and committees than in campaigning for justice. It is time for more Christians to heed the prophet Amos who, seeing the works of those who "turn justice into bitterness" and "trample on the poor", proclaimed that God no longer wants religious festivals and noisy songs, but justice to "flow like a river" (Amos 5.7,11,24).

Those in low-income countries, suffering from environmental degradation and the loss of land, are in need of the good news that Jesus Christ came to bring both salvation *and* justice. How highly do we value people suffering from malnutrition? How loud are our cries for land overseas to be restored to the dispossessed? Is it not our Christian duty to seek to eradicate 'structural sin', injustices created by people operating collectively in ways that harm the poor? Our faith without deeds is dead, just as the body without the spirit is dead (Jas. 2.26).

Tomorrow's children

One of the primary causes of environmental destruction is our short-sightedness. God, in contrast, sees through all ages; He is the Almighty "who is, and who was, and who is to come" (Rev. 1.8). As Isaiah wrote: "The Lord is the everlasting God, the Creator of the ends of the earth. He will not grow tired or weary" (Isa. 40.28).

As He gave Moses the Ten Commandments God warned that if the Israelite people worshipped idols, instead of Him, future generations would suffer. He spoke of "punishing the children for the sins of the fathers" (Exod. 20.5). The principle of justice extending between generations is similarly expressed in the Jubilee laws which, operating over fifty-year cycles, would correct any injustices which might have built up.

It is in a sense inevitable that future generations will be punished when people do not acknowledge Him and take care of His creation. Yet recognition of interconnections between generations seems a principle more readily accepted by Greens than many Christians. For example Greens often cite the saying that 'we do not inherit the Earth from our ancestors, we borrow it from our children'.

By contrast, Christians too often look backwards in time instead of speaking prophetically about the future. Some act as if the future is *entirely* predetermined and deny the hope of transforming the Earth for future generations. However, as we do not know when Christ will return, it is our responsibility to act *as if* many more generations will need a healthy planet on which to live.

Mary Evelyn Jegen beautifully expresses a sense of the interconnections between generations when she reflects upon Jesus's use of the term *Abba* to describe his intimate relationship with his Father:

> Our parents really live on in us. When I look down at my hands, I sometimes remember that the tissue that has grown organically all these years began as the union of elements from my parents' bodies. Parents do live in their children.[13]

In choosing how to use the Earth's finite resources, we are making decisions which will affect future generations and a value is effectively placed upon those as yet unborn. If we abuse the environment we devalue future generations.

The population issue is a matter of great sensitivity and controversy. The threat posed to the quality of life on Earth by the rapid growth in the global population is consequently often ignored. But population is a key factor in achieving ecological balance. At the start of this century the global population stood at 1.65 billion. According to the United Nations, it has now reached 5.2 billion. Between 1950 and 1985 it grew by an average 1.9 per cent per annum, twice the average annual rate of the previous half-century. In some countries, such as Algeria, Bangladesh, Iran, Kenya and Nigeria, the rate has been higher, sufficient to double the population roughly *every twenty-five years*.

The total is set to grow further, to 6.25 billion by the year 2000 and 8.5 billion by 2025, before stabilising – probably at around 10 billion – in the latter part of the next century. These disturbing figures already *assume* a substantial decline in fertility through increased family

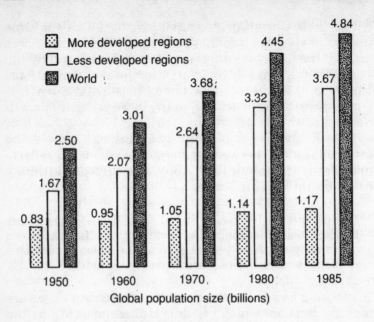

FIG. 6 GLOBAL POPULATION
Source: United Nations Population Division

planning, especially in low-income countries. Without this, the global population may grow as high as 14 billion.[14] An example of how difficult it will be to tackle the problem comes from Malaysia, where the Government is deliberately seeking to *increase* its population from 17 million to 50 million in order to expand its domestic market for industrial products.[15]

Although 90 per cent of the expected global increase will occur in low-income countries, to pour the blame on *them* would be misguided. The rich industrialised world may have less than a quarter of the world's population, but it consumes 75 per cent of the world's energy resources, 85 per cent of wood and 72 per cent of all steel produced.[16] It is *we* who are most responsible for the depletion of energy and mineral resources and for much of the world's pollution. If fingers *are* to be pointed, they might be better directed at consumption-obsessed North America, where the population is expected to rise by over one-third from 260 million in 1985 to 350 million in 2025.

The effects of population growth are most severely felt in countries where food production cannot keep pace, especially in Africa and Asia. Population pressure leads to over-cropping, over-grazing and excessive fuelwood harvesting, which in turn result in serious soil degradation. Efforts to increase food production through additional chemical inputs may well be inappropriate, being costly, energy-intensive and, ultimately, damaging to the soil structure. Often the poorest farmers are forced on to marginal land, which then deteriorates further, or they have to move to cities, frequently ending up destitute in appalling shanty towns. The problem of 'ecological refugees', people forced to move from one area to another because of environmental degradation, has become increasingly apparent.

Improved access to advice on family planning is needed in many countries, ideally integrated with better health care and education facilities. The World Fertility Survey has revealed that around half of women who want no more children lack access to effective birth control methods and facilities.

Given the frequent criticism of Roman Catholicism for its official teaching on birth control, the views of Father Sean McDonagh are worth noting. Fully acknowledging the severity of the population problem McDonagh recognises that 'extensive' family planning is needed. However, he is quick to point to the danger of coercive measures and warns that if birth control is divorced from land reform and development projects, it becomes "an oppressive tool in the hands of the rich."[17] Over-population is indeed often used as an excuse not to respond to the injustices which may underlie poverty. However, improved living standards is as much a factor in achieving population stability as birth control.

The world's population must be stabilised at the earliest opportunity if future generations are not to see their prospects of a reasonable quality of life seriously diminished. Because of the time lag involved in addressing the global problem, couples today should consider limiting their family size, and might consider adopting unwanted children rather than having more than, say, two of their own.

Whilst normally carried out for reasons related directly to the parents, as distinct from fear about global population trends, abortion raises a serious dilemma for many people. The number of abortions in Britain each year is around 170,000, of which only a very small fraction are on grounds of endangering the life of mother or child, rape, or the risk of severe mental or physical handicap. From a Christian perspective abortion for any other reason appears indefensible. In one of his Psalms David wrote of how God "knit me together in my mother's womb" (Ps. 139.13), while Jeremiah believed that he was appointed by God as a prophet even before he was born (Jer. 1.5). This suggests that in the eyes of God life begins at conception, not at birth.

In the Green movement, as elsewhere, many feminists have accepted the principle of 'a woman's right to choose'. However, as Greens claim to care most deeply about the sustainability of life and acknowledge the rights of future generations, abortion ought to be considered particularly abhorrent. What value is being placed on future life when people curtail it, fearing that it will affect their *own* quality of life? The need for self-sacrifice to improve the prospects of generations to follow is an absolutely crucial Green principle.

If life, particularly human life, has an *intrinsic* value, a value to its ultimate Creator, this raises serious questions for those who support abortion. The unborn child is not *merely* an extension of the mother; it thus has a right to exist whether or not it is wanted. Greens, of all people, would be wrong to suggest that rights only begin at birth.

Such a position seems hard for some Greens to accept, but the case needs to be made, because acceptance of abortion except for genuine health reasons is inconsistent with principles at the very heart of Green thinking. The prospect of unwanted children demands a more radical response than curtailing life between conception and birth. Often the motivation for terminating a pregnancy is a lack of support from the father or the wider community. Only when men fully share their responsibility for the child can they justifiably pronounce that it is not simply 'a woman's right to choose'.

Thus Greens and Christians alike should accept the need for steps to reduce substantially the vast number of abortions carried out annually. These should include lowering the legal time limit for abortions, in the first instance to a point below which survival in the external environment has never been possible. This must be accompanied by improved sex education, better counselling facilities, improved housing, better financial support for lone parents and more workplace nurseries. There must be no possibility of a return to illegal 'back street' abortions. Only when there is better support from the family and local community, backed by adequate government funding, will women no longer resort to abortion.

New life

Abortions on grounds other than health represent an attempt to improve people's quality of life by killing unborn children who, it is assumed, would face special difficulties in life. The logic is that if unwanted, they are likely to grow up in an insecure environment and, by implication, will not fit well into society. This really is not so very far from eugenics, the quest to improve the human species by the 'judicious mating' of those of 'good stock'. New developments in genetic engineering bring the prospect of eugenics closer.

The basic blueprint of life, found in genes contained in the DNA of every living cell, can now be altered. Since the early 1970s biologists have developed techniques which enable them to cut the threads of DNA, which carry the genetic blueprint, and stitch in other segments of DNA.

Thus they can engineer into living organisms characteristics which could not have been acquired in natural circumstances (current techniques include gene splicing, cloning and cell fusion).

Scientists are thus creating new forms of life in a way which is very different from traditional selective breeding. Organisms can be produced in days or weeks, rather than the years required for traditional breeding. Further, traditional breeding involves *whole* organisms and is limited to crossing plants and animals which are very closely *related* to each other. Genetic engineering, by contrast, allows totally unrelated species to share each other's genetic material. Transgenic animals have already been created, including a cross between a goat and sheep dubbed, pathetically, the 'geep'.

Many people do not realise how advanced this technology is, or how profound are its implications. For decades science fiction has portrayed robots working for humans. It now seems more likely that other life forms will serve us. We are, in effect, remaking nature to work for us more quickly, more efficiently, more predictably.

Genetic engineering raises crucial ethical issues, particularly when human genes are involved. It may enable improved treatment for burns, provide inexpensive insulin and synthetic antibodies, and offer cures for hereditary diseases and genetic defects. But there are worrying aspects. A genetically engineered virus may be developed for use as a vaccine, for example, but what if it should later prove unstable or capable of mutating? Are the potential medical benefits simply being touted as a panacea to gain public support for a much wider range of applications?

Vital ethical questions have not yet been adequately addressed. For example, there appears no sharp line between correcting genetic defects and enhancing genetic make-up. Genetic manipulation of living organisms may help sufferers from diabetes or sickle-cell anemia, but where is the dividing line between this and, say, using the same technology to reduce the number of people who suffer from an 'inadequate' intellect or a poor physique?

Scientists are, perhaps, in danger of making false assumptions about the possibility of human perfection. Instead of accepting the life which God has allowed to be created in our fallen world, we set about seeking to re-create ourselves in our own image. If society is willing to allow abortion for unborn children liable to be mentally handicapped, why should it not allow genetic engineering of other people liable to be born with other characteristics deemed imperfect?

The possibility of eugenic trends in medicine is, of course, deeply disturbing, and the commercialisation of human genes, cells and tissues is already a very real prospect. This includes linking human genes with those of other species. For example, human genes are being implanted into sheep in order to produce special milk for pharmaceutical purposes.

In other instances the aim is to affect, intentionally, another species. In May 1988 the newsletter of Compassion in World Farming had on its front page a pig. This may not seem unusual, except that it was one of the first transgenic pigs, born in America with a human growth gene implanted into its genetic make-up. It was intended to be fast-growing with excellent meat quality. Instead, the newsletter reported, it turned out a cripple, excessively hairy, lethargic, riddled with arthritis and apparently impotent.[18]

New genetically manipulated organisms have many potential applications, not just in medicine but in other areas. Some of these may be acceptable, but others are certainly not. In agriculture super-poisonous viruses are being developed for use as pesticides, toxin genes for making plants distasteful to pests, and crops which would grow in areas which are currently too dry or too saline to support agriculture. Reports indicate that the first genetically engineered tomatoes could be on sale in Britain by 1993 and in America there is a prospect of radical changes to agriculture, including the use of transgenic livestock by the late 1990s.

Other areas of genetic engineering research include

waste management (where genetically manipulated organisms may be used as toxic waste-disposal agents), water treatment (to remove pesticides and heavy metals), resource recovery (to concentrate minerals from low-grade ores and mine tailings), and pollution control (such as oil dispersal).

The Church throughout the world has been slow to address the genetic engineering issue. In creating new, genetically-altered life forms, human dominion reaches a new level. Michael Fox, Vice-President of The Humane Society of the United States and a leading writer on genetic engineering, questions provocatively whether a society which accepts genetically altered animals as new life forms thereby seeks to assume dominion over God.[19]

It seems instinctively unnatural to violate species boundaries through genetic engineering. In Old Testament legislation there is a warning: "Do not mate different kinds of animals" (Lev. 19.19). This was given as part of a series of instructions which affirm a divinely established order. Andrew Linzey, a leading Christian authority on animal welfare, draws a principle which summarises well the proper relationship between humans, God and animals:

> Animals have a God-given right to be animals. The natural life of a Spirit-filled creature is a gift from God. When we take over the life of an animal to the extent of distorting its natural life for no other purpose than our own gain, we fall into sin. There is no clearer blasphemy before God than the perversion of his creatures.[20]

Although traditional selective breeding similarly alters characteristics of species, this is achieved in a more gradual process, at a pace limited by nature's reproductive cycles. Moreover, it does not allow for genes to be exchanged between unrelated species. These restraints are particularly significant as regards animals, because they allow them their integrity, which gives them a certain dignity. They are what God created them to be. They have a particular God-given place in the global ecosystem. If species exist *only* through human choice, their worth is dependent on commercial, recreational or aesthetic value to humans; the instrumental value of the species is a condition of its existence.

The development of transgenic species is to judge other species as not good enough. What does this say about the Creator of all living species? Should we not concentrate our scientific efforts on conserving endangered species before engineering transgenic ones? Wesley Granberg-Michaelson, who works at the World Council of Churches, one of few Christian bodies studying genetic engineering, writes:

> Our energies are more faithfully exercised through nurturing and protecting present species rather than presuming to rearrange their genes. Crossing species lines in the creation of new forms of life amounts to a new form of technological blasphemy.[21]

Owning life

Genetic engineering is not merely a modern application of the accepted principle that nature may be used for the benefit of humankind. It is of a different order of magnitude, because people are controlling the most basic characteristics of life. Such total control is a form of ownership.

Not surprisingly, therefore, patents are now applied to genetically engineered living organisms. The US Supreme Court ruled in 1980 that new life forms could be patented, and in 1987 the US Patent and Trademark Office formally decided that 'non-naturally occurring, non-human multi-cellular organisms including animals' could receive patents. Countries in the European Community are expected to adopt national legislation to make life patentable by 1991. In April 1988 Harvard University was issued with the first such patent, for a mouse genetically engineered to be predisposed to develop cancer, through the insertion of cancer genes at the embryonic stage.

The patenting of life is effectively an extension of intellectual property rights to living species. Restricting access to particular species, it may perhaps be regarded as the ultimate privatisation, the privatisation of life.

From a Christian perspective, the patenting of life directly contravenes the principle that all life belongs to God (Ps. 24.1). The Bible teaches that we do not own even ourselves; our bodies are not ours to possess (1 Cor. 6.20). Wesley Granberg-Michaelson suggests that "if we are to regard our bodies and all creation not as our own, but as the place where God dwells, then their genetic design rightly remains in God's hands rather than our own."[22]

Genetic engineering devalues life to no more than groups of particular chemical substances capable of reproduction. Freda Rajotte, a colleague of Granberg-Michaelson at the World Council of Churches, has suggested that life becomes viewed as "merely a collection of isolated, self-replicating entities to be re-programmed and reorganized at will, instead of as intrinsic parts of God's holistic and wondrous creation."[23]

Certain solutions proposed by genetic engineering are a mere 'technological fix'. For example, to give crops resistance to hazardous or toxic environmental conditions, such as tolerance to herbicide or acid rain, may enable bad practice to continue. Such problems should instead be addressed at *source*, by decreasing the use of chemicals, or preventing pollution emissions. Another example relates to speculation about the possibility of creating a wingless, beakless chicken for battery cage life. The proper solution is surely to increase the size of the cage, not to manipulate the poor chicken!

As a science, ecology is relatively young and, as a report of the Royal Commission on Environmental Pollution pointed out, knowledge of the interactions of species in natural ecological systems is often extremely limited. The relationship between living and non-living factors in an environment is highly complex. Thus predicting the behaviour of *ordinary* species is not always easy; with genetically manipulated organisms it will be even more difficult. What if an engineered bacterium which is totally harmless in itself is able to pass on an inserted gene to other bacteria where its expression causes unforeseen hazards? Another possibility is that herbicide-resistant, drought-resistant crops might spread their resistance to weeds, resulting in mutated weed species overrunning cropland. The prospect of continuing evolutionary modification and habitat change and the difficulty of monitoring after the organisms are released into the environment are further problems.

One implication for industry and agriculture is a further concentration of power into fewer companies and farms. Most of the necessary research has been done by a handful of companies in the chemical and pharmaceutical sectors; Monsanto, for example, has spent over $1,000 million on research.[24] Such companies do not want competitors to reap the return on their investment and a desire for monopoly ownership of genetic stock explains the pressure for patenting. Moreover, most genetically engineered plants so far tested have been herbicide-resistant and developed for sale in conjunction with a brand name chemical weedkiller.

Stability and balance in nature demands a diversity of species, but genetic engineering is likely to accelerate the pace of change in the opposite direction. Attempts will be made to boost the image of genetically engineered species to give them a superior status. Large businesses tend to favour narrow uniform ranges of products. Because of supermarket demand, for example, only nine varieties of apple are commonly sold in Britain, though several thousand, mostly grown in small quantities, exist.

The point of perversion

The motivation for genetic manipulation of farm animals is to make them more 'productive' – to grow faster, leaner or larger, and to produce more milk, eggs or offspring. In dairy cow herds a genetically engineered bovine growth hormone, bovine somatotropin (BST), is being tested in Britain and other EEC countries. If administered regularly, it increases milk yields by 7 to 14 per cent. In an ominous sign of contempt to public sensitivity the British Government is allowing milk from the trials to go unlabelled into the public milk supply. There are certainly side effects on the health of the cow and, quite possibly, on humans. If it is truly safe, why the secrecy? The BST trials have started a dangerous trend. There is now serious speculation about the prospect of cows with hugely extended rumps to provide the cuts of meat that people prefer.[25]

Animals are liable to suffer from developmental, structural and physiological problems as a result of being pushed to the limits of their productive capacity. How responsible is it to expose them to potential harm and cause them to suffer, even unintentionally, through genetic manipulation?

The aim may be to reduce food costs for the consumer and raise profits for manufacturers, research scientists and farmers, but what is the *moral* price of such cost-cutting? Such practices both reflect and reinforce the perception of animals as a mere commodity. They reduce animals to living factories. And is it really possible to feel comfortable eating pork which contains human genetic material?

In summary, evolution of species by natural selection is increasingly giving way to evolution by human selection. The changes in prospect represent a major step towards transforming the natural world into a synthetic world. There is no clearer indication of the broken relationship between humans and the rest of nature than the desire to own legally, exploit fully and maximise the productive yield of other life forms. What, then, should Green Christians call for?

There is a mentality in the industrialised world that if something *can* be done, then it *has* to be done. When the forces of technology become so strong as to be deterministic, they take the form of an idol. We are in danger of losing control to such idolatry.

Scientists and politicians are fully aware that the public are, in the words of a leading professor, 'very docile and very ignorant' about genetic engineering.[26] There needs to be a much stronger ethical input into the debate, perhaps through some kind of 'bioethics forum'; so far there has been negligible progress towards this. Such a forum might help to curb technological excesses by pointing to proper ethical constraints on science and technology, such as a respect for life, compassion for animals, and a degree of humility.

We should also seek more adequate legislation, covering three areas. First, a ban on the transgenic manipulation of animals. Animals have their own integrity and to step from traditional breeding to creating new transgenic species is to cross an unacceptable threshold. Second, an end to patents on genetically engineered living organisms, on the grounds that to own a species is to breach the biblical principle that all of life belongs to God. Scientists and others who deserve financial recompense for acceptable genetic engineering work should receive it in other forms. And third, a moratorium on the deliberate commercial release of genetically engineered living organisms into the environment for, say, five years. This caution is necessary while uncertainties and potential risks are minimised, public awareness is raised, and to allow for adequate ethical debate to take place. In the event of eventual commercial development all genetically engineered products should be labelled and their producers forced to take adequate insurance cover against accidents.

Our power over the gene has been likened to that over the atom by Professor Bill Stewart, a member of the Royal Commission on Environmental Pollution. He has said that genetic engineering will have as important an impact over the next forty years as splitting the atom.

There are certainly important parallels. There is massive investment and huge risk involved and currently the public have no insurance against disastrous unforeseen consequences. As with nuclear technology, genetic engineering is liable to be abused by those who seek its development for military uses. The US Pentagon is already thought to be using genetic engineering technology to develop more lethal germ weapons, raising the prospect of a global biotechnological arms race. The pace at which genetic engineering is allowed to advance should follow public acceptance of the risks involved. However there is every sign so far that developments will take place too quickly and public confidence will be lost, a mistake made with nuclear power.

Nuclear power – technological idolatry?

By comparison with nuclear technology, which has been in use in the energy and military sectors for approaching fifty years, genetic engineering is relatively new. The nuclear industry does not inspire confidence in human capacity to use new technology responsibly. Although advocates of nuclear energy argue that it is safe, cheap and necessary, the evidence points firmly in the opposite direction.[27]

There are now several hundred nuclear reactors which operate to supply energy in at least twenty-six countries. Hundreds more propel submarines, and dozens of spacecraft in orbit around the Earth are nuclear-powered. However, many countries throughout the world have been forced to reconsider their programmes because of exorbitant costs and safety considerations in the aftermath of the Chernobyl nuclear reactor accident. Even if the risk of an accident *were* infinitesimal the case for nuclear power falls, because it is not the *magnitude of the risk* that is most significant but the *scale of the potential threat*.

The disastrous accident in April 1986 at Chernobyl in the Soviet Union confirmed fears of the inherently grave danger in nuclear technology. Three years after the disaster churches in Minsk held services to pay tribute to the

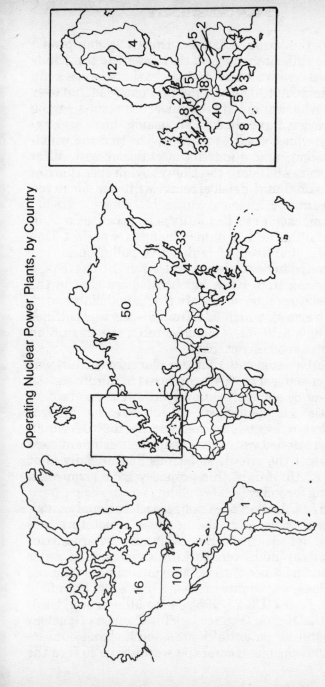

Operating Nuclear Power Plants, by Country

Numerals indicate the number of operable nuclear power plants.

FIG. 7 NUCLEAR POWER PLANTS
Source: Atomic Industrial Forum

victims. At the main Catholic church 1,000 people
mourned the suffering, many of them wearing armbands
with radioactive symbols. Although there were only
thirty-one immediate deaths it has now emerged that over
250 people who worked there or were involved in the
rescue operation have died.[28] Thousands more are expected to die over the next twenty years from radiation-
induced cancers, and hundreds of children will suffer
hereditary disease. Before the Chernobyl disaster Soviet
authorities said that the risk of an accident was one in ten
thousand years.

No nuclear reactor can be totally safe, because no technology is infallible and no human beings are perfect. One
of the immediate effects of radioactive pollution is that
water becomes dangerous to drink. Dr Yuri Stscherbak, a
Soviet physician from Kiev, has pointed out that in the
book of Revelation John writes of a star called Wormwood,
meaning bitterness, which falls from the sky and pollutes
the water (Rev. 8.10–11). Coincidentally, the Ukrainian
word for wormwood is *chernobyl*.

Dr Stscherbak suggests that the Wormwood 'star' was
sent as a menacing sign, "demanding us to think over the
very survival of our civilisation before it is too late."[29]
Great caution is demanded in interpreting biblical
prophecy, but it is at least noteworthy that Jeremiah
prophesied 'poisoned water' as a form of punishment used
by God against the sinful, idolatrous and ungodly (Jer.
8.14; 9.15; 23.15). Might this prophecy have acquired a
new meaning for today?

Radioactive pollution does not respect national boundaries. Several years after the accident agriculture was
still affected not only in the Soviet Union but in countries
such as Norway and even Britain, thousands of miles
away. Chernobyl was not an isolated incident but followed
a series of lesser accidents and near misses, at Sellafield
(UK, 1957), Fermi (USA, 1966), Three Mile Island (USA,
1979), and La Hague (France, 1980). The use of nuclear
power threatens a potentially profound international injustice in that people around the world have to face the

threat of another serious accident and in many regions they do not receive the energy produced.

Questions of justice similarly arise with the problem of disposing of nuclear waste. When potential nuclear waste dumps were first identified in Britain the Government received such vociferous local opposition, including objections from clergy and its own political supporters, that the plans were dropped. The continued use of an energy source when there is no acceptable means of disposing of its waste products is deplorable. No true caretaker of the Earth should find acceptable a technology which creates radioactive waste which remains dangerous for many thousands of years.

Claims that nuclear power improves people's material wellbeing suggest questionable motives. The potential threat to the environment is more significant than the promise of more affluence for the already rich. Even if nuclear power *was* to increase our affluence, no amount of prosperity could justify the radioactive waste.

In fact, the case for nuclear power has collapsed on *economic* grounds. For many years industrialists and politicians claimed that nuclear power was relatively cheap, but there is now a consensus that it has proved more expensive than alternatives. The stark reality of the true cost of nuclear power was brought home in 1989 when the British Government withdrew nuclear reactors from its electricity privatisation programme because it became apparent that businesses would not invest in them. As with the disguised connections between nuclear power and nuclear weapons, officials had been guilty of distorting the truth. The words of Paul apply: "They exchanged the truth of God for a lie, and worshipped and served created things rather than the Creator" (Rom. 1.25).

As nuclear power is phased out, energy needs obviously have to be met. Many people suffer from 'fuel poverty', an inability to pay for adequate heating. The claim that nuclear power would help the world's poor is, however, a cruel distortion of the truth. In industrial countries poor people would be far better off by a redistribution of income and wealth, while in low-income countries renewable energy sources, such as solar power, are far more appropriate. The needs of the poor should be conquered by economic *justice*, not energy *profligacy*. Nor is it credible to suggest that nuclear power offers a solution to the greenhouse effect – a Church of Scotland report cites research which showed that it offers a 'slow and ineffective' response to global warming compared with investing in energy efficiency.[30]

Huge amounts of energy are currently wasted in industry, offices, homes and through private transport. Investment in energy conservation is far more cost-effective than new sources of power generation. Many people's basic inclination is, however, to consume rather than conserve. Adequate incentives are needed to encourage change, which should include grant aid for energy-saving equipment and energy prices which truly reflect long-term supplies.

There *are* many safe and economic alternatives to nuclear power. Not all nations are maintaining their nuclear programmes. After holding referendums Sweden pledged itself to phase out its reactors and Austria decided not to put its sole reactor into operation. In America no new nuclear plants have been commissioned since 1979 and several dozen have been cancelled.

In addition to fossil fuel sources, such as coal and oil, safer renewable energy sources are available – wind, wave, solar, biomass, tidal, geothermal and hydroelectric power. All have *some* environmental effects, of course, but none threaten the kind of damage witnessed at Chernobyl, a catastrophe which could well be repeated elsewhere.

The sheer scale and complexity of nuclear technology is awe-inspiring. This partly explains why nuclear power is another form of industrial idol, commanding reverence from materialism and technology. It has become subject to almost unquestioning trust, inspiring its worshippers so profoundly that for many years dismantling it seemed inconceivable. However confidence has gradually fallen as claims that it would become 'too cheap to meter' and has no military connection were exposed as untrue. Attempts have been made to contrive new justification for its continued use, relating to global warming. However, choosing between catastrophic risks is not the only option. Nuclear energy should be swiftly phased out.

Some Christians may argue that, because God structured the possibility of nuclear fission into creation, it must therefore be intended for our use. Discovering this energy source was part of our mandate to develop the world; we are therefore free to use it. Anything structured into creation, they argue, cannot be evil.

The 'lawfulness' of nature, in this case the creation of heat energy through splitting atoms, is indeed part of the structure of God's creation. But different responses to such laws are open to us. To be faithful caretakers of creation we must restrain ourselves from harmful activities. Using nature's potential to create highly toxic substances destroys its intrinsic goodness. The fact that such restraint has proved so difficult in the past is a reflection of people's unwillingness to accept boundaries or limits on their activities.

Playing God

Public officials now acknowledge that nuclear power and nuclear weapons are linked more closely than the public was once led to believe. It has long been known that the nuclear power programme arose directly out of the development of nuclear weapons, but the transfer of plutonium from British nuclear reactors to the military sector was hidden by officials and politicians by lies and distortions over many years, and was only admitted by the Chairman of the Central Electricity Generating Board in 1986. The international transfer of nuclear technology, supposedly for civil purposes, is now acknowledged to be a serious threat to attempts at preventing nuclear arms proliferation.

There is a parable which runs as follows. It was late

October and Terry the Tortoise, aware that the cold weather was approaching, decided that it was time to hibernate. All the signs were that it would be a tough winter ahead and he would need to be well protected. He saw a pile of sticks being gathered in the garden and rested under them. As the pile grew higher day by day Terry felt more and more secure. What excellent protection, he thought. The pile grew ever higher. Then, one evening, when Terry felt close to sleep, a match was struck. The entire pile burned to the ground and Terry perished. He had forgotten the dangers of Bonfire Night.[31]

The aim of the story is to show how, sometimes, those who consider themselves to be well protected have a false sense of security. People leave their reason behind, blind themselves to the true situation and become rather too comfortable. Or they simply fail to pay enough attention to what is going on around them.

Although political leaders try to convince ordinary people that their military strategies are making the world secure, the reality is that despite reduced tension between East and West we remain under a grave nuclear threat. The world's nuclear arsenal is equivalent to *one million* bombs of the size of the first one dropped, which killed nearly 100,000 people in Hiroshima in August 1945. Today, American missiles *alone* could destroy the world's entire population twelve times over.

The sheer scale of the power which political élites assume has meant that "the nuclear threat epitomizes humanity's desire to claim God's power and seize the creation."[32] Never before have we had the capacity to virtually destroy the planet through warfare. Now we face the prospect of a 'nuclear winter'.

A nuclear winter would be triggered by the use of less than one per cent of this huge global nuclear arsenal. In such an event, the smoke, soot, dust and other debris lifted into the atmosphere would virtually eliminate sunlight over the affected continents. The consequent darkness would last for many months and halt photosynthesis, the process which allows vegetation to grow. Temperatures would plunge as low as −40 °C, making survival virtually impossible for many forms of life. The preceding nuclear war alone might be expected to kill two billion people, but a similar number could subsequently freeze or starve to death. Nuclear weapons are the greatest of all threats to life.

Our willingness to destroy life on such a scale says much about how we value it. Jonathan Schell argued in an influential book on the nuclear threat, *The Fate of the Earth*, that to conceive of destruction through a nuclear holocaust not only implies that life is not sacred but that it is utterly worthless. Life, as a totality, would self-evidently be *dispensable*. Greens have always opposed nuclear weapons because as caretakers of the planet we cannot envisage any conceivable situation which could *ever* justify their use because of the irrevocable damage that would be done. Christians have regrettably been more equivocal. It is our responsibility to ask if nuclear weapons are themselves *inherently* evil and whether it is a sin against God to possess such weaponry.

The arms race is not simply an unfortunate occurrence in an otherwise healthy world, but the inevitable result of exploitative and aggressive cultures. Material growth and military growth go hand in hand. They are part of the same dominant world view which sees big as beautiful, produces according to demand rather than need (hence there being sufficient nuclear weapons to destroy the world several times over), and which tolerates destructiveness.

Connections between the exploitation of resources for economic growth and the expansion of the arms race are now recognised by governments and international agencies. The Brundtland Report, for example, pointed out:

Environmental stress is both a cause and an effect of political tension and military conflict. Nations have often fought to assert or resist control over raw materials, energy supplies, land, river basins, sea passages, and other key environmental resources. Such conflicts are likely to increase as these resources become scarcer and competition for them increases.[33]

The influence of aggressive masculinity on Western culture contributes to the strength of the military sector. Being militarily strong allows national politicians the opportunity to play the role of a tough street fighter without the risk of getting (literally, at least) a bloody nose. In such macho-politics, underlying the politicians' strength is *physical* strength. It is part of the traditional bully boy's proud threat: "I'm strong, so I get what I want." In reality, of course, it takes much, much more strength to *refuse* to play such games. Men *instinctively* strike back if hit; it takes a special inner strength to enable them to resist.

Militarism also feeds on belief in national or racial supremacy, which is often disguised as patriotism. The negative view of Russians encouraged by Western governments in the NATO alliance over many years was a calculated attempt to stir up fear of the 'outsider'. It is in marked contrast with Jesus's teaching on the proper treatment of strangers, to invite them in and offer hospitality (Matt. 25.31–46).

Following the phoney logic that only nuclear weapons can ensure peace implies that global security should increase as more countries have nuclear weapons. If Britain keeps its independent nuclear deterrent we cannot, with integrity, argue that other nations should not acquire the same. It really is nationalistic nonsense to claim that nuclear weapons are safer in British hands than those of other countries. But so long as Britain and other nuclear states do not actively disarm, other countries will seek their own nuclear weapons. The Nuclear Non-Proliferation Treaty, which is intended to prevent an escalation of the nuclear threat, has not been signed by France, China, Argentina, Brazil, Israel, India, Pakistan, South Africa or Spain. All these countries have either acquired, or are believed to be close to acquiring, nuclear weapons. If *Britain* is safer with nuclear weapons these countries, and others, can make similar claims.

By the late 1980s global military spending exceeded $1,000 billion annually, a sum equivalent to the combined gross national income of China, India and all African countries south of the Sahara.[34] A major objection to extravagant expenditure on nuclear weapons is that it represents a misguided stewardship of resources. We are *already killing people* through possessing, operating and upgrading nuclear weaponry because this diverts physical resources, human skills and financial capital from feeding the hungry and caring for the sick. Claims that nuclear weapons enable reductions in expenditure on conventional weapons would be more convincing if the military budgets of the nuclear states were in fact falling.

Defence and disarmament cannot be properly considered in isolation from other issues. A lasting solution to military security is impossible unless other initiatives are taken to bring about a more just and co-operative world. As East-West tension subsides there are increasingly calls for resources earmarked for military expenditure to be used instead to tackle global environmental problems. The Brundtland Report listed four programmes to tackle the most urgent environmental problems; these related to tropical forests, desertification, water supplies and family planning. The report claimed that they could be implemented with the equivalent of less than *one month's* global military spending.[35]

Advocates of nuclear deterrence argue, however, that 'nuclear weapons cannot be disinvented'. This is appalling logic, as many other problems (such as, say, adultery), cannot be disinvented – but they are, nonetheless, indefensible by Christian standards. The choice of whether or not to *apply* military technology is open. Our capability to manufacture nuclear bombs will always exist in the form of knowledge, but the world will be a much safer place if the danger is in the form of scientific writings on paper instead of nuclear warheads targeted towards people.

Christians should set a lead and call – persistently – for nuclear disarmament. We are to follow Jesus as the 'light of the world' (Matt. 5.14; John 8.12), and work towards the

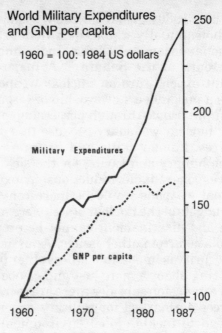

(GNP = Gross National Product)

FIG. 8 MILITARY EXPENDITURE
Source: Ruth Sivard, *World Military and Social Expenditures 1989*,
(World Priorities Inc., 1989)

fulfilment of the prophecy of the coming of a world where nations "beat their swords into ploughshares and their spears into pruning hooks" (Isa. 2.4; Mic. 4.3). Too many Christians mistakenly continue to resist this gospel, this good news, by opposing unconditional, independent nuclear disarmament.

In consequence the reaction of the Church to the nuclear threat has often been equivocal. For example, in 1983 the Church of England General Synod published *The Church and the Bomb*, a report which was a well-judged and timely contribution to the debate. However its conclusions, which included a call for Britain to renounce its independent nuclear deterrent, were not approved by

Synod. A further report was commissioned, though this time a bishop with a reputation for advocating nuclear deterrence was chosen to chair the working group responsible. Predictably, the subsequent report, *Peacemaking in a Nuclear Age*, was far more sympathetic to nuclear deterrence than its predecessor and understandably attracted criticism from peace campaigners.

A traditional Christian approach on warfare is the concept of the 'just war'. According to just war principles non-combatants must not be *indiscriminately* killed, even in retaliation, and the evil and damage which the war entails must be *proportionate* to the injustice and injuries which it aims to overcome or avert. However, with nuclear weapons these conditions are unlikely to be met. Anyone who tolerates the possession of such weapons must accept a possibility of mass indiscriminate slaughter. And the history of warfare suggests that once a battle commences it is extraordinarily difficult to contain. The prospect of a limited nuclear exchange is thus slim. There is no such thing as a 'just nuclear war'.

Christians are, in stark contrast to the logic of military combat, called to love our enemies (Matt. 5.44). Peter's epistle teaches us to "turn from evil and do good" and to "seek peace and pursue it" (1 Pet. 3.11). Love surely cannot be offered to others so long as we target weapons on them. The evil which should truly concern us most is not that which our 'enemies' threaten to do to us, but what we might do to them.

We are also called to love our neighbours (Matt. 5.43; cf. Lev. 19.18). In past centuries this may have meant people living in the immediate community, but economic and environmental interrelationships demand that we offer love to literally all inhabitants of the planet. Our neighbours are people who live in the Soviet Union or Eastern Europe just as much as those living in America or Western Europe.

The argument that it is acceptable to *possess* nuclear weapons because we would never *use* them is flawed. Countries within the NATO alliance have adopted a policy which explicitly allows for the 'first use' of nuclear weapons. In any case, retaliation once attacked would equally be evil. Advocates of a strategy of nuclear 'bluff' should note that Christians are taught to speak honestly and plainly (Matt. 5.33–7). Furthermore, even a willingness to consider using nuclear weapons is corrupting, just as the anger which precedes murder is wrong and the man who looks lustfully at a woman has already committed adultery in his heart (Matt. 5.21–30). Being willing to possess such weaponry is to live by no higher standards than the perceived enemy.

Nuclear weapons cannot ever provide people with a true sense of contented security because they will remain aware of the horrifying potential, however remote, of a nuclear holocaust. Many Christians find difficulty in discarding their faith in nuclear weapons, though they often resort to arguments for their retention which have no explicitly Christian basis. Of course no one should deny the difficulty of trusting perceived 'enemies', particularly in the light of numerous international atrocities in past years. But Christianity teaches that we are to trust in *God*, not weapons.

David was no pacifist but his faith was very clearly *directed*: "Some trust in chariots and some in horses, but we trust in the name of the Lord our God. They are brought to their knees and fall, but we rise up and stand firm" (Ps. 20.7–8). Isaiah and Hosea, too, condemned those who trusted in the strength of their armies rather than in God (Isa. 31.1; Hos. 10.12–13). Old Testament writers did not consider the size of an army to be the determining factor in winning wars (Ps. 33.16–17; 44.3; Prov. 21.31). The Law expressly *forbade* the king from acquiring great numbers of horses (Deut. 17.16; cf. Isa. 2.7; 30.16; 31.1). Thus when Gideon was about to face the Midianites, he was instructed by God *not* to have a large army, but to reduce it from 22,000 to a mere 300 in order that Israel could not boast that her own strength had saved her (Judg. 7.2). If only arms reductions in the modern world could be of a similar magnitude!

There *are* alternatives to nuclear arms escalation. Citizens could be trained in 'social defence', involving various techniques of planned non-co-operation and civil disobedience, to communicate to potential aggressors that in the event of invasion the country could become ungovernable. Furthermore, the case for countries to become neutral has been strengthened by recent political change in Eastern Europe.

The Christian's model character is Jesus Christ, who offered no defence to his accusers and allowed violence to be done to him which he could have prevented by inflicting violence upon others (Matt. 27.27–31; Mark 15.4–5). He did not fight but, as Isaiah prophesied, was "led like a lamb to the slaughter" (Isa. 53.7). We must not fear suffering. Jesus taught his disciples not to fear those who may attack the body but are unable to reach the soul (Matt. 10.28). If we truly love the Creator there can be no justification for threatening to destroy His creation.

Some Christians cling to the hope that in a crisis God would intervene to prevent a nuclear holocaust and console themselves that, if not, nuclear war must be part of a divine plan. They want the power that nuclear weapons offer but, at the same time, cannot face the *responsibility* of having this awesome power. They have free will and the collective ability to achieve nuclear disarmament but pass responsibility to politicians, the military, God, predestination – anyone or anything but themselves. But free will means that the future is in *our* hands. We *can* choose to rid the world of the nuclear threat.

The fatalism which is so disempowering to many ordinary people is contrary to the hope of Christians who, of all people, should believe in the possibility of change. We are called to be *peacemakers*, not merely *peacekeepers* (Matt. 5.9; Heb. 12.14). One of the most disturbing aspects of the nuclear threat is that most people are not sensitive to it except when a new generation of weapons is introduced, or relations between the 'superpowers' deteriorate. We must persist until the threat disappears, which will only be when nuclear weapons are no longer deployed.

To conclude, the nuclear states now have the ability to destroy God's creation, to extinguish ourselves and most other life on Earth. This demands that we consciously imagine the effect of nuclear warfare, because – unlike global problems, such as rainforest destruction and starvation – actual images of the reality of a nuclear holocaust do not regularly confront us. If we do not *face up* to this potential horror we may never be sufficiently motivated to act to prevent it. Escapism is no alternative to militarism. What kind of atrocity are those who approve of the possession of nuclear arms willing to contemplate? Is mass murder of the innocent ever tolerable? We must bring an end to the nuclear age.

Summary

A desire to sustain life motivates Christians and Greens alike. Nature is intrinsically good and we should neither live as ascetics nor despoil it. To truly love our neighbours, our concern should extend beyond immediate and local interests to embrace people in other continents and future generations. Campaigning on behalf of the world's poor and the children of the future are important expressions of this concern.

Genetic engineering and nuclear technology raise vital ethical questions relating to the responsible use of our substantial powers. The possibility of altering the basic characteristics of species and the risk of radioactive pollution through an accident or warfare demand great wisdom of decision-makers. However the Church has yet to address adequately the vital ethical issues raised and provide a moral lead to guide public policy.

Advances in genetic engineering are rapidly taking place and commercial developments should be legally restrained while safety and ethical questions are considered further. Greens seek a non-nuclear future, believing that nuclear weapons and nuclear power pose unprecedented threats to life. Many Christians see them as manifesting a form of idolatry. We need to learn to accept limitations on our activities, identifying the boundaries established by God.

1 Peter Bunyard and Fern Morgan-Grenville (eds.), *The Green Alternative*, p. x.
2 See, for example, Gen. 15.15; Judg. 8.32; 1 Chron. 29.28; Ps. 91.16; Prov. 3.16, 9.11; Isa. 65.20.
3 Eugene Heideman, 'Beyond Dung', *Third Way*, February 1986, p. 26.
4 Cited in Andrew Linzey and Tom Regan (eds), *Compassion for Animals*, p. 9.
5 Cited in Wesley Granberg-Michaelson, *A Worldly Spirituality*, p. 68.
6 Cited in Keith Thomas, *Man and the Natural World*, p. 302.
7 'Oxfam and the Environment' brochure, quoted in Jonathon Porritt and David Winner, *The Coming of the Greens*, p. 38.
8 World Commission on Environment and Development, *Our Common Future*, p. 3.
9 ibid., pp. 109, 118.
10 Sean McDonagh, *To Care for the Earth*, p. 8.
11 World Commission on Environment and Development, pp. 29–30.
12 Ghillean Prance, 'Missionaries as Earthkeepers' in *Radix 14* No. 3, November–December 1982, pp. 24–5.
13 Wesley Granberg-Michaelson (ed.), *Tending the Garden*, p. 94.
14 Nafis Sadik, *The State of World Population 1989*, New York: United Nations Population Fund, 1989, p. 2.
15 Jonathon Porritt and David Winner, p. 223.
16 Nafis Sadik, p. 1.
17 Sean McDonagh, p. 183.
18 *Agscene*, Newsletter of Compassion in World Farming, May 1988. Another genetically manipulated pig, implanted with a cow's growth hormone, had difficulty in walking, and suffered from arthritis and visual impairment. Clive Hollands, Biological Council Lecture, September 1987.
19 Michael Fox, *Catholic Worker*, June–July 1987.
20 Andrew Linzey, *Christianity and the Rights of Animals*, p. 112.
21 Granberg-Michaelson, *A Worldly Spirituality*, pp. 192–3.
22 ibid., p. 196.
23 Speech by Freda Rajotte, 'Deliberate Release into the Environment of Genetically Engineered Organisms', February 1989.

24 Speech by Earle E. Harbison, 'Biotechnology – A World Economic Revolution', March 1989.
25 *Meat Trades Journal*, 30th April 1987, cited by Clive Hollands, Biological Council Lecture, 10th September 1987.
26 Peter Campbell, cited in *Agscene*, May 1988, p. 3.
27 See 'Nuclear Reactions', *Christian Arena*, Vol. 40, No. 3, UCCF, September 1987.
28 *The Times*, 9th November 1989.
29 *Forum*, World Council of Churches, No. 5, January 1989, p. 5.
30 David Pullinger (ed.), *Scorching Heat and Drought*, p. 68.
31 Adapted from Nicholas Humphrey's 1981 Bronowski Memorial Lecture, in Jonathon Porritt, *Seeing Green*, p. 144.
32 Granberg-Michaelson, *A Worldly Spirituality*, p. 177.
33 World Commission on Environment and Development, p. 290.
34 ibid., p. 297.
35 ibid., p. 303.

7

'MEAT IS MURDER':
An abuse of animals?

People often hold double standards about animals.[1] They like to watch them in the wild on television, but each year hundreds of thousands of pets are thrown into the streets and end up as strays. They are sentimental about animals, yet many are guilty of abusing them. They claim to be animal lovers, but the majority eat flesh from their dead bodies with hardly a second thought.

The ill-treatment of animals is widespread. Anglican theologian Andrew Linzey, a leading Christian authority on animal welfare, estimates that through farming and animal experimentation alone approximately 100 billion animals are killed throughout the world each year.[2] (The human population, by comparison, numbers around five billion.) Much cruelty occurs in the process of food production, through factory farming, the transportation of live animals (often overseas), and brutal slaughterhouse practices; other sources include animal experimentation, the fur trade, circuses, zoos, abuse of pets, and blood sports such as fox hunting.

All manner of questions are raised by such abuse. Were animals created solely for the benefit of humankind? If not, what kind of constraints are placed upon us? Does each species of animal have a 'natural' life which should be respected and, if so, are any changes to this acceptable? Do animals have 'rights'? Is it fair to say, in the popular vegetarians' catchphrase, that 'meat is murder'? This chapter explores such questions from a Christian perspective.

Biblical insights

As shown in Chapter Five, God values His whole creation. His desire that people should treat animals with respect is evident from the Old Testament in particular, which provides guidelines for our behaviour. These are summarised in the proverb: "A righteous man cares for the needs of his animal" (Prov. 12.10).

Certain Old Testament laws were evidently framed in order to prevent cruelty to animals. The Israelites were told to help animals in trouble, even if they belonged to other people (Deut. 22.4). The tradition of draining blood from animals not only has deep symbolic significance, but would have prevented the practice of cutting a limb off a live animal for meat (Gen. 9.4). If people took young birds from a nest the mother bird was not to be taken with the young; this would not only preserve the bird population but would also be in their own interest, as bird life was important in keeping down numerous insect pests (Deut. 22.6–7). Animals were not to be over-exerted. The Israelites were instructed not to plough fields using an ox and donkey tied together, which would cause a strain between the animals (Deut. 22.10).

The commandment for people not to work on the Sabbath is well known but it is questionable whether many people are aware that it applies also to animals (Exod. 20.10; 23.12). Although they could be used by people, animals' lives were to be respected. For example, when a young calf, lamb or goat was to be sacrificed it could not be taken from its mother during the first seven days of its life (Lev. 22.26–7). Such a law clearly took account of the parent-offspring bond between animals.

The New Testament builds upon Old Testament teaching, although it includes, by comparison, relatively few direct references to animals. But God's care for creation was *assumed* throughout Jesus's ministry. Jesus observed, for example, that God feeds the birds and is concerned about the lives of sparrows (Matt. 6.26; 10.29; Luke 12.6, 24).

Animal sacrifices will, of course, be pointed out by some as an example of cruelty sanctioned by God. However the sacrificial system had fallen into disrepute and was beginning to wane even before the coming of Christ, and from then onwards animal sacrifice represented a form of unnecessary bloodshed (as, indeed, some regard the killing of animals today).[3] Old Testament prophets had pointed to an end of the need for animal sacrifices (Isa. 1.11–17; Mic. 6.6–8; Hos. 6.6). Jesus reiterated this teaching, and the early Christians taught that after his death and resurrection animal sacrifices no longer served any purpose as a reminder of people's guilt (Matt. 9.13; 12.7; Mark 12.28 –34; Heb. 10.5–10).

Wrongful attitudes have sometimes occurred when Christians have misinterpreted the Bible. Paul asks in connection with the Old Testament law not to muzzle oxen while treading out the grain: "Is it about oxen that God is concerned? Surely he says this for us, doesn't he?" (1 Cor. 9.9–10; cf. Deut. 25.4). This has been taken to mean that God does *not* literally care for oxen, or indeed other animals, but is only concerned about humans. However such an interpretation ignores the original basis of the Old Testament text, which is that God *does* care for animals. It is precisely because the principle (that workers deserve food) applies to *animals* that it *also* applies to humans. Paul believed that the apostles deserved to have their material needs met and this teaching is quite properly used to encourage responsible giving for the Church's needs. But the underlying principle relating to animal welfare is *equally* valid.

Indeed the intellectual basis of campaigns against cruelty to animals initially grew out of Christian teaching concerning the need to take care of God's creation.

The Christian legacy

Historical studies such as Professor Keith Thomas's *Man and the Natural World* and E. S. Turner's *All Heaven in a Rage* reveal startling examples of past cruelty and misunderstanding. Staging competitions between animals, for example, is a long-established tradition. Cock-fights were popular from the twelfth century onward and horses, bulls, bears and even tigers were 'baited' (tethered to a stake and then attacked by one or more dogs) from the thirteenth century. In bull-baiting the bull would endeavour to toss the dog into a crowd of spectators while the dog made for the bull's nose, often in the process tearing off its ears or skin. Opposition emerged by the sixteenth century, but such activities only came to an end through an Act of Parliament in 1835.

The Puritans objected to baiting and other such 'sports' because of gambling. But they also expressed concern at the suffering and viewed cruel sports as taking pleasure in the consequences of the fall – there was a prevailing belief that all animals had been tame until the fall. According to historian Keith Thomas: "Puritans lamented the readiness of dogs to fight with bears because they saw it as the result of the fall and therefore a reminder of Man's sin."[4] An earlier historian, Thomas Macaulay, had been more cynical and sneered at their opposition to bear-baiting, suggesting that it was not because of the pain suffered by bears but because of the pleasure given to those watching!

Until the late seventeenth century it was not generally thought that God was concerned for the wellbeing of the non-human creation, although there were notable exceptions such as St Francis. However this slowly began to change; in 1691 taxonomist John Ray wrote critically of the common belief that humans were the only species of value in creation and that other species were valuable only if they could be used in some way by humans, and identified a trend among more intelligent people away from such thinking.[5]

Thus from the eighteenth century people's arguments for greater concern for the welfare of animals tended to be explicitly supported by religious teachings and by the latter part of the century many considered cruelty a blasphemy, an insult to God. The Old Testament was the authority most frequently cited by propagandists.

Thomas argues against those who have suggested that religious sceptics initiated the animal welfare movement and that Christians only tagged on at the end of the eighteenth century.[6] Even in its early stages clerics were often ahead of lay opinion, and an essential role was played first by Puritans, Dissenters and Quakers, and later, by Methodists and Evangelicals. John Wesley, for example, condemned brutal sports and taught children not to cause needless harm to any living creature, although Anglicans were, according to E. S. Turner, less forthcoming: "In the Anglican Church a vicar who expressed undue solicitude for animals was liable to be suspected of Methodism, or premature senility."[7]

Christians were often at the forefront of new organisations formed to secure the wellbeing of animals. It was a minister, the Reverend Arthur Broome, who convened the meeting which resulted in the setting up of the RSPCA in 1824; evangelical social reformer William Wilberforce and two other clergymen were on its committee. In its early years the Society passed a rule making Christian loyalty explicit – not entirely without controversy, as it led to the resignation of the honorary Secretary, Lewis Gompertz, who happened to be a Jew.

When there was the first public outcry at animal experimentation prominent Christians were again involved. The National Anti-Vivisection Society was formed in 1875 after Francis Cobbe gained the support of Lord Shaftesbury, another Christian reformer, and the Archbishop of York. Cardinal Manning was involved, notwithstanding the prevailing Catholic orthodoxy, and indeed he attempted in vain to prevent the wrecking amendments that seriously weakened the 1876 Cruelty to Animals Act, which for the first time regulated painful experiments on animals.

England had by this time become known as 'the Hell of Horses' because of the suffering caused in the early stages of the Industrial Revolution to horses and donkeys used in woollen mills, breweries, coal mines and railway shunting yards. According to Turner:

These were dire days for the horse. Expansion of industry, the building of railways, the multiplication of highways, the reshaping of cities – none of this was possible without horse-power. There was scarcely a tunnel, a bridge or an embankment which was not a monument to cruelty. If contractors were behind schedule, professional horse-floggers would be called in.[8]

Dogs, too, suffered appalling abuse. They were used to pull carts with freight, carrying fish, for example, between ports and railheads. They were even used to transport people. Their journeys lasted up to fifty miles and for the latter half their paws were torn open, being unsuitable for such tasks, leaving a trail of blood on the highway. Eventually dogcarts were outlawed in 1854.

This fractured relationship between people and animals has continued into recent times. In the early 1950s myxomatosis, a disease lethal to rabbits, was deliberately introduced in several countries, including Australia, France and Britain, to reduce the rabbit population. The disease killed literally millions of rabbits in a slow and often tortuous death, graphically described by one witness who spoke of "a wretched creature, sightless, nearly hairless, and half its entrails exposed, battering itself against the wall of a house."[9] So terrible was the sight of such suffering that the RSPCA organised 'mercy squads' to shoot diseased victims. The motive of this cruel destruction was quite unashamedly to increase farmers' incomes; in other words, for the sake of human affluence.

Horses, dogs and rabbits were not alone in suffering; these are just a few selective examples of abuse to animals. The millions of animals used in experiments should not be forgotten, nor the countless otters, foxes, hares and other wild animals killed in hunting. What factors are to blame?

'Ain't got no soul'

How we treat animals reflects how we perceive them. If whales are seen as large vessels which are full of oil, and chickens as complex machines for converting grain into flesh it is no wonder that they are exploited. They should be treated very differently if seen as feeling, independent beings with souls, into which God has breathed life.

Ill-treatment towards animals has taken place because they are so often valued simply in terms of their usefulness to humans. They are viewed as 'commodities' to be bought and sold, 'tools' for scientific research and 'units of production' in farming.[10] Underlying this is a belief that they are not Spirit-filled beings created by God, but that their bodies represent no more than living, soulless machinery.

Earlier this century Professor C. S. Lewis called for Christians to rethink their attitudes to animals in the context of the debate on vivisection. He exposed the false logic of recognising similarities between the human and non-human creation but not opposing vivisection:

> Once the old Christian idea of a total difference in kind between man and beast has been abandoned, then no argument for experiments on animals can be found which is not also an argument for experiments on inferior men. If we cut up beasts simply because they cannot prevent us and because we are backing up our own side in the struggle for existence, it is only logical to cut up imbeciles, criminals, enemies or capitalists for the same reason.[11]

Comparisons between humans and other animals in terms of anatomy, speech and reason have always led to dispute. Similarly, the question of whether animals have souls is an unresolved question which has vexed theologians over centuries.

Potentially, at least, the answer is significant, as it may affect how people treat animals. Some believe that because they do not have souls animals lack fundamental intrinsic value and are not worthy subjects of moral concern. Others, however, have argued the reverse, that if animals lack souls and do not have a compensatory afterlife they deserve our *special* consideration. For example in a pamphlet on vivisection, published in 1947, Lewis argued that if animals lack souls, in the sense of having no moral responsibilities and immortality, the infliction of pain on them is even *harder* to justify. It would mean that they cannot deserve pain, nor profit morally from the discipline of pain, nor be recompensed by happiness in another life.[12]

The Bible says little about the ultimate fate of *individual* animals. The writer of Ecclesiastes addresses the question, but leaves the answer open:

> Man's fate is like that of the animals; the same fate awaits them both: As one dies, so dies the other. All have the same breath; man has no advantage over the animal. Everything is meaningless. All go to the same place; all come from dust; and to dust all return. Who knows if the spirit of man rises upward and if the spirit of the animal goes down into the earth? (Eccles. 3.19–21)

In the theology of Aquinas and other medieval scholars the process of redemption applied to humans, the four material elements and the heavenly bodies, but not to other creatures.[13] Such theology emphasised the lack of rationality in animals and paved the way for subsequent beliefs which reinforced their low status, such as the idea that they lack sufficient self-consciousness to experience pain. This freed people from sensing guilt and fear that they were causing suffering. It also helped them to rationalise any apparent signs of distress. They reasoned that either animals did not feel pain or, if they did, that this was of no concern to God.

Early Protestant writers questioned this understanding. Some concluded that the guilt of humans and the innocence of animals meant that the latter should be treated with compassion. One writer in the seventeenth century observed that people should not misuse them because "if there be any defect or untowardness in their nature or any want of duty or observance in them towards us, our sin hath been and is the cause and occasion of it."[14]

In the eighteenth century the thoughts of Methodist

John Wesley on the general deliverance made a notable impression. According to Wesley, Paul's teaching in Romans was not to be interpreted to mean that the whole creation was to be *annihilated* because this term could not be equated with 'deliverance' ('liberation' in the modern NIV translation). Wesley believed that animals would be restored to recompense them for their suffering and that they would "enjoy happiness suited to their state".[15] Thus he preached:

> The whole brute creation will then, undoubtedly, be restored, not only to the vigour, strength, and swiftness which they had at their creation, but to a far higher degree of each than they ever enjoyed. They will be restored, not only to that measure of understanding which they had in paradise, but to a degree of it as much higher than that, as the understanding of an elephant is beyond that of a worm.[16]

Belief in animal souls became much more common in the Victorian era, partly because pet-owning increased and pet owners were unable to accept that a just God would allow their pets to be doomed to oblivion. The debate was also stimulated by Charles Darwin's ideas, which presented the controversy starkly: If humans evolved directly from other animals, either those animals, too, had immortal souls, or humans did not.

Historically, however, most Christians have in general devoted little energy to considering the fate of animals; our main concern has been human salvation. The Protestant tradition in the West has in this regard followed the teaching of reformer John Calvin, who taught that animals should be handled 'gently' and with respect and that people should not abuse them 'beyond measure'.[17] However he also believed that Christians should accept uncertainty and not speculate upon whether animals will be immortal. His theology was based firmly on the assumption that humans were at the centre of God's creation and the rest of nature was created for our benefit.

If all creatures which ever existed *are* subject to

redemption, this, it has been suggested, may raise questions relating to space. In *Evil and the God of Love* theologian John Hick questioned the very possibility of an animal afterlife in the light of millions upon millions of individual animals which have existed since sentient life first appeared. Other theologians have speculated as to whether each *species* is represented in heaven (as in the ark), as distinct from each single creature. According to Hick, in the absence of a conscious awareness of past suffering a 'zoological paradise' would lack any real compensatory value for such creatures.[18] Lewis similarly questioned the meaning of immortality for individual animals: "If the life of a newt is merely a succession of sensations, what should we mean by saying that God may recall to life the newt that died today?"[19]

Were such a zoological paradise to exist, potential conflicts might be thought likely between different creatures, although, asked where millions of mosquitos might find their final place, Lewis deftly replied that a heaven for mosquitos and a hell for humans could easily be combined!

Rights over animals?

Much of the debate on the treatment of animals has focused on the concept of animal rights. As long ago as the middle of the eighteenth century when Thomas Paine was preparing his famous work *The Rights of Man*, others were arguing that flies had no less a right to life, liberty and enjoyment. It was not long before calls were made for the state to acknowledge the rights of animals in law and the concept of the 'common rights of nature' had emerged.

Discussion of animal rights heightened towards the end of the eighteenth century. Perhaps the most famous statement concerning the welfare of animals, that of the political philosopher Jeremy Bentham, was written in 1789, three years prior to the publication of *The Rights of Man*. Bentham wrote of the right of animals to protection from suffering. His case was made without reference to God's will or intention but on utilitarian grounds, the aim of maximising their happiness:

> The day *may* come, when the rest of the animal creation may acquire those rights which could never have been withdrawn from them but by the hand of tyranny . . . The question is not, Can they *reason*? nor, Can they *talk*? but, Can they *suffer*?[20]

Shortly afterwards John Lawrence, a farmer and supporter of hunting, nonetheless proposed "that the Rights of Beasts be formally acknowledged by the State and that a law be framed upon that principle to guard and protect them from acts of flagrant and wanton cruelty."[21] The earliest successful legislation concerning animals was passed in 1822 (though it was in fact approved in the context of safeguarding animals as the property of humans, not protecting them from suffering).

Rights may be defined briefly as 'just claims'. In theory they are entitlements conferred upon humans, animals, and perhaps even other forms of life, or the planet itself. American writer Theodore Roszak has argued that the needs of the planet are united with the needs of the person in our quest for peace and survival, and that "the rights of the person are the rights of the planet."[22]

However, rights have to be agreed or granted; the term only makes sense in the context of decisions by a community or by God – justice needs a *reference point*. Moreover, rights have little meaning unless associated *responsibilities* are recognised. There is, necessarily, an implied norm or moral standard. We have a right to be *able* to do that which we *ought* to do. It is only if humans have a duty to take care of the Earth that other life forms are able to claim a right to proper treatment.

Talk of 'rights' is meaningless unless such rights and responsibilities can be clearly defined and recognised. The difficulty in the absence of belief in *God* is that rights must be agreed by our own species; the 'right' of humans to determine the interests of other species is a questionable concept. God as an 'external' power may make an 'objective' judgement. How, though, can rights between species be objectively defined? Does an owl have 'rights' over a mouse?

It is thus unconvincing to argue that other creatures can *themselves* claim upon humans a right to continued existence. The idea that "long-standing existence in nature is deemed to carry with it an unimpeachable right to continued existence" is inadequate, if not meaningless.[23] Over many thousands of years species have appeared and disappeared with no human cause. Who breached the 'right' of dinosaurs to exist?

Christianity can at least make some sense of 'just claims' through belief in God, who has rights as Creator. People's responsibility for the environment is derived through God and any claim of rights for animals and for ourselves is in the context of *God's* right to have what He has created, honoured and respected. Any rights that humans claim are only valid in relation to God, in Linzey's term 'theos-rights' (literally, God-rights).

This is very different from claiming that rights exist autonomously. Rights may be claimed by God, not by animals. It would be wrong of Christians to attempt to consider animals in themselves, apart from God, as no part of creation may be properly understood except in relation to God. Linzey writes that 'theos-rights' are "concerned with the defence of God-given spiritual capacities exhibited within his creation and realised through his covenant relationship with them, and not with any capacities which may be claimed by the creature itself in defence of its own status."[24]

No clear dividing lines exist, of course, to make it easy to weigh up the relative value of different forms of life. However, the Bible suggests that there is a 'spiritual continuity' between humans and other living creatures. God's covenant was with animals made of 'flesh' (Gen. 9.9–10). Flesh has special significance in the Bible. It is alive with God's spirit which breathes life into animals and birds (Gen. 2.7; cf. Gen. 1.30; Ps. 104.30). The fact that Christ became flesh affirmed its special value (John 1.14).

The writer of Ecclesiastes compares the fate of the spirit of animals with that of humans, though he concludes that the answer cannot be known with certainty (Eccles. 3.19–21). Joel and the Psalms liken the cries of animals with a spirit yearning for God (Joel 1.20; Ps. 42.1).

Linzey proposes, tentatively, that 'theos-rights' may be conferred on humans and certain other creatures (mammals and birds, but not fish) on the grounds that these are "Spirit-filled, breathing beings composed of flesh and blood."[25] They are assumed to be especially valuable by virtue of a capacity to respond to God through a degree of spiritual perception and self-consciousness.

Much of the debate on animal rights has been carried out on the basis of comparisons between humans and animals, without reference to God. Charles Darwin's books shocked Victorian Christians by pointing to similarities in social instincts and mental powers between humans and animals, such as loving, assisting, curiosity, memory, imitation, reason, and sympathy for each other. Most people, especially Christians, had hitherto seen the differences between them as absolutely fundamental. It was ironic, then, that Darwin's claim that humans were more closely linked with the animal kingdom than hitherto believed gave impetus to experimentation on animals (Darwin himself had no objections to such experiments, though he considered an anaesthetic necessary). In contrast Lewis Gompertz, a prominent animal welfare campaigner, responded that "groping for truth with a knife was no different, morally, from groping for truth with a rack and thumbscrew".[26] More recently Peter Singer, too, has exposed apparent contradictions in Darwin's logic: "Darwin continued to dine on the flesh of those beings who, he had said, were capable of love, memory, curiosity, reason, and sympathy for each other."[27]

Most people today believe that our responsibility to other creatures cannot be as great as to our own species; to use theologian Karl Barth's example, if faced with saving a cat or a child from an oncoming train people have an *instinctive* reaction to accord the latter greater importance. Similarly, few of the millions of people who suffer from malaria or bilharzia can be expected to offer sympathy for the mosquitos and snails which transmit these diseases which cause so much suffering.

However the differences between humans and animals are not sufficient to accord fundamental rights to one but not to the other. If variations in intelligence between *humans* do not change basic 'theos-rights' or justify exploitation, nor should differences in intelligence between humans and animals.

In summary, animals have rights as defined by Linzey and this bestows upon them a *fundamental moral status*. Our behaviour towards them is not a matter of mere taste or convenience, but a matter of justice by virtue of their *Creator's* right. It is morally wrong to ill-treat animals not only because of its effect on them but because their Creator is thereby treated with contempt.

Animal 'theos-rights' are valid in the same way as human 'theos-rights', because humans and other animals are subjects of common creation bound together in the same covenant relationship. But the rights belong to *God*.

Mere machines

Demands for animal rights have increased partly out of a growing appreciation that animals are much more in-telligent than was once believed. However we are still suffering the legacy of the eighteenth-century French philosopher René Descartes, whose thinking has proved perhaps the strongest influence on the debate relating to the intelligence and sensitivity of animals.

According to Descartes a strict division could be drawn between mind and matter, which was an essential basis of dualistic thought. Animals' bodies were seen as operating like mere machines. People were distinguished from other species by virtue of possessing a rational soul, which was essentially independent of the body.

Descartes justified such thinking by people's capacity for speech and a belief that people acted through *knowledge* and not merely as a result of the disposition of their bodily organs. Descartes thereby responded to those who pointed to similarities between human bodies and those of other animals by suggesting that the latter operated purely mechanically, through 'natural impulse'. They had the necessary organs (parrots, for example, could speak), but lacked thought.

As animals were viewed as insensitive, unthinking machines, it is hardly surprising that they were treated accordingly. Thus Descartes's contemporaries argued that "the cry of a beaten dog was no more evidence of the brute's suffering than was the sound of an organ proof that the instrument felt pain when struck."[28] They dissected cats "without mercy, laughing at any compassion for them, and calling their screams the noise of breaking machinery."[29]

It was such reasoning that led Ruth Harrison to choose *Animal Machines* as the title of her critical and highly influential book, questioning the morality of factory farming. The publicity which followed its publication led the Government to establish the Brambell Committee in 1964 to produce a code of conduct for farm animal welfare. Yet the Ministry of Agriculture's initial reaction to Harrison's book was that animals would not thrive if suffering, and that boredom is not cruelty. Even then the treatment of farm animals as machines found willing defenders, and in the past quarter of a century official attitudes often seem to have changed surprisingly little.

Factory life

Factory farming provides perhaps the clearest example of the routine abuse of animals, a form of industrialised production which is cruel, unnatural and unhealthy, and for this reason is considered here in detail. It is perpetuated only because consumers are willing to purchase its produce. Few people give any consideration to the lives of chickens when they buy eggs or choose a joint of meat for the 'Sunday roast'. Most who do would probably like to believe that the chicken spent its life merrily pecking food off the ground as it wandered around an idyllic farmyard. Sadly, the truth is very different.

On a modern British farm the broiler chickens which are reared for meat are typically crowded in huge flocks in a highly artificial environment. At any point in time there are over 425 million broiler chickens, owned by around two thousand farmers. The average flock is around 22,000 birds, although a half of all broiler chickens live in flocks of over 100,000 birds. In modern turkey units the flocks typically number 20,000. There are 35 to 40 million egg-laying hens which live in battery cages, often in even larger, windowless buildings. Flocks of up to 80,000 birds are common and, in one or two cases, number almost 1,000,000 birds.[30]

Cruelty often arises from the fact that factory-farmed animals are isolated and therefore alienated from a natural living environment. Mark Gold, Director of Animal Aid, has graphically described the condition of many egg-laying hens at the end of their service, noting that they are frequently found with a combination of raw necks, deformed feet, tattered feathers, pale combs, abscesses and sores.[31]

Around 96 per cent of egg-laying hens are kept in cages measuring 20 inches by 18 inches with four or more birds in each cage. As this gives each of them a width of four inches of cage and a chicken's wing span is 30 inches, they cannot spread even a single wing, let alone two. In other countries, such as Norway and Denmark, the minimum space allowance, though still inadequate, is up to 50 per cent higher. In Switzerland and Finland limits are imposed on the size of livestock holdings, which deters intensive practices, and in Sweden new legislation may well bring a total end to factory farming. Curiously, Britain's The Protection of Birds Act of 1954, which demands that birds kept in cages and other receptacles can stretch their wings freely, specifically *excludes* poultry.

These chickens obviously cannot express instinctive behaviour such as dustbathing, wing flapping, preening, and scratching in the ground for food. In their units temperatures are kept artificially high, and the light intensity is maintained for up to seventeen hours per day to lengthen their active day. According to Compassion in World Farming, attempts are being made to breed out of the chicken the need for a stimulating environment and the aim is to reduce the activity of the hen's mind to that of an 'egg-laying vegetable'.

Broiler chickens fare little better. From the outset they are unmothered. Most are 'protected' from natural sunlight to keep them docile and never see the light of day. They stand permanently on sloping wire mesh in artificially warmed buildings and are mechanically fed instead of being allowed to gather food by pecking. Many are beak-trimmed to prevent the feather-pecking (and even cannibalism) which may occur in a stressful environment. When taken for slaughter, rough handling of their unnaturally brittle bones often results in wings and legs being broken. A survey in 1989 found that nearly a third of battery hens had freshly broken bones prior to slaughter, twice the proportion for free-range hens.

The Bishop of Salisbury, John Baker, has attacked the unthinking, unfeeling manner in which chickens are treated. Preaching at a service held by Animal Christian Concern in 1986, he was concerned at people's ignorance of the true nature of such creatures and spoke of the 'blasphemy' and 'sacrilege' of making the lives of chickens so unfortunate and their 'cruel and terrifying death'. Addressing those who would point to the apparent harsh conditions faced by wild animals he added: "It is in the battery shed and the broiler house, not in the wild, that we find the true parallel to Auschwitz."[32]

The fate of pigs is equally unsatisfactory. According to the RSPCA, Government codes of practice are ignored by the majority of pig producers. Some 400,000 breeding sows, 60 to 70 per cent of the total, are kept in close confinement systems where they are denied exercise through the use of tethers and girdles. They lack companionship and sometimes have inadequate light. Natural instincts like rooting and nest building are obviously frustrated. Weaning periods are shortened and the sows quickly put to boar. In consequence they may spend up to forty weeks of the year chained to the floor, alone and virtually immobile, lying on concrete with minimal straw.

The early-weaned piglets likewise suffer a barren, unnatural environment. Those weaned at three weeks are kept in battery cages with subdued lighting until they have grown sufficiently to be put in fattening pens. In these pens overcrowding, dim lighting and inadequate floor surfaces are very common. In such an environment tail-biting often occurs and, to combat it, pigs' tails are often docked.

Pigs kept in a more natural state would, in contrast, spend up to six hours each day rooting – not just for food but out of inquisitiveness. They would tend to live in small herds in light woodland with access to water in which to wallow. Many authorities claim that pigs are as intelligent as cats and dogs.

Natural mating is becoming increasingly rare for cattle; around two-thirds of dairy cow pregnancies are now accounted for by artificial insemination. Free-range suckling beef herds are under threat, as new developments in 'embryo transfer' bring closer the prospect of wholly beef-bred calves being implanted into dairy cows.

Neither do cattle escape the horrors of intensive farming methods. Veal production is notoriously cruel, although some of the worst abuse, calves reared in small wooden crates, is being phased out in Britain. Even so, when calves are reared for veal they are fed on special low-iron diets in order to produce pale, tender meat. Cows kept for milk production undergo a continuous cycle of pregnancies, producing a calf (or twin calves) annually in order to produce milk for ten months of the year. The calf is removed from the mother at three or four days old because her 'milk flow' will otherwise adapt to the calf's needs, much less than the high level expected of a modern commercial milk producer. Despite already excessive milk production there are continually attempts to increase normal milk yields. In 'zero-grazing' systems cattle are kept permanently under cover and fed a concentrated diet and, as noted in the previous chapter, dairy cows have been injected with the genetically engineered BST growth hormone to increase milk yields further even though they are already overstretched.

Farm animals which are living in reasonably natural conditions and are well cared for should be healthy. However, special health problems arise in the artificial factory farm environment. Disease spreads quickly. One of the regular tasks of broilerhouse workers is to clear out dead and dying chickens. Indeed in modern automated units workers press buttons to ensure that light, heat and feed systems are operating effectively, and may only physically handle chickens if they are infected or about to be sent for slaughter. This surely cannot be equated with the biblical idea of *shalom*, or 'right relationships'.

Many farm animals suffer stress-related disease because of their living conditions. According to Mark Gold, without inputs from the pharmaceutical industry, factory farming would collapse in an epidemic of infectious diseases:

> Anti-stress sedatives; energy boosters to encourage animals to eat more; hormones to encourage speedy fattening, to regulate when animals give birth or to encourage conception rates, and antibiotics to fight mounting problems with disease: to the drug industry, factory farming is good news.[33]

Perhaps the most callous disregard for animal welfare is in slaughterhouses where 'execution follows life imprisonment' and death is often painful, frightening and undignified.[34] In recent years the Government's own advisory committee (the Farm Animal Welfare Council) and EEC inspectors have each criticised slaughterhouse conditions.

It might be said that at least people can afford to eat more meat than in the past. This is questionable, but if true, the reason is quite simple. Factory farming without doubt reduces costs, which explains why the price of chicken and pork has fallen relative to that of beef and lamb over recent decades. The price of cruelty is paid for by the farm animals, not the customer.

Objections to factory farming are instinctive to people because the conditions are so unnatural. People share many characteristics with other animals and thereby have an intuitive sense of the wrongness of rearing animals in bad conditions. It is difficult to make such an environment satisfactory for, say, chickens, because they are not in natural conditions and there is consequently a need for very careful regulation, through temperature and lighting controls, to prevent restlessness, aggressiveness and other abnormal behaviour. The factory farm industry needs animals to be like machines which fit in more conveniently with *their* machines. God chose instead to create unique *living creatures* which vary in size and temperament.

One thing is absolutely certain. Factory farming has not occurred by *chance*; the motivation is maximum productivity and maximum profit. In modern factory farm conditions chickens reach four pounds in seven weeks, compared with thirteen weeks in the 1940s. Battery-caged hens lay on average around 250 eggs annually, compared to around 200 eggs for free-range hens. Sows produce five litters over a two-year period instead of four when weaning periods are shortened from eight weeks to three weeks. Quicker 'production' means higher 'throughput' – and greater profits.

Vegetarian Christianity

Having described the infliction of suffering on farm animals, it is appropriate to reflect upon the ethics of killing for food. Is it true, as William Blake wrote, that:

The lamb misused breeds public strife,
And yet forgives the butcher's knife.[35]

Public attitudes towards animals have thankfully improved since the seventeenth century, when a small but notable trend towards vegetarianism emerged in Britain. At that time it was still a popular custom for people to wage bets to bite the heads off chickens and sparrows and to eat them, or even fox cubs and cats, alive. By the end of the eighteenth century there was an articulate vegetarian movement and even people who ate meat preferred an animal's more recognisable features to be concealed. People began to feel a revulsion towards the butchery involved in producing meat.

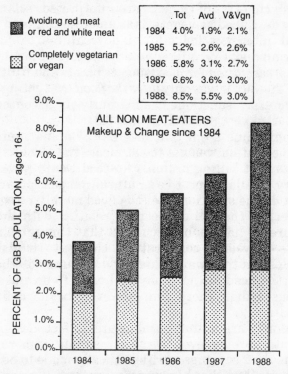

	Tot	Avd	V&Vgn
1984	4.0%	1.9%	2.1%
1985	5.2%	2.6%	2.6%
1986	5.8%	3.1%	2.7%
1987	6.6%	3.6%	3.0%
1988	8.5%	5.5%	3.0%

Avoiding red meat or red and white meat

Completely vegetarian or vegan

ALL NON MEAT-EATERS
Makeup & Change since 1984

PERCENT OF GB POPULATION, aged 16+

FIG. 9 VEGETARIANISM IN BRITAIN
Source: *Gallup Survey* conducted for the Realeat Company

The current growth of interest in vegetarianism is remarkable; one in three people are actively cutting back on their meat consumption. Some people regard the killing of any animal for food as morally wrong, while others object merely to current practices of factory farming, drug injections and inhumane slaughter. Many believe that a diet based on meat consumption is a contributory factor in causing world hunger. Meat consumption is also reduced for health reasons and some believe there to be a considerable value in abstaining from meat as part of their spiritual development.

Such explanations need to be explored from a Christian perspective. The tradition that humans were originally vegetarians is ancient and worldwide.[36] However literally the early chapters of Genesis are interpreted, Adam and Eve are described as vegetarians and this points to God's original intention for all living creatures to have a vegetarian diet. God offered Adam and Eve (and all other animals) *vegetation* for food, such as plants and fruit trees (Gen. 1.29–30). It was only *after the flood* that eating meat was expressly sanctioned, apparently as a concession, though Abel kept flocks (Gen. 4.2; 9.3).

It would thus seem that originally our natural God-given inclination was not to eat meat. The Genesis story suggests that killing animals for food would have been contrary to Adam and Eve's natural compassion and the explicit divine sanction after the flood merely recognised the effect of the fall on people's relation with the rest of nature. It has been speculated that through the fall people's physical constitution changed, fruits and herbs lost nutritional value, or the curse of the soil caused the need for hard physical work to be aided by a meat-based diet; there can, however, be no definitive explanation.

Some may argue that humans are, in fact, *designed* to eat meat. However, even if true, it makes little more sense to argue that, say, pigs were specifically made to be eaten by humans than that humans were created to be eaten by crocodiles. Our *ability* to eat meat is not an adequate criterion to judge whether it is acceptable, and it is, of course, perfectly *possible* for most people to live as vegetarians!

In biblical times eating meat was considered acceptable to God. In the time of Abraham, Isaac and Jacob the Israelites lived as nomads, herding animals, and they probably had substantial meat in their diet. When they later settled in Canaan they practised mixed farming and because supply was limited they probably ate rather less – perhaps only on special occasions, including celebrations and religious festivals, and normally as part of a sacrificial offering.

There were various restrictions. Eating certain types of animals or birds was forbidden, possibly for health reasons or, perhaps, to give the Israelites a sense of their separate identity (Lev. 11.1–47; Deut. 14.1–21). There also was a special ritual in killing animals in which the blood was drained out (Gen. 9.4; Lev. 17.13–14; Deut. 12.16). However within these limits the Israelites were allowed to eat as much meat as they wanted (Deut. 12.15).

Jesus certainly ate fish (Matt. 14.17–20; Luke 24.42–3). Though there is no conclusive evidence, in all probability he also ate meat. Had he been a vegetarian it is remarkable that the Gospels do not explicitly record this fact. The apostle Paul avoided proscribing what other Christians should eat although his own principle was that "everything God created is good, and nothing is to be rejected if it is received with thanksgiving" (1 Tim. 4.3–4) and "no food is unclean in itself" (Rom. 14.14).

The main controversies appear to have been whether Jewish converts to Christianity should eat only kosher meat and whether meat which might have been sacrificed to idols was acceptable. Paul told the people that they could eat anything sold in the meat market (1 Cor. 10.25). He evidently believed that those who abstained from meat had a weak faith: "One man's faith allows him to eat everything, but another man, whose faith is weak, eats only vegetables" (Rom. 14.2). His main intention in these teachings, however, was the importance of looking beyond the physical dimension to life. He wanted the early Christians to understand that what *really* mattered was that they should act in love. It was if they were liable to offend others by eating meat that they should abstain (Rom. 14.13–21); he had nothing to say on the rights, or otherwise, of animals.

Clearly there is no explicit, God-given *law* concerning vegetarianism. Many Christians have accepted the viewpoint expressed by John Calvin in his commentary on Genesis, that God "has laid open to us the earth and the air, in order that we may thence take food as from his storehouse."[37] Calvin wrote of the 'tyranny of vegetarianism' and suggested that "atrocious injury is done to God, when we give such license to men as to allow them to pronounce that unlawful which God designs to be lawful, and to bind consciences which the word of God sets free, with their fictitious laws."[38]

However circumstances today are very different from those of biblical times and the Bible *should* be understood in the context in which it was written. There may indeed be no biblical law as such, but Christians ought to reflect seriously upon the implications of eating meat in the present age. As shown above, current methods of producing meat are frequently immoral and people who purchase meat which originates from factory farms are helping to perpetuate this cruelty.

In past eras meat may have been *necessary* to people's diet. They may have lacked information about healthy vegetarian diets and may not have had easy access to certain essential vegetarian food. This is often no longer the case, and as Andrew Linzey argues, it is *needless destruction* of animals that is sinful. Where there is not true need, to kill animals for food is immoral:

> Christian vegetarians do not have to claim that it is always and absolutely wrong to kill in order to eat. It could well be that there were, and are, some situations in which meat-eating was and is essential in order to survive. Geographical considerations alone make it difficult to envisage life in

Palestine at the time of Christ without some primitive fishing industry. But the crucial point is that where we are *free to do otherwise* the killing of Spirit-filled individuals requires moral justification.[39]

The fact that agricultural produce is traded on inter-national markets means that the diets of people in the industrialised world affect the lives of the starving. Over one-third of all the grain produced in the world is current-ly fed to animals. Those agricultural systems in which livestock production is dominant tend to be relatively inefficient in terms of protein produced per unit of input. When the land is used instead to grow cereals to feed direct to humans, the result is much better. Thus in theory, at least, if people ate less meat more food would be available for the starving.

Obviously the situation should not be over-simplified. If less land was devoted to rearing livestock and this re-sulted in more grain, the extra grain would not *automati-cally* reach the mouths of the starving; wise and radical political decisions are needed to ensure this. Moreover a sudden increase in grain supplies may have the effect of lowering prices and harming local producers in the poor nations. Thus price guarantees are needed to encourage producers and ensure that crops are planted for future years. The solution rests not just in our choice of diet but in national and international political decisions.

It is quite wrong, for example, that countries in the EEC import millions of tonnes of animal feed each year, the majority of which comes from low-income countries whose populations are frequently malnourished. Factory farm-ing is even spreading to low-income countries in Africa and Asia. In the context of eradicating hunger this is absolutely appalling, because grain has first to be fed to the poultry, which makes the process of providing nourishment to the starving much less efficient.

If Christians are to stand out as 'the light of the world' we must make an effort not to contribute personally to animal abuse or to a system which helps to perpetuate global malnutrition. We must sensitise our consciences to determine the acceptable use of animals.

Most people do not *need* meat; a vegetarian diet can provide adequate nutrition. Lord Soper was right when he said that although Jesus Christ was not a vegetarian, he probably would be in today's world.[40] In all but exceptional circumstances, Christians ought to avoid eating meat from animals reared in a manner which is utterly immoral; we should either become vegetarians or, at least, minimise our meat consumption. Those who do not wish immediately to become vegetarian but want to avoid meat from factory farms will find a small but growing number of suppliers of 'real meat' from more humane producers.

Even so vegetarians certainly cannot claim that they are not 'using' animals. Dairy calves are removed so that the cow's milk can be used for humans, and the majority of beef is a by-product of *dairy* herds. People who proudly refuse beef but not cow's milk ought also to consider the likely fate of the millions of male calves born annually in dairy herds! Similarly, some 40 million male chicks are born annually from egg-laying hens. These are not of the genetic strain which fatten quickly for the meat market and are consequently destroyed when one day old, normally by gassing or suffocating. Some people thus go further than vegetarianism – vegans, for example, reject all food derived from animals and, strictly speaking, any by-products of slaughter. It is a logical step for those who believe that humans should not impose their will in any way upon animals.

This can, however, be taken to extremes. Should we abstain from beer and wine because dried blood is used in fining? Or stop painting because the bristles in brushes come from pigs? Do we no longer play tennis and refuse surgical stitching to those in hospital because 'catgut' comes from sheeps' intestines? And stop licking postage stamps because most glues have their origin in offal which originates from the slaughterhouse?

There are, of course, no simple answers to such questions. The Bible explicitly sanctions our use of other creatures, but indicates our duty to take responsible care of them. What is imperative, therefore, is that we become fully informed about our use of animals, recognise the value of each creature to God, and are sensitive to our consciences.

Making the change

In the light of the continued ill-treatment of animals, the ambivalent attitude of many Christians is a matter of great shame. We should be active in campaigning for change. Rapid reform should be our aim, although meat-eaters ought not to be expected to become totally vegetarian overnight, nor all animal experimentation ended immediately if this will *genuinely* cause a substantial increase in pain inflicted upon humans. But there should be a ban on the export of live farm animals for slaughter, voluntary codes on animal welfare should be made mandatory and factory farming brought to an end. Imports of furs, skins and products from endangered species should be prohibited, all cruel sports banned, and substantial reductions made in experiments on animals. Christians too often tend to regard animal welfare as a fringe issue, which is largely unconnected with their faith, and comment by Church leaders on the issue is unfortunately rare.[41]

There are, in some quarters, signs of a new sense of responsibility. For example the past two Archbishops of Canterbury have publicly called for proper stewardship of animals. Addressing the RSPCA in 1977 Archbishop Coggan spoke of people's duty to respect the rights (his term) of animals, and in 1981 Archbishop Runcie issued a statement saying that he is 'abhorred' by hens in battery cages and veal calves in crates. He has also stated that many experiments carried out on animals cannot be ethically justified. Occasionally other Church leaders, too, have spoken out. Some of them, including Edward Carpenter, former Dean of Westminster, have been prominent in the animal welfare movement for many years. The *Animals and Ethics* report, produced in 1980 by an ecumenical group of theologians and biologists which he convened, made an important statement defending the 'basic behavioural needs' of animals.

Meanwhile Pope John Paul II has called upon Catholics to reflect on St Francis's example of meekness towards and sincere love of animals. He said in 1983 that "it is necessary and urgent to abandon ill-considered forms of a dominating custody of all creatures . . . so that animals may be considered and treated in a Franciscan way, as brothers and sisters." (However it should be noted that he continues to refer to animals as 'irrational' and 'inferior' creatures.)

This more hopeful picture has to be set against evidence of continued conservatism. For example, the Church of England's report, *Our Responsibility for the Living Environment*, made some curious assertions which seemed to defend current vivisection practices.[42]

The Church Commissioners, who own around 425 farms on behalf of the Church of England, issue an agreement to their tenant farmers which states that they should comply with Government codes relating to the welfare of farm animals and should not allow them "to be caused unnecessary pain or unnecessary distress." The adjective 'unnecessary' could, of course, hide a multitude of sins. Only a handful of the tenant farmers on Church Commissioners' land were still using intensive units by the start of the 1990s, following lobbying by Christian animal welfare campaigners. But the Church Commissioners have so far resisted pressure to make this situation permanent by introducing a clause into all new contracts, claiming that Charity Law prohibits this, despite lobbying by the Christian Consultative Council for the Welfare of Animals, Animal Christian Concern, and other animal welfare campaigners for a review of the position. Intensive livestock farming on glebe land owned by dioceses was surveyed by Animal Christian Concern, and although thirty Diocesan Boards of Finance replied that none takes place, the other twelve did not answer.[43]

The Roman Catholic Church, too, has a mixed record. Several religious Orders are, or have been, directly involved in intensive farming as a means of gaining financial support. In 1989 it was revealed that nuns at a convent in Daventry were keeping 10,000 chickens in factory farm conditions when one of the two flocks was affected by a salmonella virus and Government regulations meant that they had to be destroyed. The nuns' resistance resulted in much media attention, although they eventually conceded defeat.

All blood sports permitted in law are currently allowed on land belonging to the Church of England unless tenants exercise a right to forbid them. The medieval Church forbade hunting by clergymen, considering it a 'carnal diversion' (although the ban appears to have been widely disregarded). Twenty years have now elapsed since in 1970 a motion passed by the Church of England's National Assembly (now General Synod) attacked hare coursing, deer hunting and otter hunting as "cruel, unjustifiable and degrading" and urged Christians to secure their speedy abolition.[44] But these practices, officially deplored by the Church, are permitted on its *own* land (although otter hunting has largely been replaced by mink hunting). The extent to which tenants allow blood sports is not known for certain, although it would be highly surprising if they do not take place. But the Church seems to be in a confused state – many local authorities and other landowners who have banned such activities are setting a better example.

Organisations using the name of St Francis, patron saint of ecology, have not always helped the cause for which he is renowned. In Spain, a nation with one of the poorer records on animal welfare, the complicity of the Church in cruelty has come under criticism. Many Church organisations and leaders have actively supported bullfighting, which involves the death of thousands of animals each year. The Archbishop of Barcelona has publicly

stated his belief that nothing definite can be said on the
subject of bullfighting from a Christian point of view.
Bullfighting supporters' clubs have even been named after
St Francis! Another bad example are nuns of the order of
St Francis who manufacture darts which injure and maim
bulls during festival celebrations in Coria, in which
the bulls are paraded through the streets and then
deliberately attacked.[45]

To conclude on a rather more positive note, services of
Thanksgiving and Blessing for animals are regularly held
in churches and cathedrals. In America an annual service
takes place at St John's Cathedral in New York City at
which even elephants and camels have been present! In
Britain services for animals have been held in recent
years at York, Truro, Salisbury and Worcester Cathedrals. Each year there are services to commemorate
the anniversary of St Francis and the nearest Sunday to
October 4th has been designated World Day of Prayer for
Animals. The services would seem to be gaining popularity – in Westminster Abbey in 1987 an estimated one
thousand people attended a service marking St Francis's
anniversary. Animal Christian Concern organises an
annual cathedral service and the Christian-based Willow
Tree Animal Sanctuary has held a 'Carols for Animals'
service at Chelmsford Cathedral each Christmas since
1977. In addition several small churches hold similar
services, often for blessing pets.

Summary

Britain has a reputation as a nation of animal lovers, but
our treatment of the animal creation is frequently bad and
occasionally scandalous. In vivisection laboratories, factory farms and slaughterhouses, animals are treated as
mere machinery. This cruelty continues because they are
valued only in terms of their usefulness to humans instead
of their worth in themselves. Contrary to popular belief,
the influence of Christianity on attitudes to animals has

by no means always been negative and several leading campaigners have been Christians.

There is no adequate justification for people refusing to use animals for their benefit, but they should be treated fairly and with compassion. As Compassion in World Farming explain: "The whole process of the domestication of animals has been the deliberate care of the individual animals concerned in such a way that they are protected from dangers such as predators, exposure and starvation. Factors which work to the detriment of the animal are controlled and the animal benefits."[46]

Where we *should* disengage from contact with animals is in any involvement with cruelty, as in factory farming. There is a very strong case for refusing to eat meat from animals reared in intensive units and Christians should seriously consider becoming vegetarian. A necessary aspect of Christian care for creation is to take active steps to reduce cruelty to animals and protect their wellbeing.

 1 For the purpose of clarity this chapter will use the term 'animals' to refer to non-human animals, though recognising that humans are themselves, of course, animals.
 2 Andrew Linzey, *Christianity and the Rights of Animals*, p. 99.
 3 ibid., p. 42. Linzey argues that the practice of sacrifice adds weight to the belief that the life of the individual animal continues after mortal death.
 4 Keith Thomas, *Man and the Natural World*, p. 157.
 5 Cited in Thomas, p. 167.
 6 ibid., pp. 180–81.
 7 E. S. Turner, *All Heaven in a Rage*, p. 161.
 8 ibid., p. 145.
 9 ibid., p. 311.
10 Linzey, p. 111.
11 Cited in Linzey, p. 115.
12 Cited in Andrew Linzey and Tom Regan (eds), *Animals and Christianity*, p. 162.
13 H. Paul Santmire, *The Travail of Nature*, p. 94. Linzey points out that Aquinas never denied the existence of animal souls, but distinguished between different types of soul. Humans alone had

rational souls and the rationality of souls determined immortality. Andrew Linzey, *Christianity and Rights*, p. 36.

14 Thomas, p. 157.
15 Cited in Linzey and Regan, p. 73.
16 ibid., p. 102.
17 Thomas, p. 154.
18 Linzey and Regan, p. 65.
19 ibid., p. 107.
20 Turner, p. 74.
21 ibid., p. 74.
22 Theodore Roszak, *Person/Planet*.
23 David Ehrenfeld, cited in Jonathon Porritt, *Seeing Green*, p. 99.
24 Andrew Linzey, *Christianity and Rights*, p. 83.
25 ibid., p. 85.
26 Cited in Turner, p. 202.
27 Peter Singer, *Animal Liberation*, p. 231.
28 Thomas, p. 33.
29 Linzey and Regan, pp. 75–6.
30 Statistics from Mark Gold, *Living Without Cruelty*, p. 8; Richard North, *The Animals Report*, p. 41; Mark Gold, *Assault and Battery*, p. 10; Compassion in World Farming, *The Place of Animals in the Farm*, Petersfield, 1984, p. 18.
31 Gold, *Assault and Battery*, p. 7.
32 Cited in *Animal Christian Concern News*, Autumn 1988. This was not the first time such a parallel has been made. In 1964, after publication of Ruth Harrison's *Animal Machines*, *The Guardian* asked: "How big a step is it from the broiler-house to Auschwitz?" See Turner, p 315.
33 Gold, *Assault and Battery*, p. 41.
34 Gold, *Living Without Cruelty*, pp. 8–9.
35 Linzey and Regan, p. 46.
36 Thomas, p. 288.
37 Linzey and Regan, p. 200.
38 ibid.
39 Linzey, *Christianity and Rights*, p. 142.
40 Cited in Linzey, *Christianity and Rights*, p. 49.
41 A Yale University survey found that people who attend religious services are more likely to have attitudes towards animals which express human dominion, or even negativity. Wesley Granberg-Michaelson (ed.), *Tending the Garden*, pp. 2–3.
42 Church of England Board for Social Responsibility, *Our Responsibility for the Living Environment*, pp. 29–33. For example, paragraph 80 implies that current practice is to minimise pain during animal experiments which may be an intention, but is certainly not what happens in practice!
43 *Animal Christian Concern News*, Summer 1988, pp. 8–10.
44 Earlier during this century the Church has faced criticism for

tolerating fox hunting, notably at the formation of the League against Cruel Sports in 1926. See Turner, p. 283.

45 Anglican Society for the Welfare of Animals *Bulletin* No. 31, Spring 1988, pp. 16–25.

46 Compassion in World Farming, *The Place of Animals*, p. 20.

8

GREEN LIVING:
Steps towards the new Earth

Christians and Greens share the hope of a future society in which people no longer believe that increased consumption provides a guarantee of a high quality of life. There is much to be gained from working together to bring an end to the destructive production processes which threaten irrevocable damage to the planet.

Greens are frequently charged with being unrealistic, idealistic and even utopian. But many Christians, far from aiming too high, have tended to lack any real breadth and depth of vision and consequently have developed a conservative complacency. Intensely aware of the destructive power of sin, they are almost devoid of any earthly hope and have resigned themselves to inevitable failure.

We should not be blindly optimistic. In William Temple's words, "assertion of Original Sin should make the Church intensely realistic and conspicuously free from Utopianism."[1] However we *should* expect commitment to Jesus Christ to have a transforming impact on Earth. Jesus taught his followers to pray: "Your kingdom come, your will be done on earth as it is in heaven" (Matt. 6.10).

Change begins with the individual, and often ignorance, fatalism or apathy have to be overcome. There are also serious political obstacles which prevent society from being transformed. Unfortunately, many people have in effect 'privatised' their Christian faith and reduced it simply to God's authority over their personal morality. Anything in the Bible relating to issues such as wealth and poverty or oppression and liberation is distorted and interpreted as referring to otherworldly concerns. God is thus elbowed out of economic life. To such people an honest appraisal of their biblical interpretation and an understanding of ecology, which reveals the significance of relationships, would offer the possibility of a deeper faith.

Many Christians, notably evangelicals (who perhaps have been most guilty in this respect), have recently sought to develop a deeper understanding of God's kingdom in which it is recognised that the Bible promises a new heaven and a new Earth where the whole creation will co-exist peacefully. At a recent gathering of evangelicals Graham Cray described *shalom* as 'wellbeing and wholeness' and argued that it should be understood in the context of *relationships* rather than subjective personal feelings.[2]

In biblical thought the coming of the kingdom marks a decisive step in history, a new era in which the Messiah reigns. When Jesus came to reveal God's kingdom it was widely misunderstood, however, as his presence signified neither the coming of political liberation nor the final judgement which many expected. Instead he has brought an era characterised by the 'provisional kingdom'. Signs of God's rule are evident but the final victory over all the forces of destruction is still awaited. This kingdom is sometimes described as 'already but not yet'. Christians are already "a new creation" (2 Cor. 5.17) but "the end of the age" has not yet come (Matt. 24.3). The kingdom is provisional because although it has broken through into the world and is offered to us, it is also resistible. It is thus a reality around us and, at the same time, a vision to live towards.

The kingdom is received in faith and is manifest in good works. Jesus's first act after his temptation, as recorded by Luke, was to fulfil Isaiah's prophecy by preaching good news to the poor and proclaiming the coming of the Jubilee, with its profound implications for liberty and justice (Luke 4.18–19, cf. Isa. 61.1,2; Lev. 25.10). He taught that our acts are evidence of faithfulness, just as a tree can be identified by its fruit (Matt. 7.15–21, cf. Jas. 2.17). Asked by followers of John the Baptist if he was the promised Messianic king, he responded by pointing to the evidence of his *works* (Matt. 11.2–5). Thus in his parable of the sheep and goats, the people for whom the kingdom is prepared are those who do good deeds such as feeding the hungry and visiting the sick (Matt. 25.34–6).

Throughout the world signs of the kingdom are evident around us. They are found when liberty is restored to those unjustly imprisoned, and when sickness gives way to improved health. They are present when racism and nationalism are overcome, and when military conflicts end and nuclear weapons are removed. They accompany each step towards proper economic and social justice. But this is a mere foretaste of the kingdom. Our hope is of a kingdom which will not just be occasionally and momentarily glimpsed but realised in its fulness, when *all* relationships will be made right.

There is, of course, no simple blueprint, but there are, at least, some arrows which point in the right direction. This concluding chapter explores how we might use such signposts as we work our way towards the kingdom. It considers practical church-based initiatives, the imperative of political change and describes how a need for Greener Christian teaching has emerged.

Ecology in the Church

Ecology has been described earlier as embracing the study not just of living species but of institutions. Thus a church can itself be viewed ecologically, in terms of the relationships which define its structure and direction. Within a church there are a multitude of internal relationships between, for example, its members and the church's equipment, energy consumption, cars and bicycles, buildings, kitchen and food, churchgrounds and so forth. Such relationships also connect to the 'outside' world, either physically, through adjacent sites and the wider environment, or in terms of other connections, such as suppliers of its equipment, the local community and the institution where its funds are invested. The site of a church is, in effect, a small ecosystem, which links into a larger ecosystem.

In most churches much more can be done to encourage a more responsible use of natural resources. All churches have financial audits and a few also carry out theological and social audits. Churches should consider developing and using an annual '*environmental audit*'.

Such an audit could identify all the resources consumed during the course of the church's activities and provide a means whereby a church could then minimise its destructive impact on the environment. It might ask the following questions:

[1] Is the church acting as a 'Green consumer' in its regular purchases?
– is the church newsletter and stationery printed on recycled paper?
– is waste recycled wherever appropriate?
– are disposable products, such as cups, plates and cutlery, ever used in the kitchen or elsewhere?
– is the choice of food and drink which is served influenced by considerations such as global poverty and factory farming?
– are other materials purchased, such as cleaning products, environmentally safe?

[2] Where are the church's funds invested? Are they with an institution which uses ethical criteria in judging where to place them, or are they in an ordinary account, perhaps indirectly contributing to arms purchases, alcohol production or animal experimentation? Do church members understand 'stewardship' in terms of annual gift days and tax-saving covenants? Or do they understand it in terms of a lifestyle which demands the appropriate use of *all* resources at their disposal?

[3] Are the church's buildings, including any halls and the minister or priest's home, used efficiently? Are they properly insulated? A specialist from one of the building

professions could be invited to give advice on reducing energy consumption (without making the church uncomfortably cold!). Could buildings be more fully utilised during weekdays? Pollution can cause considerable damage to the exterior of church buildings. Has the church considered campaigning against sources of pollution such as power station emissions and vehicles (particularly heavy lorries, which may in addition possibly cause structural damage)?

[4] Is church land used in an ecologically sound manner? Church grounds often receive inadequate care or are overmanaged; either way the potential for rich and varied plant, animal, bird and insect life is reduced. 'The Nature in Churchyards' initiative, part of The Church and Conservation Project run by the Arthur Rank Centre, helps churches to encourage diverse wildlife in their churchyards and has had remarkable success in reviving graveyards where signs of life are not, in normal circumstances, encouraged! Information and grants are made available to encourage land to be used in ways that promote wildlife. Is much of the land around the church covered in asphalt or concrete rather than soil, plants and trees, and, if so, could this be changed?

[5] A variety of other issues could be raised in the audit:
- the promotion of car-sharing, which might lead to a reduction in the proportion of churchgoers travelling to church (and elsewhere) by car. Sharing of other possessions might also be encouraged and the effects monitored.
- churches might provide suitable sites for recycling facilities such as a bottle bank or, alternatively, churchgoers could bring together items for recycling in order to save individuals making unnecessary trips to local facilities.
- jumble sales could be specifically promoted as 'Recycling sales'. They provide ideal opportunities to avoid throwing away potentially useful products and reduce expenditure on new products.

– churches could have a noticeboard which people could use to offer to share their goods with others or exchange them. People with skills in repair work and crafts could offer them to others.

What an impact churches nationwide could make if each year they carried out an environmental audit and publicised the results so that the best practices of 'Green' churches could inspire others.

Churches might also wish to reconsider how their worship and witness fits into the church's local environment. For example, experiences of worship in rather quiet, harmonious and tightly ordered services might affect the ease with which people sense God's presence in an ever-changing city environment, with its noise and bustle. Such worship may represent either a welcome contrast to the stresses of life or, more negatively, a form of escapism. A variety of worship forms is perhaps the ideal, the gentle alongside the noisy and the reflective combining with the prophetic.

Christians need to assess carefully the hymns used in services. Some make theological assumptions which, coming from the pulpit, would be viewed with considerable scepticism! Sermons about ecology are typically restricted to an annual occasion, such as Harvest Festival, rather than integrated into the church's overall teaching ministry. There is a value in occasional special services, such as a service of Thanksgiving and Blessing for Animals, but our ecological understanding needs to be developed *constantly*. This may lead to greater awareness of the cycles of the seasons which God created. These provide occasions for us to reflect upon God's activity at particular moments in time, when He breathes life into some species and takes life away from others (Ps. 104.29–30).

The significance of symbols which are used in church, such as the bread and wine for Holy Communion, is sometimes not fully appreciated. Sean McDonagh has questioned whether it is possible to celebrate a meal in memory of Jesus without being challenged to respond practically to the appalling reality of starvation and the injustices of global food production. In the Philippines, where he has worked, bread is an imported luxury food of the middle and upper classes and because the staple food of most Filipinos is rice McDonagh believes that the 'inner dynamic' of its symbolism is lost; it is alien to their culture and for that reason less satisfying. In the industrial West the use of sliced white bread and wine laced with chemical additives speaks of a different culture! Such symbols need to be wholesome and satisfying and yet linked to people's everyday experience in the world. Edward Echlin has pointed to the fact that Holy Communion includes not only bread and wine; water, fire, cloth, wax, incense, wood, metal and stone may also be tangibly present, representing the inclusion of the rest of creation.[3]

Mention has been made earlier of land possessed by the Church of England. Apart from glebe and other land owned by dioceses most Church land is owned by the Church Commissioners in order to produce income with which to pay the clergy. Its landholding totals over 160,000 acres, making it one of the nation's largest owners of agricultural land.

This investment involves conflicting interests. According to the Church Commissioners, "as a charity, our first duty is to get a proper return on our investment. Because of this, environmental issues have to be at the margin."[4] If the income from the Church's investment in land is maximised the clergy will benefit, but the Church Commissioners concede that this may be achieved at the expense of environmental objectives. Their claim that charity law demands the highest return on their investments is somewhat ironic, because the Archbishop of Canterbury and other Church leaders have publicly criticised the exclusive focus on maximising profit in modern Britain.

Of course, the problem partly arises from the fact that regular giving by churchgoers provides less than half the sum needed to pay the clergy. But is it right that the Church Commissioners are ultimately answerable to Parliament rather than to the Church of England General

Synod? A satisfactory resolution of this conflict certainly
demands more generous giving by churchgoers, but to
encourage the most environmentally sound practices may
also quite possibly demand the disestablishment of the
Church to give it the freedom to have its land farmed
according to biblical and ecological principles.

In the meantime an improved information base on
Church land is necessary. No significant independent
study has been carried out on current agricultural practices and the Church Commissioners do not even maintain
a comprehensive record of what happens to land once sold,
though some has certainly ended up under concrete.
Several dioceses are even uncertain about the site of their
landholdings.

The land provides the Church with an opportunity to set
an example of good practice – sustainable, organic
methods and, perhaps, reviving the sabbath principle.
Instead it actually has a policy of selling off its land and
investing elsewhere for a higher return. Church-owned
farms which are setting a lead are few in number, Chislet
Court Farm in Kent and Coatsway Moor Farm in Durham
being notable exceptions.

The politics of hope

Action at an individual level is important. If we are not
buying organic food, for example, we are helping to perpetuate current agrochemical-based farming practices by
purchasing its output. But people who try to develop
appropriate lifestyles often discover obstacles in their
path which can only be removed by *political* change. A
willingness to recycle waste leads nowhere if suitable
facilities are not provided. Commitment to give up driving
is less likely if public transport is infrequent and jugger-
nauts are allowed to terrorise cyclists. Seeing Green is
often easier than *being* Green!

Each of us is jointly responsible for the government
which is elected, notwithstanding the shamefully

undemocratic nature of Britain's electoral system. Traditional perceptions of Western 'democracy' and Eastern bloc 'totalitarianism' are thrown into confusion by Green Party experience. A Green representative has been elected to the Supreme Soviet, having already been elected to the Lithuanian Parliament, while in Britain in 1989 the Green Party did not gain representation in the European Parliament despite obtaining 15 per cent of the vote.

Local and central government play a critical role in taking decisions which have a major effect on the environment. Local authorities are normally responsible for proposed building developments and for planning matters such as the number of bicycle lanes and car parking spaces. They also decide whether extensive recycling facilities are to be available. Central government takes decisions on taxes and public expenditure which are similarly crucial. Taxes will affect consumption of particular resources (such as oil) and spending priorities will be made between, say, producing weapons of mass destruction and assisting countries whose people are starving and whose natural environment is being destroyed. It also sets important regulations which influence the extent of energy conservation in buildings and the acceptable level of pollution; and, directly or indirectly, it determines the availability of public transport, the size and curricula of schools, and the size of hospitals and type of health care.

Government policy affects us all. Involvement by churches in local authority planning is appropriate in certain circumstances, particularly where decisions affect church land or property, or local transport facilities. Churches could also make an input into local health and education services, to encourage holistic health care and appropriate educational curricula.

Political change is imperative if a path is to be found away from environmental destruction. While it is true that modern society has great power over nature, it is equally significant that natural resources are used as an instrument by which some people exert power over others. Most of the richest people have substantial land-holdings because this provides a secure base for their funds. The privatisation of water means that many ordinary shareholders will hold financial power in the form of control over natural resources.

Professor Paul Wilding has contrasted the 'politics of imperfection' with the 'politics of hope'. Some Christians are deeply pessimistic about human nature and sceptical about the possibility of any social improvement. This is the politics of imperfection. There is no hope because people are sinful, ignorant and irrational, and governments powerless to effect significant change. It is an essentially fatalistic approach. However Wilding indicates that "to base one's view of the world and human possibilities solely on fallen human nature is surely to make human beings rather than God determinative in the world."[5] In such a view there is little appreciation of God's power to inspire transformed attitudes and lifestyles.

The politics of hope, by contrast, recognises that although human nature is fallen, people are made in the image of God and may be transformed through His power. It recognises the social dimension to moral decisions and that society may be ordered in such a way that individuals are encouraged to take the right moral decisions. There are opportunities for progress through political change which may lead to improvements in society. Thus, Wilding concludes, "hope is not a simplistic belief that things will get better, but the conviction that things *can* be different" (his emphasis).[6]

The Old Testament does not separate social justice from private morality. Indeed, the themes of peace, justice and reconciliation cannot be understood in anything but a collective sense. Land redistribution, interest rate policy, sabbath laws; all involve the whole community. Jesus's call to love our Creator and our neighbours similarly demands looking outward from ourselves to God's creation and to others.

However, many Christians shy away from any overt

political expression of their faith. Some clergy and church-goers are cautious, fearful of creating divisions within the church and spoiling fellowship. Others mistakenly conclude that religious and political belief can somehow be separate. Such people are inclined to be individualistic, conservative in temperament and introspective, believing that faith is primarily about personal salvation and moral conduct. But if Christian faith does not touch every sphere of life it loses its power to transform society. It is rather ironic that Christian fundamentalists are often politically conservative because, taken literally, Old Testament laws on justice would be politically revolutionary![7]

One explanation for such conservatism is that some Christians have interpreted Jesus's words "my kingdom is not of this world" (John 18.36) as against involvement in politics. However, as Albert Wolters points out, the original Greek suggests that Jesus meant that his kingship and authority does not *arise out of* the perverted, fallen Earth but derives from heaven. The *rejection* of politics by Christians is indeed a profoundly political act; it is a tacit acceptance of the political status quo. People who would in this way preserve existing laws, regulations, institutions and values are taking as political a stance as those who work for political change. It is no less political to be Conservative than to be Green, Socialist, Liberal, Democrat or Republican!

This myth of political neutrality led to a national controversy in 1984 when junior Government minister John Butcher called on the clergy to give up politics for Lent and "concentrate on their major tasks of saving souls and filling churches".[8] The Bishop of Coventry retorted that the Church had a duty to speak out on important issues and that "politics is too important to be left to politicians."[9] Politics and religion cannot remain separate. Christians should be involved in politics as a testimony to the rule of God, telling the world what type of concerns the gospel brings into human experience. We must "flavour politics with the distinctive taste of the kingdom".[10]

The idea that the issue of saving the environment is somehow 'above' politics is an absurdity. It is precisely because of the magnitude of the problem, the evident need for political action, and the failure of established parties to respond promptly or with sufficient resolve that Green parties have proved necessary. A consensus to save the environment may *sound* admirable, but in reality each political party has a different ideology which invariably affects its policy proposals. Ultimately contradictions between left wing, right wing and Green ideas become apparent; political choices then have to be made between policy priorities, institutional reforms, the roles of individual and State action, and the pace of change.

The coming of the kingdom will not happen smoothly. As John Gladwin, Provost of Sheffield Cathedral, points out, "non-controversial Christianity has no ethical bite."[11] The political implications of Christianity are profound as the Christian faith should destabilise conventional expectations and worldly standards, opposing hierarchical powers in society as it reaches out to the weak, the outsider and the outcast.

Conflict with existing political authorities must therefore be expected, as experienced by the early Christians.[12] In the industrialised West few Christians are thrown into prison for their beliefs, although peace campaigners have been a notable (and admirable) exception. But elsewhere in the world – in Poland, South Africa, El Salvador, East Germany and elsewhere – Christians have been imprisoned for working for justice and proclaiming their faith. We should not expect to fit in comfortably with the rest of the world any more than Jesus, who was despised and persecuted (John 15.18–21). We are *not* to conform to society's norms (Rom. 12.2). As Richard Foster wrote in *Celebration of Discipline*, conformity to a sick society is itself a form of sickness.[13]

The Greening of politics

The starting point for Christians who are considering
involvement in politics is to analyse whether the ideology
which underlies a party's policies reflects a philosophy
based on Christian principles. How does it view our place
in creation, the purpose for living and the potential for
renewing the creation?

No political party has a monopoly of truth; none in
Britain are explicitly 'Christian' in principle, and certainly none are in practice! As Graham Cray has pointed out
"the kingdom may not be precisely identified with human
systems, concerns or aspirations."[14] It may be approached,
but is not yet fully consummated. But as the Green Party
most closely expresses in political terms the thinking
underlying this book, their ideas merit special and critical consideration.

The Green Party's constitution states that its aim is 'to
develop and implement ecological policies'. The principles
underlying its policies are thus rooted in ecology, 'the
study of the structure and function of nature'. Such study
may be on the basis of belief that all things are held
together through Christ and will be reconciled through
him or, alternatively, that the Creator is absent and the
creation is self-regulating. Either may lead people to
concern about the environment and a desire to express
this politically. However the political principles of the
Greens may be seen as consistent with Christian beliefs in
several important areas.

Firstly, Green philosophy rejects the secular humanism
which underlies the political alternatives. It regards the
separation of secular and sacred aspects to life as false,
and acknowledges a need for change so deep that it may be
properly termed 'spiritual'. Unlike a humanistic philosophy, which puts the welfare of people above all other
considerations, it is concerned for the *whole* creation.
Greens hold different faiths and the Green philosophy is
not explicitly Christian, but it flows easily out of a Christian world view and its message of hope fits well with the

prophetic biblical vision of the whole creation existing in harmony.

Secondly, Green politics is not pragmatic and short-sighted but visionary and prophetic. Greens propose fundamental institutional change rather than superficial reform. Although change should *begin* with the individual, the transformation of economic and political structures is regarded as imperative. It represents an alternative to the individualism which characterises right wing politics, the collectivism of the left and the uneasy mix of the centre. Instead of regarding the balance between private and public ownership as central to their politics, Greens put the long-term relationship between humans and the rest of nature at its heart.

And thirdly, Greens seek to reverse the materialism and militarism which other political alternatives unduly tolerate. Green politics affirms the need for responsible treatment of the Earth's resources and rejects the contemporary lust for affluence. In advocating 'nuclear pacifism' it proposes a defence stance which Christians should find considerably more acceptable than the present nuclear arms escalation through the Trident programme and our profligate military expenditure.

A particular attraction of the Green Party to many Christians is that it recognises explicitly the spiritual dimension in people's lives and values its importance. Obviously the Party does not take a dogmatic stance, as there is a need to be open to people's different 'starting points' and 'ultimate commitments' – in other words, their faith. However, many Christians are active in the party and a significant number have been candidates in elections.

The Green Party is, of course, not without weaknesses, and its underlying philosophy has not always been presented with proper clarity. In stressing the possibility of a better world supporters have sometimes failed to offer convincing proposals to counter the presence of evil – the Party has, for example, failed so far to produce an adequate policy on crime. A small minority of Greens who advocate policies on the basis of 'biocentric equality' (which virtually excludes any use of animals) have yet to be adequately challenged. And Greens who favour positive steps to reduce substantially the incidence of abortion have still to prepare clear policy proposals.

However, the Party's ecological principles and policies seem to fit more easily with the Christian understanding of caring for the whole creation than the political alternatives. That said, advocating Green politics is not *necessarily* a party political point. Members of the other parties may move in a Green direction. For example, Liberal Democrat MP Simon Hughes, a Christian who has shown sympathy towards Green politics, has said: "My politics is . . . about working with all creation, holistically, respectfully, to do all that I can to ensure that every living creature has the best possible quality of life."[15] But there remains a large gulf between what the Green Party is advocating and the proposals of other parties.

A Greener faith

Christians have a special duty to develop and communicate ecological ideas because in the industrialised world, which is primarily responsible for the damage being caused, they retain great influence. However it is clear that much Christian thought does not offer a vision capable of galvanising people's energies to respond to the environmental crises. Far from being at the forefront of the Green movement and developing its ideas, most Christians have been towards the rear. We need urgently to rethink our understanding of Christian responsibility for God's creation and to inspire practical action.

It has been argued earlier that the tendency in conservative evangelicalism to neutralise the dynamic transforming power of the gospel renders it too weak for this immense task. Similarly, neither is liberal theology or liberation theology wholly adequate.

Modern liberal theology, popularised in Britain by John Robinson and, more recently, Don Cupitt, has correctly identified problems with believing in a God 'up there', a supreme and separate Being out of reach of humankind. Its solution has effectively been to abandon belief in an autonomous God who is 'up there', or even 'out there', and to understand Him as no more than, in Paul Tillich's phrase, 'the ground of our being'. According to Robinson, "God is not outside us, yet he is profoundly transcendent."[16] The danger in such a view is that God is reduced to little more than an expression of feelings or "what for you is ultimate reality".[17]

In modern thought such as 'theistic existentialism' people attempt to make sense of the world by considering their subjective experience. In such an approach the starting point is not God, or the biosphere, but self. It emphasises the limitations on the validity of the reasoning and experience of others – each individual has to create his or her *own* understanding of God. Much modern liberal thought has thus ended up as fundamentally human-centred, concerned with a personal search for meaning in a world of despair. It has offered little concerning ecology, 'the structure and function of nature', and the fate of the environment.

Indeed to some theologians faith calls believers away from identifying with nature and the world is a profane place. Rudolf Bultmann and others believed that because God's actions in nature are no more visible to the Christian than to the unbeliever it is only legitimate to speak of God as a personal being who acts on persons.

Liberation theology emerged in the late 1960s out of the experience of Christians in Latin America and was popularised through important works by, among others, Gustavo Gutierrez and José Miguez Bonino. Although it makes no claim to be applicable to other cultures and situations, there are signs of inadequacy even in its own geographical context. In its concern for the present, liberation theology has often paid too little regard to the well-being of other species and unborn generations and to the radical transformation of the Earth after the second coming of Christ. Wesley Granberg-Michaelson is critical because "in its insistence that God's work is discovered only in the historical struggle, the foundation of creation is simply ignored. In its focus on the people's struggle, faith remains centred on human experience."[18] A new theology is needed which will aim to liberate not only the poor and the oppressed from suffering, but will go further, seeking to liberate the whole creation.

Christians need to think afresh about the future of life on our planet and develop an alternative, 'Green' theology. Green theology must not make the mistake of losing sight of the promise of the radically transformed heaven and Earth at the second coming, the kingdom of God which flesh and blood cannot inherit. Nor, equally, must it fall into the trap of conservative teaching, thereby missing the vital power of the gospel to affect people's daily experience in the contemporary world.

One alternative in which environmentally concerned Christians in several countries have developed an interest in recent years is 'creation-centred spirituality'.[19] An essential element of such thinking, the leading exponents of which are Matthew Fox and Thomas Berry, is a shift in theological emphasis from the concepts of fall and redemption to that of creation.

Creation-centred spirituality thus stresses the 'original blessing' of God in creation and focuses on the value of celebrating life and creativity instead of dwelling upon original sin. The fact that human beings are evolving is regarded as more significant than their fallen nature. Suffering is understood in terms of the birth pangs of a new creation, a necessary part of the journey to new life. Such thinking is inspired by Celtic spirituality, St Francis of Assisi and medieval mystics and saints. Its supporters are critical of much Christianity, believing that it has been responsible for undervaluing artists and prophets, not caring enough about the poor and dispossessed, and degrading attitudes towards women.

Much of Fox's work is controversial and he has recently been under investigation by the Vatican and banned from public speaking for one year. Critics of creation-centred spirituality suggest that to concentrate on the creative power of God rather than the redemptive power of Christ is wrong. One imbalance is replaced with another. Many object to the fact that the unfolding evolution of the universe is viewed as the primary source of God's revelation and Berry describes the universe as eternal and self-sustaining, a view which would seem to fall outside Christian orthodoxy.

Despite these serious questions, creation-centred spirituality is offering a thought-provoking alternative to the kind of Christianity which understates the significance of creation and consequently fails to take responsibility for the Earth. Its present formulation of ideas should be viewed cautiously and with an open mind, as they will doubtless be developed and refined. The current alternatives are flawed or inadequate. What, then, should form the basis of this 'Green theology'?

Green theology may be defined as being *centred upon God as revealed in Jesus Christ* and *concerned with the structure and function of the whole creation*. It should offer a new understanding of human 'dominion' over other creatures, encourage a growing appreciation of the intrinsic goodness of creation and seek to understand the true scope of redemption. Theologian Jürgen Moltmann writes of the need for a doctrine of creation which is "directed towards the liberation of men and women, peace with nature, and the redemption of the community of human beings and nature from negative powers, and from the forces of death."[20]

In summary Green theology will be dynamic, holistic, empowering to individuals, and life-enhancing to all species. It will be characterised by a sense of our intrinsic interdependence with all forms of life.

Though much essential work in developing Green theology may be undertaken in theological colleges and Bible schools, it must reach down from heady intellectual heights into the everyday experience of Christians.

As this new theology develops it will benefit from recent

theological insights, taking ideas from process philosophy, liberation theology and creation-centred spirituality, although it will also build upon older traditions. Throughout this book attention has been drawn to the valuable insights of the Eastern Orthodox tradition, in particular its understanding of how God took the form of human flesh in order to reconcile the whole cosmos to Himself. Christians in the West need to look critically at the impact of our culture upon how we interpret our faith.

In order to communicate fresh insights into our faith we need appropriate worship material, Bible study guides, Sunday School material, leaflets, and other resources. These are very slowly becoming available. In the United States Albert Fritsch has produced *Earthen Vessels: An Environmental Action Manual for Churches* which is intended to stimulate environmental initiatives and aimed particularly at church leaders. In Britain, although the Church of England has yet to produce such a resource, the Methodist Church has issued a slide and study pack on the theme *Making Peace with the Planet* and comprehensive material is available in CAFOD's *Renewing the Earth* Campaign Study Guide and Christian Aid's *Focus on the Earth* pack, both of which include study material, prayers and liturgies. The World Council of Churches' 'Justice, Peace and the Integrity of Creation' initiative has also provided relevant material, as has the World Wide Fund for Nature.

There is also a need to modify and refine some of the material used in churches and to introduce new activities. Various obstacles may have to be overcome. Objections may be raised if past practices are discarded and some may criticise any new emphasis on themes such as justice, peace or the environment as 'too political'. Making change in the church inevitably brings out hidden tensions.

The task of educating Christians in the significance of the Green movement and encouraging participation within it is great. However this work has commenced and numerous courses, seminars and meetings are held regularly by organisations such as Christian Ecology Link, the

Christian Rural Centre, the Open Christian College and Creation-Centred Spirituality groups.[21]

Act now!

Green Christians live in anticipation of a renewed Earth through a vision which offers inspiration to all who cherish God's precious creation. Biblical writers describe the whole creation as sharing this hope (Rom. 8.20–21). At the appointed time the sea and all the life in it will resound. The trees in the forest will sing for joy, as will the mountains. The fields, and all that live in them, will be jubilant. The rivers will clap their hands. The Earth, once filled with violence, will be full of the knowledge of the Lord (Gen. 6.13; Ps. 96.11–13; 98.7–9; Isa. 11.9; Rev. 21.1).

In the meantime God has set before us a choice between life and death, blessings and curses, just as He did, in a different context, to the Israelites some three thousand years ago. He is calling on us, as before, to "choose life", so that we and our children may live (Deut. 30.19). Just as each of us has the freedom to respond positively or negatively to our Creator, we have that same freedom in respect of His creation. The choice is *ours*. We can love God and "walk in his ways" and we will find ourselves in a land of promise (Deut. 30.15–18). But we can choose to seal the fate of ourselves and all other species on this threatened planet by squandering precious natural resources and polluting the air, land, rivers and seas.

Christians have a *special* responsibility to care for the environment, as it is typically people in countries where Christianity is the dominant religion who are most careless in using the Earth's resources. This means that we should be repentant and humble. But it also points to the great potential of Green Christianity to lead a transformation in Western culture away from selfish individualism, life-threatening militarism and profligate materialism. We can provide inspiration and hope of change.

It is time that Christians, the 'communion of saints', acknowledged the importance of the entire 'Earth community' revealed in God's covenant with all living creatures (Gen. 9.10). Too few have so far responded to the emergence of ecological ideas and acknowledged the duty to act as caretakers of the Earth. We need to ask what it truly means when the planet is in grave peril to believe in Jesus Christ, in whom "all things hold together", who "fills everything in every way", and who is "the Alpha and the Omega, the Beginning and the End" (Col. 1.17; Eph. 1.23; Rev. 21.6). Christians should recognise that by misusing the Earth we are showing contempt for our Creator. It is precious to Him; it *matters*. We must care for the whole creation and utilise our huge international network of communication to meet this responsibility. The task is now urgent.

Christians and Greens can benefit together. Christians need to listen to the message of the Green movement. In exceptional circumstances God may choose to make His will known through those who do not acknowledge Him. The circumstances of today *are* exceptional – humankind has brought the planet to the brink of a catastrophe – and the Greens are speaking words of truth about the value of the natural environment more boldly than the Church.

Greens have discovered that the key question of our age is no longer 'Why is there something rather than nothing?', but 'What is the likelihood of the continuation of life?' We may have more knowledge than ever about the existence of life on the planet, but we do not know for how much longer it will be sustained. The Green movement has acted as a quiet, prophetic voice, raising difficult questions about the process of nurturing life. Christians need to listen and learn in order to forge stronger bonds with other species, to 'make friends with the planet', and to feel at home in the world.

Similarly, Christians have much to offer Greens. Christianity provides a real sense of purpose, an alternative to allowing nature simply to run its course. It offers moral criteria which go beyond mere appeals to posterity.

The incarnation of Christ and the sacraments provide the supreme affirmation of the material world; the resurrection offers hope of life where death and decay is creation's alternative destiny.

Christianity inspires most of all through the promises of Jesus Christ, the source of all life, who came to live on Earth as a man and selflessly sacrificed his life for the sake of the whole creation. Each of us needs to search within for that same hallmark of love, a selfless willingness to enable others to be brought into existence and have life "to the full" (John 10.10). Such commitment will provide our true hope that future generations and other species may flourish.

1 Cited in Paul Wilding, *Christian Theology and the Politics of Imperfection*, Modern Churchman, p. 8.
2 Graham Cray, 'The Kingdom of God and the Mission of the Church', the Sir Norman Anderson Lecture, 1988.
3 *Catholic Gazette*, June 1989, p. 13.
4 Jill Worth, 'How Green is the Church?', *Today*, August 1989, p. 8.
5 Wilding, pp. 8–9.
6 ibid., p. 9.
7 Fundamentalists have more in common with some liberals than they might admit. They seek to remove politics from the Bible just as liberals remove the 'supernatural' element; both remove its transforming power.
8 *The Guardian*, 6th March 1984.
9 ibid.
10 John Gladwin, *God's People in God's World*, p. 122.
11 ibid., p. 119.
12 See Acts chapters 4–12, especially 4.19; 5.29; cf. Rom. 13.1.
13 Richard Foster, *Celebration of Discipline*, p. 70.
14 Graham Cray, 'The Kingdom of God and the Mission of the Church.'
15 Speech to Green Voice conference, 16th January 1988.
16 John Robinson, *Honest to God*, p. 60.
17 ibid., p. 55.
18 Wesley Granberg-Michaelson, 'Why Christians Lost an Environmental Ethic', *Epiphany*, Winter 1988, p. 48.
19 Recent articles include Edward Echlin, 'The Geo-theology of Thomas Berry', *The Month*, Aug.–Sept. 1988, pp. 822–4; Stephen

Muratore, 'The New "Teilhard" at the North American Conference on Christianity and Ecology', *Epiphany*, Winter 1988, pp. 6–14; Thomas E. Clarke, 'Theological Trends: Creational Spirituality', *The Way*, Vol. 29, No. 1, January 1989, pp. 68–80; Alan Shephard, 'Millennia of Blessings', *Green Christians*, Nov. 1989–Jan. 1990.)

20 Jürgen Moltmann, *God in Creation*, pp. 4–5.
21 An Open Christian College course on Ecology/Environmental Studies will be available from 1991; details from Jim Tickner, Open Christian College, 243 Newbridge Road, Bath, Avon BA1 3HJ.

BIBLIOGRAPHY

Biblical quotations are taken from *The Holy Bible, The New International Version* (1986 edition).

Michael Allaby, *The Eco-Activists*, Tonbridge: Charles Knight, 1971.

Rudolf Bahro, *Socialism and Survival*, London: Heretic, 1982.

Ian G. Barbour, *Issues in Science and Religion*, London: SCM, 1966.

Peter Bunyard and Fern Morgan-Grenville, *The Green Alternative*, London: Methuen, 1987.

Fritjof Capra, *The Turning Point*, London: Fontana, 1982.

Fritjof Capra and Charlene Spretnak, *Green Politics*, London: Hutchinson, 1984.

Russell Chandler, *Understanding the New Age*, London: Word, 1988.

Church of England Board for Social Responsibility, *Man in His Living Environment*, London: Church Information Office, 1970.

Church of England Board for Social Responsibility, *The Church and the Bomb*, London: Hodder and Stoughton / Church Information Office, 1982.

Church of England Board for Social Responsibility, *Our Responsibility for the Living Environment*, London: Church House Publishing, 1986.

Church of Scotland Science, Religion and Technology Project, *Where the Earth Endures*, Edinburgh: Saint Andrew Press, 1986.

Tim Cooper and David Kemball-Cook (eds), *God's Green World*, Malvern: Christian Ecology Group, 1983.

Herman E. Daly (ed.), *Economics, Ecology, Ethics*, San Francisco: Freeman, 1980.

Herman E. Daly, *Steady-State Economics*, San Francisco: Freeman, 1977.

Thomas Sieger Derr, *Ecology and Human Liberation*, Geneva: World Council of Churches, 1973.

Bill Devall and George Sessions, *Deep Ecology*, Salt Lake City: Gibbs M. Smith inc. Peregrine Smith, 1985.

Edward Echlin, *The Christian Green Heritage*, Bramcote, Notts: Grove, 1989.

HRH The Duke of Edinburgh and Michael Mann, *Survival or Extinction*, Salisbury: Michael Russell / St George's House, Windsor Castle, 1989.

Paul Ekins (ed.), *The Living Economy*, London: Routledge and Kegan Paul, 1986.

John Elkington, *The Green Capitalists*, London: Gollancz, 1987.

John Elkington and Julia Hailes, *The Green Consumer Guide*, London: Gollancz, 1988.

Robert Faricy, *Wind and Sea Obey Him*, London: SCM, 1982.

Richard Foster, *Celebration of Discipline*, London: Hodder and Stoughton, 1980.

Matthew Fox, *Original Blessing*, Santa Fe, New Mexico: Bear and Co, 1983.

The Global 2000 Report to the President, Harmondsworth: Penguin, 1982.

John Gladwin, *God's People in God's World*, Leicester: Inter-Varsity Press, 1979.

Mark Gold, *Assault and Battery*, London: Pluto, 1983.

Mark Gold, *Living Without Cruelty*, Basingstoke: Green Print / Marshall Pickering, 1988.

Bob Goudzwaard, *Idols of Our Time*, Downers Grove, Illinois: Inter-Varsity Press, 1984.

Wesley Granberg-Michaelson, *A Worldly Spirituality*, San Francisco: Harper and Row, 1984.

Wesley Granberg-Michaelson (ed.), *Tending the Garden*, Grand Rapids, Michigan: Eerdmans, 1987.

Paulos Mar Gregorios, *The Human Presence*, Madras: Christian Literature Crusade, 1978.

Green Party, *General Election Manifesto*, 1983, London: Green Party.

Green Party, *General Election Manifesto*, 1987, London: Green Party.

Green Party, *Working to Live*, London: Green Party, 1988.

Sue Grieg, Graham Pike, David Selby, *Earthrights*, London: WWF / Kogan Page, 1987.

Brian Griffiths, *Morality and the Market Place*, London: Hodder and Stoughton, 1982.

Douglas Hall, *Imaging God*, Grand Rapids, Michigan: Eerdmans / New York: Friendship Press, 1986.

Donald A. Hay, *A Christian Critique of Capitalism*, Bramcote, Notts: Grove, 1975.

James M. Houston, *I Believe in the Creator*, Grand Rapids, Michigan: Eerdmans, 1979.

Ivan Illich, *Tools for Conviviality*, London: Marion Boyars, 1985.

Keith Innes, *Caring for the Earth*, Bramcote, Notts: Grove, 1987.

Philip Joranson and Ken Butigan (eds), *Cry of the Environment*, Santa Fe, New Mexico: Bear and Co, 1984.

Mother Julian of Norwich, *Revelations of Divine Love*, Harmondsworth: Penguin, 1966.

The Lion Encyclopedia of the Bible, Tring, Herts: Lion, 1978.

Andrew Linzey, *Christianity and the Rights of Animals*, London: SPCK, 1987.

Andrew Linzey and Tom Regan (eds), *Compassion for Animals*, London: SPCK, 1988.

Andrew Linzey and Tom Regan (eds), *Animals and Christianity*, London: SPCK, 1989.

James Lovelock, *Gaia: A new look at life on Earth*, Oxford, OUP, 1979.

Roy McCloughry and Andrew Hartropp, *Debt*, Bramcote, Notts: Grove, 1988.

Sean McDonagh, *To Care for the Earth*, Geoffrey Chapman, 1986.

Sallie McFague, *Models of God*, London: SCM, 1987.

Jürgen Moltmann, *God in Creation*, London: SCM, 1985.

Hugh Montefiore (ed.), *Man and Nature*, London: Collins, 1975.

Rowland Moss, *The Earth in Our Hands*, Leicester: Inter-Varsity Press, 1982.

Norman Myers (ed.), *The Gaia Atlas of Planet Management*, London: Pan, 1985.

The New Bible Commentary, London: Inter-Varsity Fellowship, 1953.

The New Jerome Bible Commentary, London: Geoffrey Chapman, 1989.

Lesslie Newbigin, *The Other Side of 1984*, Geneva: World Council of Churches, 1983.

Max Nicholson, *The Environmental Revolution*, Hodder and Stoughton, 1969.

Charles D. Niven, *History of the Humane Movement*, London: Johnson, 1969.

Richard North, *The Animals Report*, Harmondsworth: Penguin, 1983.

Eugene P. Odum, *Fundamentals of Ecology*, Philadelphia: W. B. Saunders, 1971.

Martin Palmer, Anne Nash, Ivan Hattingh (eds), *Faith and Nature*, London: Century Hutchinson / WWF, n/d.

John Polkinghorne, *Science and Providence*, London: SPCK, 1989.

Jonathon Porritt, *Seeing Green*, Oxford: Blackwell, 1984.

Jonathon Porritt and David Winner, *The Coming of the Greens*, London: Fontana, 1988.

David Pullinger (ed.), *Scorching Heat and Drought*, Edinburgh: Saint Andrew Press, 1989.

John Robinson, *Honest to God*, London: SCM, 1963.

Theodore Roszak, *Person/Planet*, London: Gollancz, 1979.

Peter Russell, *The Awakening Ark*, London: Routledge and Kegan Paul, 1982.

H. Paul Santmire, *The Travail of Nature*, Philadelphia: Fortress, 1985.

E. F. Schumacher, *Small is Beautiful*, London: Sphere, 1973.

Walter and Dorothy Schwarz, *Breaking Through*, Bideford, Devon: Green Books, 1987.

Francis Schaeffer, *Pollution and the Death of Man*, London: Hodder and Stoughton, 1970.

Henryk Skolimowski, *Economics Today – What do we need?*, London: Green Alliance, 1980.

Ronald J. Sider, *Rich Christians in an Age of Hunger*, London: Hodder and Stoughton, 1978.

Peter Singer, *Animal Liberation*, London: Jonathan Cape, 1976.

James Sire, *The Universe Next Door*, Downers Grove, Illinois: Inter-Varsity Press, 1976.

Mike Starkey, *Born to Shop*, Eastbourne: Monarch, 1989.

John V. Taylor, *Enough is Enough*, London: SCM, 1975.

Keith Thomas, *Man and the Natural World*, Harmondsworth: Penguin, 1983.

Malcolm Torry, *Basic Income for All*, Bramcote, Notts: Grove, 1988.

E. S. Turner, *All Heaven in a Rage*, London: Michael Joseph, 1964.

John Vyvyan, *In Pity and in Anger*, London: Michael Joseph, 1969.

Brian Walsh and Richard Middleton, *The Transforming Vision*, Downers Grove, Illinois: Inter-Varsity Press, 1984.

J. A. Walter, *The Human Home*, Tring, Herts: Lion, 1982.

Barbara Ward and René Dubos, *Only One Earth*, Harmondsworth: Penguin, 1972.

Kallistos Ware, *The Orthodox Way*, Oxford: Mowbray 1979.

Martin Wiener, *English Culture and the Decline of the Industrial Spirit 1850–1980*, Cambridge: Cambridge University Press, 1981.

Loren Wilkinson (ed.), *Earthkeeping: Christian Stewardship of Natural Resources*, Grand Rapids, Michigan: Eerdmans, 1980.

Albert Wolters, *Creation Regained*, Leicester: Inter-Varsity Press, 1985.

World Commission on Environment and Development, *Our Common Future*, (The 'Brundtland Report') Oxford: OUP, 1987.

World Resources Institute / International Institute of Environment and Development / United Nations Environment Programme, *World Resources 1988/89*, New York: Basic Books, 1988.

Donald Worster, *Nature's Economy*, Garden City, New York: Anchor Press / Doubleday, 1977.

INDEX